Landmark

ADVANCED | Teacher's Book

Olivia Date, Simon Haines, & Mike Sayer

OXFORD

UNIVERSITY PRESS

OXFORD

UNIVERSITY PRESS

Great Clarendon Street, Oxford OX2 6DP

Oxford University Press is a department of the University of Oxford.
It furthers the University's objective of excellence in research, scholarship,
and education by publishing worldwide in

Oxford New York

Auckland Bangkok Buenos Aires Cape Town Chennai
Dar es Salaam Delhi Hong Kong Istanbul Karachi Kolkata
Kuala Lumpur Madrid Melbourne Mexico City Mumbai
Nairobi São Paulo Shanghai Taipei Tokyo Toronto

OXFORD and OXFORD ENGLISH are registered trade marks of
Oxford University Press in the UK and in certain other countries

ISBN 0 19 437963 9

Printed in China

Contents

How the course works

Students themselves always constitute a major resource for teachers. In addition to their existing language knowledge and skills, they bring interests, ideas, opinions, general knowledge, and life experience into the classroom. This is particularly true of advanced students, who can express themselves with greater clarity and fluency. It is important that teachers acknowledge and value this resource when teaching at this level. *Landmark Advanced* encourages this in a number of ways.

Themes students will find relevant and motivating

Success in language learning depends to a great extent on students' motivation and willingness to participate in the learning process. If we want students to learn with enthusiasm, it is important that we present them with material which they find interesting, relevant, and motivating.

In *Landmark Advanced*, great care has been taken over the selection of themes which will appeal to students. Student's Book units are based on broad themes, with the separate stages focusing on different aspects of these themes. Units are kept deliberately short to avoid 'topic fatigue', the feeling that students have said all they want to say about a particular subject, which can occur at this level.

Encouraging student participation

Wherever possible, language activities are personalized in order to encourage students to engage with the topics and contribute their knowledge, ideas, and opinions. There are regular brainstorming activities, quizzes, discussions, and debates. Tasks for pairs and groups encourage students to interact and help less outgoing students express themselves orally and so build up their self-confidence, even in large classes.

Authentic texts and unscripted recordings

All main reading texts and recordings have been selected primarily for their potential to stimulate students' interest.

Authentic texts provide a variety of challenges such as new vocabulary, idioms, and accents, while at the same time allowing students to feel connected to real life and real situations. Students are given support and realizable tasks to help them meet the challenges, improve their confidence, and develop the necessary skills for dealing with natural language outside the classroom.

A guided discovery approach to grammar

Many advanced classes include students with different levels of grammatical awareness and mixed ability in using language accurately and fluently. In *Landmark Advanced*, target language – grammar, functions, and vocabulary – is first explored in the context of reading texts and recordings. This language is then highlighted and students work through a series of concept questions to check how much they already know, or can work out, about the underlying rules and patterns.

This approach allows stronger students to check their existing knowledge and show what they know, while providing less proficient students with the opportunity to work at their own pace.

To provide the balance of challenge and consolidation appropriate for advanced learners, the target language is approached in the following ways:

- reviewing discrete grammatical items, e.g. *The conditional* (Unit 2.1)
- bringing together language items not normally studied at the same time, e.g. *Alternatives to relative clauses* (Unit 15.1)
- presenting grammar which is likely to be new to students at this level, e.g. *Fronting* (Unit 15.2)
- investigating different aspects of an 'umbrella' topic, e.g. *Emphasis* (Unit 2.2)
- taking a broadly functional approach, e.g. *Making generalizations* (Unit 7.3).

Key features of a unit

Unit structure

All units consist of two or three stages followed by *Exploring words* and *Language commentary*.

Each stage focuses on a different aspect of the overall theme of the unit. For example, in Unit 4 this theme is danger. Stage 1 is based on a road traffic incident, Stage 2 on situations where people have felt threatened, and Stage 3 on computer viruses.

Lead in

This section introduces the theme of each stage, by means of quizzes, brainstorms, and opinion questions. Where appropriate it also revises or introduces key vocabulary relevant to the topic.

Reading and listening

All the main texts and recordings are authentic and have been chosen to stimulate interest and comment from students. They are multi-purpose: engaging material helps students develop and practise their skills as well as providing examples of the target language in a clear and memorable context.

Reading texts in *Landmark Advanced* come from a variety of sources: newspapers, magazines, the Internet, works of fiction, letters, and e-mails. Listenings include interviews, conversations, vox pops (spontaneous replies from members of the public), monologues, and unscripted role plays. Although, for purposes of clarity and variety, some of the listening material is studio recorded, the speech itself is spontaneous; both recordings and tapescripts therefore include any apparent 'errors' which the speakers have made.

When reading or listening, students are often encouraged to read between the lines or interpret what they hear, rather than simply answering comprehension questions. *React and discuss* gives students the opportunity to respond to the content of the texts and passages. Students' different interpretations and reactions can provide the basis of lively discussion.

Exploring natural speech

This section, which follows most main listening activities, highlights features of natural speech that occur in the recordings. The focus may be on pronunciation, particular words and phrases, or features of conversation. The main aim is to make students aware of these features; they are not necessarily expected to incorporate them into their own speech, although some may be keen to experiment with them.

Close up

This section, which accompanies a majority of the main reading activities, helps students notice items of vocabulary or grammar which appear in the texts. This section may be referred to during or after the main reading tasks.

Language focus

This section focuses on key grammar points or functional items that have occurred in the preceding text or recording. Students are asked to look at examples of the target language and to work through a series of concept questions, discussing ideas and comparing answers in pairs or small groups. The questions are designed to help them work out rules or language patterns for themselves. They can then use the *Language commentary* to check their ideas.

If you have a less confident class, you may wish to treat this as a whole class activity, providing guidance and support where necessary.

Each *Language focus* section ends with *Exploitation*, which provides a combination of restricted and freer practice of the target language in a meaningful context.

Speaking

Speaking tasks are integrated throughout each unit, for example in *Lead in*, *React and discuss*, *Exploitation*, and *Exploring words*. Each unit also contains a section which provides the opportunity for more extended speaking. This comprises discussions, problem solving activities, roleplays, and the chance to exchange experiences and ideas.

Even at an advanced level, students can find it difficult to speak freely for extended periods and feel daunted by the prospect of speaking in front of a group. To help overcome this, the activities are structured to allow students thinking time and the opportunity to rehearse in pairs or smaller groups.

Additionally, the speaking tasks often generate ideas which help students to prepare for the writing section.

Writing

Writing tasks vary in length, from short activities that can be done in class to longer pieces which are best done as homework, where students can spend as long as they need. When appropriate to the task, students are encouraged to plan their writing paragraph-by-paragraph and to write a first draft. Further support is provided by the *Writing guidelines* at the back of the book. These include clear models of specific types of writing, together with a checklist of points to consider when planning, writing, and checking.

Exploring words

The last section of each unit, *Exploring words*, focuses on areas of vocabulary, such as:

- specific topics, e.g. *Computers and computing* (Unit 2)
- the ways in which words are combined, e.g. *Collocation* (Unit 4)
- word families, e.g. *Words and their roots* (Unit 6)
- word grammar, e.g. *Countable and uncountable nouns* (Unit 8)
- appropriacy, e.g. *Colloquial words and expressions* (Unit 7).

Students discover, organize, and practise useful words and phrases through a range of written and oral activities. *Exploring words* provides an integral, stand-alone vocabulary lesson. However, where stated in the teacher's notes, these lessons can be split up and incorporated into the main stages.

Vocabulary study is integrated throughout the units. Where appropriate, key topic vocabulary is introduced at the beginning of the stage. Texts and recordings also provide the opportunity for studying vocabulary in context (See *Exploring natural speech* and *Close up*).

Language commentary

Language commentary comes at the end of each unit and summarizes the grammar or functional language content of the unit. Easy-to-follow rules and explanations are provided as well as extra examples of the target language.

Students may use the *Language commentary* to check their answers to questions in *Language focus* sections of units or for revision and consolidation at any other time while using the course. The language of explanation is aimed at advanced level students, so commentaries can be used without help from the teacher.

In the back of the book you will find writing guidelines, tapescripts, and communication activities.

Support for teachers

Aims and overview

Each unit of the Teacher's Book begins with a clear overview of themes, main skills focus, and target grammar and vocabulary.

A step-by-step guide

For each activity in the Student's Book, the Teacher's Book contains a clear statement of aims, followed by concise, easy-to-follow procedural notes. There is a comprehensive key to all the exercises and suggested answers for open-ended questions, along with tips on student interaction and conducting feedback.

Grammar and vocabulary support

The *Language commentary* in the Student's Book is intended primarily for student reference. In some cases this means that more complex, potentially confusing aspects of particular grammar points have not been included. Additional explanations are given in the Teacher's Book, where we feel this may be helpful to the teacher. Also included are explanations of possibly unfamiliar idiomatic and colloquial language from the texts and recordings.

Where possible we have tried to help you anticipate problems your students may encounter with the target language by providing lists of common difficulties and typical errors.

Alternative ways of exploiting material

Because teachers, teaching situations, and groups of students are all different, not all teachers will want to approach activities in the same way. So, where appropriate, alternative ways of exploiting material are suggested. These relate to:

- helping less imaginative students
- alternative ways of grouping students for particular tasks – pairs, groups, mingles, etc.
- teaching monolingual classes.

Additional materials and suggested activities

To help you adapt and supplement lessons to suit your students' needs, the Teacher's Book contains extra activities, such as:

- warmers
- further practice of specific language points
- extension activities
- fun activities.

Where extra teaching materials are included, these may be photocopied for use with your classes.

Course components

Student's Book

- 18 units, each consisting of 2 or 3 stages, providing 100–120 hours of class work
- Including most tapescripts, language commentary, and communication activities

Class Cassettes

Two cassettes containing all the listening material for the Student's Book

Teacher's Book

- Aims and overview of each unit
- Support with advanced grammar and vocabulary
- Suggestions for exploiting material to suit your classes
- Extra activities and photocopiable materials

Workbook

The exercises in the Workbook are designed to help students consolidate and expand their knowledge, improve their accuracy, and build their confidence.

Each unit of the Workbook contains four sections:

Language focus

Full and varied practice of all grammar and functions from the Student's Book, including authentic texts which provide real contexts for new language

Vocabulary focus

Revises and extends key vocabulary areas from the Student's Book

Vocabulary expansion

Introduces new idioms, collocations, and a wide range of useful vocabulary using authentic reading texts

Listening

Listening exercises to improve understanding, develop skills and strategies, focus on key vocabulary, and raise awareness of features of natural speech

The Workbook includes an Introduction for students, which describes the aims of the different stages of Workbook units and incorporates useful Study tips.

Student's Cassette

- 18 unscripted listening passages to help students get used to natural speech and familiarize themselves with a wide variety of accents
- 18 recorded exercises to improve accuracy and build speaking confidence

CAE Study Pack

Designed for students who want to work towards the Cambridge *Certificate of Advanced English* while following a general advanced level course

- free-standing self-study workbook with two audio CDs
- introduction to the five papers of the examination
- tasks to develop and practise skills, techniques, and strategies
- exam tips to help improve examination performance
- a complete practice exam
- user-friendly reference key which gives information on what's right and why

Although a free-standing resource, the study pack is thematically linked to the units in *Landmark Advanced*.

1 Influences

Theme: famous and ordinary people, beliefs, and their influence on us

1.1 20th century people

People who influenced the 20th century

- **Reading:** gist and specific information
- **Language focus:** discourse markers
- **Listening:** prompt for discussion
- **Speaking:** reaching a consensus and presenting ideas

1.2 My influences

People talk about individuals who have been an influence on them

- **Listening:** gist and specific information
- **Exploring natural speech:** pronunciation of unstressed syllables
- **Vocabulary:** two-part adjectives (*hard-hitting, low-flying*)
- **Speaking:** discussion
- **Writing:** a personal profile

1.3 *-isms*

Influential movements and beliefs

- **Reading:** matching text and summary
- **Language focus:** *all, both, either, neither, none*
- **Other input:** comparison language
- **Speaking:** 'inventing' a new *-ism*

Exploring words

Why we are like we are: personality and temperament

Workbook

- **Language focus:** discourse markers *all, both, either, neither, none*
- **Vocabulary focus:** *-isms*; describing people – metaphors and idioms
- **Vocabulary expansion:** adjectival suffixes; adverbs
- **Listening:** influences

1.1 20th century people p.6

Stage 1 includes a reading text which is a reaction to *Time* magazine's list of 100 people who influenced the 20th century, and contextualizes discourse markers.

Lead in

Aim *To get students thinking and talking about the theme of the lesson and, particularly with new classes, to break the ice and provide an opportunity to talk about ideas, attitudes, and beliefs.*

1–2 Introduce the activity briefly: ask students to look at the pictures and the five categories.

- Ask them to complete tasks 1 and 2 in pairs.
- Monitor but do not interrupt. Students are getting to know each other as well as finding the answers to the task.
- Conduct whole-class feedback to see which of the people they know. Supply answers as necessary.

Glossary

Titan – someone of great size or strength, from the Greek mythological character. Adjective – titanic. Often used as in this text, i.e. a person of great importance: *Henry Ford was a **titan** of industry.*
Icon – In this usage means someone who is uncritically admired. *The singer Madonna is an **icon** to many young people.*

1	Leaders and Revolutionaries	Mohandas Ghandi / Pope John Paul II
	Artists and Entertainers	Picasso / Oprah Winfrey
	Builders and Titans	Henry Ford / Bill Gates
	Scientists and Thinkers	Sigmund Freud / Albert Einstein
	Heroes and Icons	Marilyn Monroe / Pelé
2	Albert Einstein	

Note

The answers given here are those that *Time* magazine listed, but there is certainly room for discussion and disagreement. Marilyn Monroe and Pelé could be entertainers; Oprah Winfrey might be considered an icon. Encourage students to discuss and defend their answers – this is good for their English! There is a full list of *Time* magazine's people on p.17.

Reading

Aim *To extend vocabulary, practise paraphrasing skills, and encourage students to react personally to the letter, which is one person's written reaction to the* Time *magazine list.*

1 Ask students to work individually without worrying at this stage about difficult vocabulary.

- When most have finished, ask students to compare and discuss their answers in pairs for a few minutes.
- There is no need for whole-class feedback at this point.

Close up

Aim *To extend vocabulary and to focus students' attention on the differences between formal and informal language.*

- Ask students to do this individually or in pairs. Encourage them to make guesses from context rather than rely on their dictionaries.
- Check answers with the whole class.

> **1.12** *figures* = people (as in *public figures / a cult figure*); other meanings:
> 1 body shape – *She's got a slim figure.*
> 2 numbers – *He earns a six-figure salary.*
> 3 a diagram or illustration in a book – *Figure 16 shows how a computer keyboard works.*
> 4 to think / calculate – *I figure we'll arrive at about midnight.* (informal conversation and American English)
> **1.16** met
> **1.17** *ethnic minority* = a group within a larger population which is a racial minority
> *ethnic cleansing* = the policy or practice of killing or driving out of an area the people of one race or religion by those of another
> *ethnology* = the comparative study of human people
> **1.22** Leave out the word *whom*

Note

Whom is virtually non-existent in spoken English today. It is sometimes used in written English to add weight or seriousness to the language: 'He was someone for whom I am sure we all had the deepest regard' rather than 'He was someone who I am sure we all had respect for'.

2 Ask students to complete the task individually or in pairs.

- Check answers and encourage a whole-class discussion.

> **Possible answers**
> **a** most people on the lists were American / the list was unbalanced, biased
> **b** including a wider range of people / people from the Third World, more from the early part of the 20th century, fewer from contemporary pop culture
> **c** he was ethnocentric, he didn't know much about people of his parents' generation, he rated people he liked as more important than those he disliked

Language focus: discourse markers   p.7

Aim *To expose students to a wide variety of discourse markers, both formal and informal, and encourage them to extend their range by practising a few of them.*

Discourse markers help us understand how spoken language or a written text is constructed and so how a speaker's or writer's thoughts are linked.

It is **not** a good idea to ask students to practise all the discourse markers presented; this would be overwhelming and daunting. They need to build up their range gradually, by recognizing and identifying markers when they come across them and by gradually using more themselves.

Discourse markers often present difficulties, even for advanced students (and native speakers!). Students may not understand what a particular word or phrase really means, they may not recognize how formal or informal the discourse marker is, they may place it incorrectly in the sentence, and they may simply have a very limited range which they consequently overuse. This section will help them become more confident and competent users of these common linguistic devices.

1 With books closed, ask students what they understand by 'discourse markers'. Write up any that they know, and point out that discourse markers can be informal (*well, anyway, I mean*) as well as formal (*nevertheless, therefore*). Ask them to think about the discourse markers they use in their own language, and those they use in English.

- Explain the aims for this section: in *Language focus*, they will look at examples of language from the context they have just studied. They will then do tasks which will help them to check and expand their knowledge of the language area.
- Students answer this question individually or in pairs.
- Check answers with the whole class.

> **a** *Nevertheless* introduces a contrast.
> **b** *Here are* introduces examples.

2–3 Ask students to complete task 2 in pairs. (They will need to copy the chart into their notebooks.)

- Set a time limit. Monitor, but don't spend too long with each pair. You will probably need to go over the answers with the whole class.
- Check answers to 2, and ask students to think about 3 as you go through their answers.
- Use the Language commentary on p.13 for further explanations and example sentences.

2

Purpose of words or phrases	Examples
• Adding information	*in addition; another thing is; as well as that; on top of that; what's more*
• Balancing contrasting ideas	*whereas; while*
• Changing the subject	*anyway; incidentally*
• Concluding / summing up	*to sum up; in short*
• Pointing out a contrast	*however; despite this*
• Giving examples	*for example; for instance*
• Logical consequence	*therefore; so*
• Making something clear	*in other words; I mean; what I mean is; actually; as a matter of fact*
• Showing your attitude	*to be honest; frankly; quite honestly*
• Structuring and sequencing	*to start with; firstly; lastly; at first; eventually; in the end; then*

3 Most of these markers could be used in informal conversation, although you are unlikely to use: *in addition, however, despite this, therefore, firstly, lastly*. They would be more likely to be used in formal writing.

Exploitation

Aim *To provide controlled practice in using some of the discourse markers.*

1 Outline the task. Explain that the students should only add the discourse markers in bold type because the others are already in their table.

• Check answers quickly with the whole class. Set a time limit.

> See table above

2 Ask students to do this individually. Sometimes more than one answer is possible.

• Students check their answers in pairs. Monitor this stage so that you can give individual attention where necessary and spot confusion or mistakes that are general.

• Check answers with the whole class.

> Where more than one choice is possible, the first answer given is the better.
> 1 To start with / At first
> 2 However / Despite this
> 3 Despite this / However
> 4 Actually / As a matter of fact
> 5 Anyway
> 6 so
> 7 At first / To start with
> 8 Then
> 9 Eventually / In the end
> 10 In the end / Eventually / So
> 11 for instance
> 12 whereas
> 13 quite honestly
> 14 As a matter of fact
> 15 What I mean is

Speaking

Aim *To practise listening for key information and to develop informal discussion skills.*

1 Outline the task briefly. Allow students time to read through the lists and check that they know what they refer to.

• Play the recording.

Note

Throughout *Landmark Advanced*, recordings and transcripts are of spontaneous speech. They therefore include any grammatical slips and errors which the speakers have made.

1.1

Speaker 1 For me the key event of the 20th century would have to be the erm, coming down of the Berlin Wall. …
Worst idea of the 20th century must be the the motor car, I think.

Speaker 2 I think the most important event of the 20th century was er the er breaking down of the Berlin Wall and the er union of the two Germanies and the integration of the ex-Communist countries into the erm shall we say 'free world'? And I think one of the worst ideas of the 20th century was beside Cold War was Communism, state socialism.

Speaker 3 Erm I would say some of the key events of the 20th century would be erm, the first things that spring to mind are the wars, so the First World War and the Second World War and the Vietnam War erm, man on the moon, and scientific advances, the discovery of DNA which has huge implications now …
Erm I don't know if I'd call it really the worst idea of the 20th century but I think possibly cars or or motorized transport would come would come fairly close …

Speaker 4 … I think I would list all the wars – the First World War, the Second World War, Vietnam, I think all the wars. Erm …
Intertwined with the hundred key events, cos although the First World War the Second World War were key events, they were also bad ideas, Hitler's idea to eliminate the Jews, for example, would be one of the worst ideas …

• Students compare their answers in pairs.

• Play the recording again if necessary.

> **Speaker 1:** the coming down of the Berlin Wall; the motor car
> **Speaker 2:** the Berlin Wall; the Cold War
> **Speaker 3:** the First World War; Second World War; the Vietnam War; man on the moon; DNA; cars
> **Speaker 4:** all the wars; Hitler's idea to eliminate the Jews

Note

Elvis Presley – American pop singer 1935–1977, famous as a pop icon and for making rock 'n' roll popular in the 1950s.
First landing on the moon – 1969. The American Neil Armstrong was the first person to walk on the moon.
World War II – 1939–1945. A global war was fought in the air, on land, and at sea. By the end of the war 45 million people had died.
US civil rights movement – Led by Martin Luther King (1929–1968) to establish equal rights for black people. Civil Rights Act was passed in 1964.
Prohibition – 1920–1933. Period in USA when it was illegal to manufacture or sell alcohol. Led to huge trade in illegal, home-made alcohol and people who sold it – 'bootleggers'.
Message T-shirts – refers to T-shirts printed with messages on them, e.g. I ♥ London.
Suntans – The idea that it was attractive / desirable to get a suntan was a 20th century phenomenon.
Videophones – Refers to phones with video monitor so that you can see the person you are talking to.

2 Give students five minutes to think of things to include in the two lists.

3 Students work in small groups to agree their 'Top 5' lists. Set a time limit.

4 Each group should choose one member to present their list to the class. Set a time limit.

• Ask the groups listening to note down each 'Top 5' and see how many ideas they have in common. (This helps to ensure they listen to each other.)

• If your class would benefit from some extra informal writing practice, you could use the following activity in class or as homework. If possible, ask students to send it by e-mail to other members of the class.

Write an e-mail to the editor of *Time* magazine commenting on the four *Worst Ideas of the Century* listed on p.7 and arguing for the inclusion of one of your own ideas.

Write quickly and informally – in other words, a typical e-mail.

Use informal discourse markers of these four types:
– Pointing out a contrast
– Giving examples
– Showing your attitude
– Structuring and sequencing
Write 80–100 words.
Give / send your e-mail to someone else in the class.

1.2 My influences p.8

Stage 2 introduces listening to spontaneous speech, and provides vocabulary and skills work.

Lead in

Aim *To encourage students to think and talk about types of people who have personal influence.*

1–2 Students work in pairs or small groups to look at the pictures and discuss the questions. Alternatively:

• Introduce the theme with books closed. Write the words 'My influences' on the board and ask students to suggest various people / groups of people who influence us. Write up their suggestions in note form, perhaps in a 'bubble diagram': write the word *influences* in a central bubble, and add the categories they suggest such as *family, teachers, friends, famous people* in smaller bubbles radiating from it. You then elicit from the students the specific influences, and also perhaps when they were influential. Write these on the board radiating out from the appropriate bubble (see diagram).

• Ask students to discuss the suggestions in pairs or small groups. Set a time limit.

• It is not necessary to conduct a group feedback unless the students would like to.

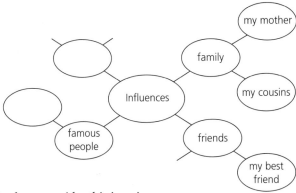

3 Students consider this in pairs.

• Check answers.

---

1 Possible influences:
Family: parents; grandparents; older siblings
Outside: teachers; sports personalities; pop stars; school friends; priests; national leaders

2 They represent the kind of person you would like to be.
They lead the kind of life you'd like for yourself.
They seem happy or successful.
They are interested in you. They advise and help you.

3 A role model is someone you attempt to emulate – a very strong influence.

Listening

Aim *To practise the skill of listening to informal, natural speech in order to obtain specific information.*

Glossary
_____
smart – intelligent, clever (US English)

1 Explain the task briefly then play the recording.

1.2

Speaker 1 I'd say one person that really influenced me when I was growing up was erm a teacher. Now I'd moved schools at a time when not many children were moving across to a new school – it was sort of in the middle of a, in the middle of a term, I think it was and erm, I didn't know anyone obviously and I was feeling a little bit unsure of myself and er the physical education teacher was called Ralph which is my name and he was very popular – he was a really sort of tall guy, you know, er he was er ranked in the country for his tennis playing and I loved tennis and I really sort of admired him and because I had the s..., the same name I thought that there may be some connection and erm you know, I sort of you know would watch him and see what he was up to and then he actually took me under his wing a little bit and gave me some extra coaching, tennis coaching, and erm it was great, but it taught me a lot about sportsmanship and a lot of values and things that were to do with with with sport and sport-related which was you know something I was very much into when I was a child and er it was really useful and very beneficial even now.

Speaker 2 … erm well, I'm influenced I suppose by by my parents and friends and stuff and I base, well my role model might be, I think probably my brother because he's he's always erm really confident and relaxed and I seem seem to get a bit stressed and I dunno, tied up and he'll come home and watch TV and phone up his friends and stuff and if he's got an exam he won't really care – he'll just go out and enjoy himself and I'm a bit more conscientious so I sort of look up to him and I I see that he's always enjoying himself – but he's still got time to, you know he still does well, and he's got a good job and he he works hard, so he he is probably the person that I look up to most …

Speaker 3 I'd have to say one of the people who has has had a great influence on me would be Barbara Walters, believe it or not. Erm I just remember as a little girl er turning on the TV and there not being a whole lot of women er giving the news, I mean hard-hitting news, and I remember watching Barbara Walters be right up there with all the the other male news anchors and thinking 'Wow if she can do it then I can definitely do it!' and er I just always loved er watching her stories and the questions that she would ask and for me she was just a smart woman erm that I could you know flip on the TV and see her and she was a real inspiration and made me feel like as a woman as a young girl I could really do whatever I wanted to do – so she was a role model for me in that way.

- Students compare their answers in pairs.
- If they haven't got all the answers, play the recording again. This is more helpful than merely giving them the answers; it encourages them to develop their own self-reliant listening strategies.

> **a** Speaker 1 – teacher
> Speaker 2 – older brother
> Speaker 3 – successful public figure, the American TV newsreader Barbara Walters
> **b** They were all inspired to improve or develop in some way by someone older and more successful than themselves.

2 Ask students to read the questions carefully.

- Suggest they work in pairs to see if there are any questions they can already answer.
- Play the recording again.
- Students check their answers and compare in their pairs.
- Repeat as necessary (probably two or three times) and conduct whole-class feedback.

Note

Barbara Walters has received many awards for her broadcast journalism and interviews. She became the first woman to co-host national network news in the United States when she joined ABC News in 1976. She had previously worked on NBC's *Today* programme.

> **a** He admired him, felt protected by him, grateful because he learned a lot from him.
> **b** The speaker had moved schools at an unusual time and felt unsure of himself at his new school. He identified with the teacher partly because they shared the same first name.
> **c** The older brother is laid back and confident. The younger brother is conscientious and feels more stressed.
> **d** He enjoys himself but is still successful.
> **e** She was a successful woman in an otherwise male world.
> **f** The speaker realizes that if her role model can succeed, so can she.

Exploring natural speech   p.9

This section focuses on the sound 'schwa' /ə/. Students will have come across this before, but even advanced students sometimes find it difficult to believe, or accept, that natural English reduces so many vowel sounds to this 'schwa'. The aim is to help students recognize this so that they can focus on the other sounds, which in turn helps them to make sense of faster speech.

1 Outline the task briefly and give students time to read the sentences carefully. Ask them to predict what the missing words might be and compare answers in pairs.

2 Play the recording and ask students to check their answers. (This is not included in the tapescript section of the Student's Book.) You may wish to explain to students that the extracts from recordings which appear in their books are of unscripted speech, and therefore include any apparent 'errors' which the speakers have made.

1.3

a I'd say one person that really influenced me when I was growing up was erm a teacher. Now I'd moved schools at a time when not many children were moving across to a new school …

b 'Wow if she can do it then I can definitely do it!' and er I just always loved er watching her stories and the questions that she would ask and for me she was just a smart woman …

c … and she was a real inspiration and made me feel like as a woman as a young girl I could really do whatever I wanted to do …

d … so she was a role model for me in that way.

> **a** that; was; a; were; a
> **b** can; can; and; and; that; for; was; a
> **c** was; to
> **d** that

- When they have the correct answers, play the recording again and ask them to think about the question.
- Check answers and discuss with the whole class. Explain that the 'schwa' is the most common vowel sound in English.

> All words in **a–c** contain the 'schwa' sound. The vowel sound is unstressed.
> *that* in **d** does not contain the 'schwa' sound. When *that* is used as a determiner, the vowel is never weakened.

Vocabulary: two-part adjectives

Aim *To introduce students to some common two-part adjectives and to develop their ability to use them descriptively.*

1 Introduce the task briefly and ask students to look at the two lists of words. Check that they understand them.

- Students complete the task in pairs. Give them enough time to have a go but not to reach the point when they are struggling. Several combinations are logically possible, but are not used in English.
- Check answers with the whole class.

hard-hitting	= forceful, strong, powerful
easy-going	= calm, relaxed
long-suffering	= puts up with trouble patiently
fast-growing	
slow-moving	
clean-living	= honest, upright character
low-flying	
loose-fitting	= fits loosely, baggy

2 Suggest that students complete the task in pairs.

- Check answers with the whole class.

> hard-hitting documentary / film / speech /
> easy-going company / family / patient / politician / student /
> teacher / wife
> long-suffering patient / politician / student / teacher / wife
> fast-growing business / company / family
> slow-moving film / plane / story / traffic
> clean-living family / politician / student / teacher / wife
> low-flying plane
> loose-fitting jacket / jeans

3 Ask students to complete the task in pairs.

- Check answers with the whole class.

> **a** long-running   **e** smooth-talking
> **b** sweet-smelling
> **c** fast-flowing
> **d** important-looking

- For further practice you could write up a selection of two-word adjectives from questions 1, 2, and 3. Students work in small groups to categorize a selection of the two-word adjectives into 'positive', 'negative', or 'it depends'. This will probably provoke considerable discussion (is *easy-going* always positive? From whose perspective?) and should therefore help students to remember the adjectives.

- Check answers with the whole class.

  ▶ There is an extra activity on p.140 which practises metaphors to describe people.

Speaking

Aim *To give students the opportunity to practise the language learned and discuss the theme of the lesson more freely. It also provides them with useful preparation for the writing task.*

1–2 Ask students to complete the tasks in pairs or small groups.

- Alternatively, do question 1 yourself first. Tell the class about someone who has been your role model, and what influence this person has had on your personality, ideas and beliefs, career or education. Talking to the class yourself like this is sometimes referred to as 'live listening'. Used carefully – i.e. speaking naturally, not for too long, and encouraging reaction and follow-up questions – it can provide extremely useful and motivating listening and speaking practice.

- Now ask the students to do the same, in small groups.

- There is no need for whole-class feedback as this is a personal speaking activity. Only ask for feedback if you feel it is necessary to round off this stage of the lesson.

Writing

Aim *To develop students' semi-formal writing skills and to consolidate the theme.*

As this is the first unit, you could take the opportunity to run through the advantages of the process approach to writing.

This should include:

- Planning
- Writing a first draft (quickly)
- Checking for errors of grammar, vocabulary, spelling, style
- Writing an accurate final version

Make sure students are aware of and refer to the Writing guidelines at the back of their books on p.150.

1 Outline the task briefly. It follows on very clearly from the speaking.

- Run through the outline plan with the class. You could ask students to note down any adjectives they would use to describe this person's qualities, as well as examples which illustrate them, for example:

  My maths teacher
  Qualities   Examples
  patient   *helped me to understand the basics of maths /*
           spent time with me after school / never lost his
           temper with me
  kind   *always encouraged me even when I got low*
           marks

- Students work individually to produce their plan in class time.

2 If there is not time for task 2 in class, set it for homework, but make sure the students understand that a fellow student will be looking at it before you do. Remind them also that this is a draft, to be done quickly, and set a time limit.

3 Students work in pairs. Give them time to read each other's work through. They may first need to clarify problems caused by handwriting.

- Students help each other to improve their drafts. Set a time limit, e.g. five minutes to read each draft, and time these stages fairly strictly.

- Clarify requirements for final profile, number of words, title, layout.

4 Students discuss their ideas for improvements, then work individually to write their profiles.

Stage 3 consists of a reading text and work on *all, both, either, neither, none*, followed by a light-hearted design task.

Lead in

Aim *To prepare for the reading task by getting students thinking about beliefs, qualities, and movements.*

1 Books closed. Set the task as a brainstorming activity with the whole class to begin with, writing up a few -*isms* as they think of them. Then once the students have got the idea, they should work in groups and write down as many words as they can. Set a time limit.

• Do a quick oral group feedback, and write up the words offered.

2 Put the categories on the board and ask students to group their -*isms* under these headings. They should keep their books closed.

> **Examples**
> **Political or religious beliefs**
> *Communism; Socialism; Conservatism; Marxism; Liberalism; Feminism*
> *Hinduism; Buddhism; Judaism; Sikhism*
> **Attitudes and abstract qualities**
> *fanaticism; radicalism; racism; sexism; cynicism; stoicism; idealism*
> **Creative movements**
> *Cubism; Expressionism; Impressionism; Surrealism; Modernism; Classicism*

Reading

Aim *To develop the theme of attitudes, beliefs, and movements, practise intensive reading skills, and extend vocabulary.*

1 Quickly check the words in the list if they did not come up in *Lead in*, then ask the whole class to look at Paragraph A and give them time to work out which -*ism* it refers to (materialism). Show them how there are clues in the writing (*the only thing that really exists in the world is* **matter** ...).

• Ask the students to do the rest of the task individually, then compare their answers.

• Check briefly with whole class, going over the pronunciation of the -*isms* as you do so. It is useful to ask the students to mark the word stress and then practise saying it. If the stress is in the right place, the other vowels will tend to become shorter and sound more accurate.

> **A** Materialism /məˈtɪərɪəlɪzm/   **B** Behaviourism /bɪˈheɪvjərɪzm/
> **C** Buddhism /ˈbʊdɪzm/   **D** Nihilism / nihilists /ˈnaɪɪlɪzm/
> **E** Anarchism /ˈænəkɪzm/·   **F** Pacifism /ˈpæsɪfɪzm/

Close up

Aim *To develop and practise intensive reading skills.*

• Ask students to do this individually or in pairs. Encourage them to make guesses from context rather than rely on their dictionaries.

• Check answers with whole class.

> 1.2 idealist
> 1.3 for example
> 1.4 to found
> 1.13 believes
> 1.17 the end of one century and the beginning of the next
> 1.21 to seek

2 Put the students into pairs for this task.

> **a** D   **b** B   **c** E   **d** F   **e** A   **f** C

• If you want to give students an opportunity to talk about the article more freely, write these discussion questions on the board:

What do you personally associate with the -*isms* you have read about?

What's your opinion of them?

Language focus: *all, both, either, neither, none*   p.11

These are very familiar to many students at advanced level, but they can still cause problems, e.g. with word order, or singular / plural verbs, so the aim here is to review both meaning and use and to ensure that students can use them appropriately and correctly. Choosing the right form of the verb that follows these words often makes students (and native speakers!) feel insecure. (*Neither is / are from England – 'is' is correct, but many people say 'are'.*)

1 Outline the task briefly.

• Ask students to work individually or in pairs. Refer them to the Language commentary on p.13.

• Check answers with the whole class.

> **a** both
> **b** 1 either / neither / none
>   2 both
>   3 all

2 Check answers with the whole class.

> all / both

> Note
> ―――――――――――――――――――――
> *either* and *neither* are followed by singular verbs, which sometimes causes difficulty. You might want to remind them that *everything* and *nothing* are also followed by singular verbs.

3 Ask students to complete this task in pairs.

• Check answers with the whole class.

> **1** all / are   **2** none / is   **3** both / end   **4** neither / is

▶ There is an extra activity on p.140 which can be used after task **3** for extra individual practice in class.

Exploitation

Aim *To give further semi-controlled practice in using all / none, etc. in context, and also to give the students free, informal speaking practice.*

1 a Outline the task briefly. You might like to assign different lists to different pairs or groups of students. Emphasize the need to find as many different, complex, comparisons as possible, and encourage them to do so.

> *Paris and London are both cities.* – too simple

> *Paris and London are both important cultural and financial centres. They are both built on major rivers, and neither of them is on the coast.* – better

- Monitor, but there is no need for whole-class feedback.

b You can ask students who finish sooner to do this, or the whole class if you feel they still need the practice.

2 Focus attention on the Comparison language in the box.

- Demonstrate the task using yourself and another student, then ask the class to do this in pairs.

- Monitor and encourage students to discuss all the areas suggested and to go into some depth with their questions and answers.

- While they are still interested and there is still a buzz of activity ask them to join with another pair to find out what they all have in common.

- In all speaking activities it is difficult to gauge when to stop and move on. As a general rule it is better to try and move on just *before* the level of interest dips.

Speaking

This activity gives some light-hearted speaking practice focusing on inventing a new *-ism* and describing its features to the rest of the class.

1 Encourage a short general class discussion on the *-isms* that are important to the students, or the students' country/ies. You may need to start the discussion so be prepared with some ideas.

2 Read through the task with the students, making sure they understand what they have to do.

- Put the students into small groups of three or four and set a time limit. Monitor and help as necessary, making sure each group notes down its key ideas.

- Give each group a set time (short) to present their *-ism* to the rest of the class. You could ask the class to vote on the best / most amusing / most original if you feel it is appropriate.

- You could also look at these sayings or *-isms* that became associated with particular well-known people, often politicians or comedians. Write the following examples on the board and go through them with the whole class to make sure they get the point of the humour.

Bushism: *More and more of our imports come from overseas.* (George W. Bush)
Goldwynism: *Any man who goes to a psychiatrist should have his head examined.* (Sam Goldwyn)
I can answer you in two words: im-possible. (Sam Goldwyn)

- Students work in pairs or small groups to discuss what these famous people's *-isms* tell us about the people themselves, and whether there are any typical sayings like them associated with people from their country. They could also make up some *-isms* of this kind of their own.

- Ask students to tell them to the rest of the class, explaining them if necessary.

Exploring words   p.12

Aim *To extend students' vocabulary connected with personality and mood and to raise awareness of the quite subtle distinctions between similar words. There is also the opportunity for students to discuss personality and so extend their speaking skills.*

1 a Outline the task quickly and check answers. *Temperament* may be a new word and the subtle distinctions between the four may need some help. What is most important here is that any possible mother tongue interference is dealt with (in some languages, for example, *temperament* is negative).

> The difference between these words is very difficult to describe or explain. They can be seen as a difference in layers of presentation to the world, with *nature* at the deepest level and *mood* at the most superficial.
> So *nature* is the way we fundamentally are; people are described as having a nice or an unpleasant nature.
> *Temperament* is a manifestation of this nature in the way we behave, similar to *disposition*, so people have a pleasant / calm / aggressive temperament.
> *Character* suggests something fuller than temperament; a combination of our fundamental nature, which gives us our temperament, together with other qualities, so character gives a more multi-faceted description of a person: decent / honourable / fastidious / gregarious, etc.
> *Mood* is used to describe the way we are feeling at a particular moment: in a good / bad mood, irritable / relaxed, etc.

b Ask students to look at questions 1–4 in the questionnaire first. Go over any difficult vocabulary.

- Play the recording.

1.4
1

W1 Well, I'd like to think that I'm a quite strong person, would you say?

W2 Yeah, yeah, you know your own mind.

W1 Good, I'm glad you agree with me on that. Erm I have been accused of being I suppose, a bit self-centred sometimes.

W2 Everyone's like that though. OK.

W1   OK. Erm, the last two.

W2   Ah, you're dependable.

W1   Yeah. I'd say (definitely). I'm always there on time, aren't I?

W2   Yeah.

W1   Yeah, dependable.

2

M   Er, I'd say, I'm I'm quite an excitable person actually.

W   Definitely, you do get a bit overexcited at times.

M   I do, I do get a bit carried away. I'm maybe I should try some meditation to calm down.

W   Maybe, what about, what about the second two?

M   Oh all right, erm …

W   You're quite easy-going, though.

M   I'm very easy-going …

W   Quite laid back.

M   Yeah very laid back. I I should learn to be more difficult, really. I (should) go to difficult classes or something.

W   Erm.

M   I'd like to be more passionate about things. (Yeah, yeah) I think, erm I think more oomph …

W   Yeah, you lack a bit of passion. Bit of ambition.

M   I'm a bit too cautious perhaps.

W   So, I suppose cautious will do.

M   Yeah. I am cautious.

3

W1   Erm …

W2   Well, I think that's answered it really.

W1   What? Timid?

W2   Yes. Timid, definitely. We'll choose timid.

W1   Timid. And – er oh, I'm not gloomy.

W2   No, definitely not, you're always in a good mood.

W1   So …

W2   Sunny.

W1   Sunny.

W2   Definitely, yeah.

W1   OK.

W2   And, agreeable or moody?

W1   Do you think I'm moody?

W2   Not at all, no.

W1   Really? I'm not moody, am I?

W2   No.

W1   No, I think I'm quite agreeable.

W2   Definitely.

W1   OK.

4

W   So, what sort of mood are you in then?

M   I am in a good mood.

W   Good.

M   Definitely in a good mood.

W   OK.

M   I have a smile on my face.

W   Right, and are you, do you think you're in a carefree mood or a thoughtful mood?

M   I would edge towards carefree, but …

W   Right.

M   … that sounds a bit lacksadaisical, but no I do, I'm not feeling terribly pensive or thoughtful.

W   OK.

M   And …

W   And well obviously if you're in a good mood, you're probably feeling optimistic.

M   I am …

W   Yeah.

M   No definitely feeling optimistic. It's it's the middle of the week, there's lots of things happening. It's good.

W   Good.

- Students check their answers in pairs.
- Play the recording again if necessary.

Glossary

---

lackadaisical – not showing enough care and attention. (The speaker adds a redundant 's' to this word.)

1	strong, self-centred, dependable
2	excitable, easy-going, cautious
3	timid, sunny, agreeable
4	good, carefree, optimistic

c   Outline the task briefly and set a time limit for individuals to answer the questions.

- Put students in pairs to discuss and compare their answers.

d   Ask students to draw themselves a table with two columns: **Adjectives** and **Nouns**, and to write the asterisked adjectives in the adjectives column.

- In their pairs, they try and work out the related nouns.

Adjectives	Nouns
strong	strength
weak	weakness
independent	independence
self-centred	self-centredness
calm	calm / calmness
excitable	excitement / excitability
cautious	caution
assertive	assertion / assertiveness
timid	timidity
moody	mood / moodiness
thoughtful	thought / thoughtfulness
optimistic	optimism
pessimistic	pessimism

e   This task will work best if your students know most of the adjectives here so encourage them to use dictionaries. Alternatively, select just a few adjectives for them to work on in the way suggested.

- Ask students to do this together in pairs. It is probably a good idea for them to draw up three columns in their notebooks and record the adjectives under the headings *positive*, *negative*, and *neutral*. They may want another column *it depends*.

Note

Differences of opinion are a good thing! They provoke discussion, which helps the language become more memorable.

Possible answers

affectionate – positive
aggressive – usually negative, though when someone is described as being an 'aggressive defender of human rights' for example, this may be seen as a more positive attribute.
ambitious – may be positive or negative depending on context and culture
determined – positive
emotional – often negative, carrying the suggestion of not being in control; sometimes positive, meaning not afraid to show one's feelings
energetic – positive
frank – generally positive
hypocritical – negative
logical – neutral
loyal – positive
malicious – negative
modest – positive, though sometimes slightly negative, e.g. *a modest salary, of modest ability*
narrow-minded – negative
obstinate – negative
possessive – negative
practical – neutral
protective – positive; *over-protective* is negative
rational – generally positive
reserved – neutral
selfish – negative
sensitive – can be positive or negative
truthful – positive

2 a Ask students to do this individually or in pairs, but to check their answers in pairs.

• Then check answers with the whole class.

affect = verb
effect = noun
open to = willing to accept an idea / suggestion
prone to = likely to do something, usually negative, e.g. *prone to accidents*. Note also *accident-prone*.
mood = the frame of mind you are in, may be good or bad
temper = bad mood, often sudden and quick

b Ask students to do this individually first before comparing answers in pairs.

• Check answers with the whole class.

1 effect (*effect* is a noun / *affect* is a verb)
2 prone (note that this is followed by the preposition *to*)
3 swings (*mood swings* collocate, *mood turns* do not)
4 keep (you *keep your temper* but *hold your tongue*)
5 temper (the opposite of *keep your temper* – you could say *Jack was in a terrible mood*, but not that he *lost his mood*)
6 restrain (*restrain* is *to hold back*, *constrain* is *to confine* and is more commonly used in the passive: *He was constrained by the four walls of his room.*)
7 regain (He might *reclaim his lost suitcase*, but not *his composure*)
8 composure (*to regain composure* collocates; otherwise you could say *He was calm again* / *He became calm again* / *His calmness returned*)

3 a Outline the task briefly. Students could make notes under the three headings: *colleague*, *holiday companion*, *friend* and attribute five qualities to each.

• Give students enough time to think about this quietly on their own before sharing ideas with their partner.

b Ask students to discuss their answers with another pair (i.e. in groups of four), to see how much overlap / difference there is in their ideas.

• You could round up the lesson with a group feedback.

Complete *Time Magazine* list:

Albert Einstein: Person of the Century

He was the iconic 20th-century scientist, the bumbling professor with the German accent, a comic cliché in a thousand films. Instantly recognizable, like Charlie Chaplin's Little Tramp, Albert Einstein's shaggy haired visage was as familiar to ordinary people as to the matrons who fluttered about him in salons from Berlin to Hollywood. Yet he was unfathomably profound – the genius among geniuses who discovered, merely by thinking about it, that the universe was not as it seemed.

Leaders and Revolutionaries

Theodore Roosevelt; Vladimir Ilyich Lenin; Margaret Sanger; Mao Zedong; Winston Churchill; Franklin Delano Roosevelt; Eleanor Roosevelt; Adolf Hitler; Mohandas Gandhi; David Ben-Gurion Ho Chi Minh; Martin Luther King; Ayatullah Ruhollah Khomeini; Margaret Thatcher; Lech Walesa; Ronald Reagan; Mikhail Gorbachev; Pope John Paul II; The Unknown Rebel; Nelson Mandela

Artists and Entertainers

Pablo Picasso; Martha Graham; Le Corbusier; Igor Stravinsky; Coco Chanel; James Joyce; T.S. Eliot; Louis Armstrong; Charlie Chaplin; Marlon Brando; Rodgers & Hammerstein; Frank Sinatra; Lucille Ball; The Beatles; Bob Dylan; Aretha Franklin; Jim Henson; Steven Spielberg; Bart Simpson; Oprah Winfrey

Builders and Titans

Henry Ford; David Sarnoff; Charles Merrill; Willis Carrier; Lucky Luciano; William Levitt; Leo Burnett; Ray Kroc; Pete Rozelle; Sam Walton; Louis B. Mayer; Amadeo Giannini; Stephen Bechtel; Walt Disney; Juan Trippe; Walter Reuther; Thomas Watson, Jr.; Estee Lauder; Akio Morita; Bill Gates

Scientists and Thinkers

Sigmund Freud; Leo Baekeland; Wilbur & Orville Wright; Albert Einstein; Alexander Fleming; Robert Goddard; Jonas Salk; Edwin Hubble; Ludwig Wittgenstein; Jean Piaget; Enrico Fermi; Louis, Mary & Richard Leakey; Philo Farnsworth; Kurt Gödel; Rachel Carson; William Shockley; Alan Turing; John Maynard Keynes; James Watson & Francis Crick; Tim Berners-Lee

Heroes and Icons

Emmeline Pankhurst; Helen Keller; Charles Lindbergh; Bill Wilson; The American G.I.; Jackie Robinson; Anne Frank; Billy Graham; Edmund Hillary & Tenzing Norgay; Rosa Parks; Che Guevara; Marilyn Monroe; The Kennedys; Muhammad Ali; Bruce Lee; Pelé; Harvey Milk; Mother Teresa; Diana, Princess of Wales; Andrei Sakharov

2 Infernal machines

Theme: the relationship between people and machines

2.1 Computers and cars

A humorous comparison of computers and cars

- **Reading:** intensive – gap-filling
- **Language focus:** the conditional – *if* sentences
- **Speaking:** discussion – making future predictions

2.2 Computers and you

People talk about the role of computers in their lives

- **Listening:** gist and specific information
- **Vocabulary:** *make* and *do*
- **Language focus:** emphasis
- **Speaking:** arguing for and against

Exploring words

Computers and computing

Workbook

- **Language focus:** the conditional; emphasis
- **Vocabulary focus:** *make* and *do*
- **Vocabulary expansion:** formal and informal language
- **Listening:** a short story

2.1 Computers and cars   p.14

Stage 1 revises conditionals within the context of comparing cars and computers.

Lead in

Aim *To get the students interested in the theme of the lesson by means of a personalized speaking activity involving categorizing.*

- Check that students know the words for the items in the photographs.
- Discuss the first photograph as a class to get the students started, then ask them to do the task in pairs.
- Conduct a whole-class feedback. Ask the students to justify their ideas.

Reading

Aim *To provide practice of intensive reading.*

The students have to read the text closely to insert phrases into the appropriate spaces. It also previews, and creates a context for, the use of conditionals.

1 Start this part of the lesson by asking the students to read the title and introductory paragraph of the reading text. Ask them one or two open questions in feedback: *Do you think computers are reliable? Which are more reliable – cars or computers?*

Note

Bill Gates is the founder of *Microsoft*, the world's biggest computer software company, and *General Motors* is the largest car producer in the United States.

- Write these words on the board and ask students to work in pairs to put them into two groups: **car words** and **computer words**. Some words can go in both groups.

  airbags / battery / carburettor / crash / disk drive / engine / hard drive / headlights / keyboard / monitor / mouse / warning lights / windows / windscreen wiper / mirror

Glossary

carburettor – the apparatus in an engine that mixes fuel and air.

Car words:
airbags / battery / carburettor / crash / engine / headlights / warning lights / windows / windscreen wiper / mirror
Computer words:
battery / crash / disk drive / (search) engine / hard drive / keyboard / monitor / mouse / warning lights / windows

- Tell the students they are going to make a list of possible computer faults. Elicit one or two examples, then put the students in pairs to make their lists. You could do this activity as a pyramid discussion: the students make a list in pairs, then add to their list by comparing with another pair in a group of four. Finally, pull all their ideas together by writing a class list on the board.

> **Possible computer faults:**
> crash / lose work / disk gets stuck / can't connect to Internet / will not print / everything freezes / cursor disappears / get a virus / can't open a file

2 With the whole class read through the first point in the text comparing cars with computers. Ask students to look at the list of sentence completions a to j, and elicit the correct completion of the first point (*b*).

- Ask the students what clues helped them work out the answer. For example, the grammatical clue is that *would* is followed by an infinitive without *to*, so only a, b, d, f, and i are grammatically possible.

- Ask the students to work individually to read the text and complete the sentences. Let them check their answers with a partner before conducting a whole class feedback.

> **1** b **2** i **3** g **4** d **5** h **6** f **7** c **8** e
> **9** j **10** a

Close up

- Put students in pairs to do the exercise. Encourage them to make guesses from context rather than rely on their dictionaries.

- Monitor closely to see what problems they have, but don't tell them the answers before the whole-class feedback at the end.

> **1.14** *manoeuvre* is of French origin and is pronounced /mənuːvə/; *army manoeuvres* are large-scale exercises by armed forces.
> **1.26** *such as* is followed by a noun. Other similar expressions: *like / for example / for instance*
> **1.28** IBM / Time / Macintosh, etc.
> *make* is used to describe cars.

Language focus: the conditional   p.15

Aim *To review and practise first, second, third (past), and mixed conditionals.*

This area of grammar is probably not new for the students. Consequently, the focus of the exercises is to activate the students' knowledge by getting them to match rules to examples, and to encourage them to think about why they might choose to use different conditional forms. It also checks their ability to use alternative conjunctions to *if*.

Difficulties at this level may still include problems with the complex form, in particular using *will* and *would* after *if*, for example, **If I will / would have enough money, I will / would go on holiday.* The pronunciation of *I'll* /aɪl/ and *I'd* /aɪd/ may be difficult for some students. However, the main problem is

likely to be a confusion as to whether a conditional is possible or improbable. Point out that this is often dependent on the point of view of the speaker. After doing exercise 3, you could compare two sentences on the board:

> *If I get a new computer, I'll give you my old one.*
> *If I got a new computer, I'd give you my old one.*

Ask the students to tell you in which context they might use each sentence. A possible answer is that in the first the context might be that he/she is planning or saving up to buy a new computer, whereas in the second he/she has no plans to change. Make sure you watch out for errors with these two forms in the exploitation section.

1 Complete the first sentence as a class, as an example. To focus them on the task, ask them why the second conditional form is used here.

> **a** was; would regularly stop
> The answer is that a car is not like a PC, and unlikely ever to be so. Consequently, we use this form to show that the condition is purely hypothetical. There is little or no possibility that it will be fulfilled.

- Put the students in pairs to complete the other sentence, then let them check their answers by looking back at the article.

> **b** fitted; might not work

2 Ask the students to complete this task in pairs.

- Check as a class. You may wish to refer the students to the Language commentary on p.19.

> **a** Second conditional
> **b** C something unreal or hypothetical
> The whole article is based on the first idea: *If a car was really like a PC ...* Of course, a car is not really like a PC.

3 Ask the students to complete this task individually, then check their answers in pairs.

- Check answers with the whole class.

> **a** B **b** A **c** C **d** D

- At this stage, if you think your students need reminding, you may wish to check the form here:

> **a** Past perfect form / *would+have+*past participle
> **b** Present simple form / *will+*infinitive
> **c** Past simple form / *would+*infinitive
> **d** Past simple form / *would+*infinitive

Note

Tense and time are not the same thing here. The past form is used to refer to something hypothetical about the present or future, not the past. The past perfect form is used to refer to something hypothetical about the past.

4 Ask the students to complete this task individually, then check in pairs.

- Check answers with the whole class.

5 Do the first as an example, then ask the students to complete the task in pairs.

- Check as a class. You may wish to refer the students to the Language commentary on p.19.

Note

Unless may cause a problem. It generally means *except if*, and cannot always replace *if ... not*. Compare these examples:
> *If the weather **isn't** sunny, we'll stay at home.*
> ***Unless** the weather is sunny, we'll stay at home.*
In other words, *we'll stay at home **except if** it's sunny*.
> *If the weather **isn't** sunny, I'll be really surprised.*
> ****Unless** the weather is sunny, I'll be really surprised.*
In other words, *I'll be surprised **in the situation that** it isn't sunny.*
Here, *if ... not* does not mean *except if*, so cannot be replaced by *unless*.

Exploitation

Aim *To test the students' ability to use the grammar accurately and fluently. They have to use their imagination, personalize the language, and think up appropriate vocabulary to use.*

1 Ask the students to complete the sentences, and compare them with a partner. They could correct each other's errors at this stage.

- In the feedback, ask one or two students to give you an example for each sentence.

Possible answers
a ... you'd better start working harder.
b ... if I had checked the car brakes.
c ... I could get out and see my friends. / I hadn't broken my leg.
d ... we wouldn't be having to ask you so many questions now.
e ... we're going to go on strike.
f ... you fill it up with petrol.
g ... you let me use it from time to time.

2 Start with a class brainstorm to generate ideas, for example:

- If children were like computers, they would remember everything / they would do what we told them / we could switch them off.

- If the government was like a computer, it would send us lots of junk mail / you could switch it off after four years.

- If planes were like computers, they would fly you to your destination at the press of a button, but you would have to wait in an in-box for ages before someone opened it and let you out.

- Then put the students in pairs or small groups to do the activity. Monitor, prompt, and note down any errors the students make as they speak to each other.

- Do a whole-class feedback, eliciting and encouraging interesting or humorous examples.

- Do an error feedback (if there were any!). Write any errors students made on the board (anonymously). Ask the students to suggest corrections.

Discussion

Aim *To improve the students' ability to express themselves fluently and to practise some of the language from the lesson.*

1 Put the students in groups of three or four to do activity 1.

- Do a brief whole-class feedback. This activity should set the students up to do the next task, which requires more imagination.

2 If your students have difficulty in coming up with ideas, elicit one or two from the class before getting them to continue in their groups.

- Monitor and help with ideas.

- Students express their ideas as newspaper headlines.

2.2 Computers and you p.16

Stage 2 uses the context of people describing their relationships with computers to contextualize the way we use emphasis in natural speech.

Lead in

Aim *To get the students talking about computers by means of a personalized speaking activity involving a questionnaire.*

- Ask the students to complete both parts of the questionnaire individually, then put them in pairs or groups to compare their answers.

- Do a whole-class feedback.

- Alternatively, do the second part of the questionnaire as a mingle. Ask the students first to complete it individually, then circulate and ask all the other students in the class which things they use a computer for. They could ask follow-up questions, for example: *What sort of work do you do on the computer?* Once they have finished, you could ask students to work in pairs to briefly tabulate their findings, and then present them as percentages, for example, *80% of the class use computers at work.*

Listening

Aim *To listen first for gist, and then for specific information.*

- If you wish, you could do exercises **1** and **2** of *Exploring words* (p.18) as a lead-in or follow-up to the listening activity.

Glossary

Word – word-processing package

1 Focus the students on the task and play the recording.

2.1

Speaker 1 Erm computers really equal work in my mind, erm. That's not to say I don't like them. I do. I love, love using them and I can't believe the sort of progress I personally have made in my use of it in the last, well, two years, since working here. Erm, I would like one at home in some ways, I mean, mainly just as an information source, rather than having to make phone calls all the time – I'd much rather be on e-mail or the Internet, erm – I really like using the Internet actually and would like to do it more erm. I wonder what else I'd use it for if I had one at home. I probably would end up working at home which is not a good thing in my mind – so not in that sense erm, but yeah, I'm not really into computer games or anything like that, but I guess I could be converted.

Speaker 2 Computers – incredibly important for work erm – where I just completely take them for granted – if one went wrong I wouldn't know what to do with it at all erm, but basically I just use it as a sort of glorified typewriter and for sending e-mails to friends erm and I have got a computer at home which probably hasn't been turned on, I would guess for at least a year now erm and is under a blanket.

Speaker 3 I suppose the, most of the contact I have with computers is at work. Erm and they are vital for for the kind of work I do – erm communication between different people via e-mail, erm writing up documents erm and researching on the Internet – I suppose these are, are the main uses. I really only use Word erm when I'm creating a document myself because I'm not, I'm not a computer wizard. Erm at home I do have a computer but I use it very little erm, I suppose erm the most it's used for at home is is games and I'm not very good at them, so so I don't play.

Speaker 4 Computers are very important to me, cos I couldn't do my job without one really – I'm a designer and I basically sit in front of a computer for most of my working day and then I haven't got my own computer at home but my housemates do and I have used them at home as well, so my life is erm pretty much revolving round computers some of the time but I could live without one and erm maybe I quite appreciate living without one some of the time.

Speaker 5 I'm not sure how important computers are to me really. I think I need to use one at work but only really for for word-processing. I tend not to use one at home although we've got one. E-mail clearly is a very important part of what you can do with a computer at the moment and I must say that I think it's a wonderful invention, but if we didn't have e-mail then I'm sure I'd go back to communicating in the ways we used to and in fact I think in a way it would almost be good if if I did and chose to write letters to people and telephone people rather than rely on e-mail which is very easy in a way – it's it's a very good thing to have but it also makes you fairly lazy, I think.

Speaker 1
Where? work
Why? Internet
Speaker 2
Where? work
Why? word-processing / e-mail
Speaker 3
Where? work
Why? e-mail / word processing
Where? home
Why? games
Speaker 4
Where? work
Why? design tasks
Speaker 5
Where? work
Why? word-processing / e-mail

2 Read through the phrases with the students and check vocabulary. Then play the recording again.

a Speaker 4   **b** Speaker 3   **c** Speaker 2   **d** Speaker 5
e Speaker 1

- You could follow up this task by asking the students if any of the speakers has a similar experience to themselves of using computers.

Exploring natural speech

Aim *To practise* I suppose *in natural speech.*

1 Ask the students to look at the examples and discuss the question in pairs.

> *I suppose* has a similar meaning to *I believe* or *I imagine*. It is used frequently here as a filler, partly to give the speaker thinking time, and partly to signal to the listener that the speaker is thinking up her ideas and opinions as she goes along. She isn't sure about what she is saying – it's just what she thinks.

2 Play the recording for the students to listen and repeat for pronunciation. *Suppose* is pronounced /səˈpəʊz/ with a weak 'schwa' sound on the first syllable and strong stress on the second syllable. (This is not included in the tapescript section of the Student's Book.)

2.2

a I suppose most of the contact I have with computers is at work.

b I suppose these are, are the main uses.

c Erm I suppose erm the most it's used for at home is – is games.

3 Model the activity with a strong student, then put the students in pairs to practise.

- Monitor and correct errors in use and pronunciation.

> This activity requires the students' own answers, but they should start their answers like this:
> **a** I suppose I mostly use it for …
> **b** I suppose I send about … e-mails a day.
> **c** I suppose I like … / The aspects I like are …

React and discuss

- You could do this as a whole-class discussion, or in small groups with a whole-class feedback at the end.

Vocabulary: *make* and *do*

Aim *To practise the use of* make *and* do.

Make and *do* are confusing for students of many nationalities because their use is often contrary to the use in their first language or can be translated with one verb. If you have a monolingual class, try to make a list of examples of your students' common errors before the class. Or you could start the lesson by eliciting confusions that the students are aware of.

- Read through the rules with the students as a class.

a Put the students in pairs to complete the extracts.

> **1** made **2** make **3** do **4** do

b Students make their lists individually, then compare with their partner. Elicit the students' collocations and list them on the board.

> **Some common expressions**
> *make:* an offer, an excuse, money, sure, fun of, a decision, the most of, room for, a go of (something), certain, a discovery, a suggestion, a choice, an effort, an enquiry, a bed
> *do:* an exam, (someone) a favour, damage, (your) best, (your) duty, business, good, housework, nothing

▶ If your students need more practice with *make* and *do*, there is an extra gap-fill exercise on p.140 which can be done in class, or for homework.

Language focus: emphasis   p.17

Aim *To make the students aware of how spoken English uses extra auxiliary verbs, adverbs, word order, and specific emphatic words and phrases to emphasize ideas.*

The main problem at this level is that students are simply unused to manipulating grammar, particularly auxiliary verbs, to express emphasis in English. It requires a certain feel and confidence in English to do this. So be aware that this may seem strange to students and difficult to do. The approach here is very much one of finding out how it works. Don't expect too much fluency from students. There is further practice in later units.

Auxiliary verbs for emphasis in English are particularly difficult because we use such a range, and students have to work out whether it is *am, do, did, have, will, would, could*, etc. If you have a monolingual class, reflect on how auxiliaries are or are not used for emphasis in the students' own language. In certain languages, auxiliaries are not used in this way.

1 Start with books closed. Write the word *emphasis* on the board, and ask the students to give you different ways that we use to emphasize ideas when we are speaking.

- Check the students understand the ways listed in exercise **1** by asking for an example of each.
- Put the students in pairs, and ask them to listen to and read the extracts, and underline any examples of emphasis. (This does not appear in the tapescript section of the Student's Book.)

> **2.3**
>
> a Computers really equal work in my mind, erm. That's not to say I don't like them. I do.
>
> b They really frustrate me, computers do.
>
> c Computers – incredibly important for work erm – if one went wrong, I wouldn't know what to do with it at all erm, …
>
> d E-mail clearly is a very important part of what you can do with a computer at the moment and I must say that I think it's a wonderful invention, but …
>
> e He hasn't got a clue about what to do if his computer crashes, Paul hasn't.
>
> f You always accuse me of not answering your e-mails. I do reply to them – eventually.

- Do a whole-class feedback. Refer the students to the Language commentary on p.19.

> a *really* = adverb; *I do* = extra auxiliary verb
> b *really* = adverb; *computers do* (at end) = word order; also the auxiliary verb *do*
> c *incredibly* = adverb; *at all* = emphatic phrase
> d *clearly* = adverb; *I must say* = emphatic phrase
> e *Paul hasn't* = word order
> f *I do reply* = extra auxiliary verb

2 Do the first as an example, then put the students in pairs to do this exercise.

> a not / enjoy / do   d fair / do
> b amazes   e expect / listening / have
> c say / brilliant   f always / accusing / listening / say / do

3 Play the recording for the students to check their answers. Then students take it in turns to practise saying the sentences with their partners. Alternatively, play the recording again, and pause it after each phrase for the students to repeat. (This does not appear in the tapescript section of the Student's Book.)

> **2.4**
>
> a That's not to say I don't enjoy driving. I do.
>
> b It really amazes me, the Internet does.
>
> c I must say I think they're brilliant, the latest computer games.
>
> d That's not fair – I do work hard.
>
> e I expect you think I haven't been listening. Well I have.
>
> f You're always accusing me of not listening to what you say. I do listen.

Exploitation

Aim *To practise grammatical ways of emphasizing.*

It is difficult for students to integrate these grammatical ways of emphasizing into their speech. Consequently, the activities in this section are quite guided and accuracy-focused, and expect students to come up with language from prompts. Give the students plenty of preparation time here.

1 Put the students in pairs to prepare and write responses in each conversation. Monitor and help with ideas and corrections.

- When they have finished, give the students time to practise their conversations in pairs, taking it in turns to be **A** and **B**.

- Ask some pairs to act out one or two conversations for the class. Ask the other students whether they have emphasized the auxiliary verbs correctly.

> **Possible answers**
> b I do (put petrol in the car occasionally).
> c I do. I really like them.
> d I did (remind you) but you weren't listening.
> e I would.
> f (Well) I am (hungry).

2 Do one as an example, then put the students in pairs or threes to prepare this exercise.

- Get some students to say the sentences with different stress for the class to comment on.

> **Possible answers**
> a You must be joking. / You are joking, aren't you?
> b It really is true. / You may think it isn't true, but it is.
> c They're brilliant, computers are. / Computers are really brilliant, they are.
> d I do understand, really. / I really do understand.
> e I really do think it was difficult, and you agree with me, I know you do.

Speaking

Aim *To get the students using the functional language of arguing for and against, and using emphasis, in a group discussion.*

If you wish, you could do exercises 3–5 of *Exploring words* (SB p.18) before this speaking activity.

1 Make sure students understand the instructions. Set a time limit for them to prepare their arguments individually. Monitor and help with ideas.

- Give students time to think about how to present their ideas, using the expressions in the box.

2 Students present their ideas to their group. Set a time limit for this, and also for any discussion which follows. Monitor and listen for errors.

3 After groups have voted, you may wish to do an error feedback on the board, focusing on how students used the expressions in the box and emphasis in their arguments.

- Here is an alternative way of organizing this activity, which should work well if you have a vocal class with strong opinions:

- If your class is not too big, put the statement on the board and ask which students agree or disagree with it.

- If you get a fairly even split, put the students in groups of four. Each group has to prepare a persuasive argument *for* or *against*, depending on the group's point of view. (If you don't get an even split, you may need to persuade one or two

students to change their allegiance, from *for* to *against*, or vice versa.)

- Monitor and help with ideas as above.

- Split the class so that two from a *for* group join two from an *against* group. This results in more interaction and a more realistic opinion gap for this activity.

- Monitor the activity and do an error feedback as above.

Exploring words p.18

Aim *To expand the students' vocabulary around the topic of computers.*

This lesson could be worked through as a whole. It does, however, split easily into two parts, each of which could be incorporated into the main part of the unit. Exercises 1 and 2 could be used as a lead-in or follow-up to the listening activity in Stage 2. Exercises 3 to 5 could be done before the speaking activity at the end of Stage 2 to make a reading / vocabulary / speaking lesson. Exercises 1 and 4 could be set as homework.

1 Ask the students to complete the sentences.

> a send; e-mail
> b surf; Web or Internet
> c websites; visit
> d sit; terminal; log on; Internet
> e join or visit; chat room
> f back up; files

2 Put the students in pairs to discuss the questions. Monitor and check they are using the appropriate collocations from exercise 1. These are deliberately avoided in the questions.

3 Use the opening question to encourage a brief discussion. If your students have experience of using e-mail at work, ask about their company's policy or any personal experiences.

- Set the gist question, and ask the students to read the passage.

4 Focus on the example then ask the students to match the words.

> a derogatory / insulting / complimentary
> b private / confidential / public
> c informal / casual / formal
> d speedy / rapid / slow
> e inappropriate / improper / fitting
> f scandalous / outrageous / inoffensive
> g complicated / complex / simple
> h legitimate / official / unlawful

5 Put the students in groups to discuss the questions. Monitor and encourage them to use the vocabulary from this lesson.

Theme: questions with no clear answer

3.1 Caught in the rain

Is it better to walk or run when it rains?

- **Listening:** context-setting
- **Reading:** intensive for gap-filling and specific information
- **Language focus:** *wish*

3.2 Time travel

People talk about where they would go if they could travel in time

- **Listening:** context-setting and specific information
- **Exploring natural speech:** contractions
- **Language focus:** speculating and imagining (*would, might, could, Imagine, Suppose,* etc.)
- **Speaking:** role play interview
- **Writing:** a formal letter

3.3 Saving a language

Can dying languages be saved?

- **Vocabulary:** words to describe language (*dialect, mother tongue*)
- **Reading:** matching and specific information
- **Vocabulary:** adjective–noun collocations
- **Speaking:** role play

Exploring words

Crime and punishment

Workbook

- **Language focus:** *wish*; *if only*; other ways of expressing wishes; speculating and imagining
- **Vocabulary focus:** noun–adjective collocations
- **Vocabulary expansion:** adjectives to describe size; collocations – noun + *of* + noun, *hot* and *cold*, etc.
- **Listening:** rain

3.1 Caught in the rain   p.20

Stage 1 introduces the first 'open question', and provides an initial context for the *Language focus* (*wish*).

Lead in

Aim *To introduce the topic and prepare for the reading and Language focus.*

1 You could do this with books closed. Write the words *damp*, *soaked*, and *wet* up on the board and ask students to order them, either as a whole class, or in pairs.

- You could add these words / expressions to the lists if you think your class can cope with more vocabulary.

  saturated, wet through, soaked to the skin, drenched dash, walk briskly, dawdle, sprint

  a damp / wet / soaked / drenched / saturated / wet through / soaked to the skin
  b dawdle / stroll / walk / walk briskly / run / dash / sprint

2 Have a brief whole-class discussion on this question. The listening and reading explore this in depth; use this opportunity to set the scene.

3 Outline the task briefly.

- Play the recording.

3.1

W   Oh I know I got absolutely soaked – I wish I'd brought my umbrella – I can't believe it, but I …

M1 Oh – what this morning?

W   Yeah yeah – but it occurred to me actually – cos I was running down the street to try and get into the office and erm, as I say, I arrived drenched but erm someone said to me – when I got into the office – was saying oh well, you know, I mean you don't achieve anything more by by running cos you're still going to get just as wet …

M2 Yes.

M1 Well it's about a ten-minute walk isn't it, so …

W   Well, no no, that's not the …

M1 … by running you'll do it in five, so you're not going to achieve anything – you're still going to be wet.

M2 Yeah.

W   Yeah, but no the idea that, you know, you're by running in it you're, you're still – as much rain is falling on you as if you were walking – mind you it would have gone totally against the grain just to have strolled down the road.

- Ask students to check their answers together.

- Play the recording again if necessary.

> a She forgot her umbrella, so she ran to her office to try to avoid getting too wet.
> b No definite answer is given in the conversation. Obviously, the woman speaker thought she would get less wet by running, but a colleague at work told her it didn't make any difference whether she ran or walked.

4 Ask students to do this in pairs.

- If necessary, play the recording again so that they can hear the relevant sections.

> a I suddenly realized
> b but

▶ There is an extra activity practising the phrases on p.141.

Reading

Aim *To give students practice at reading a text intensively at word, sentence, and paragraph level.*

1 a Read the instructions and ask students to work individually or in pairs. If individually, ask them to check their answers in pairs.

- Conduct a whole-class feedback.

> Weather / rain / problem / downpour / walk / run

b Brainstorm ideas from the whole class. Put them into pairs to discuss their answers.

- Ask for ideas from the whole class but don't say whether they are right or not. They will find out when they read the article.

2 Give students time to read the article quietly on their own.

- When most are ready ask them to check with their partner whether their predictions were right.

3 Ask students to do this individually, then compare their answers in pairs. Conduct a brief whole-class feedback.

> a False. You get just as wet if you run as if you walk.
> b False. It falls directly onto the top surface (head and shoulders) and then you also run into it with the front of your body.
> c True. They used 'idealized cuboid people'.
> d True. If we were caught in a terrible storm, it would be a good idea to make a dash for it.
> e False. Scientists are 'baffled' by why most people prefer to run.

4 Put the students into pairs.

- Outline the task briefly, making sure students know they should prepare clear explanations in their pairs first, (writing brief notes if they want to), before trying to explain these to another pair.

- Monitor and help as necessary.

- When they are ready, ask the pairs to team up and work in groups of four.

- The pairs read their explanations to each other and decide which is clearer.

- You could then conduct a whole-class feedback to find the best answer, deciding as you are going through why one answer / word / phrase is better than another.

> **Possible answers**
> a It is pointless to run in the rain because you get just as wet running as you do walking. This is because you get wetter from the raindrops in front of you, than you do from the raindrops that fall on your head.
> b The scientists used idealized cuboid people because it was easier to calculate the differences between the top and the front surfaces of a cube than to use real people.

Language focus: *wish*   p.21

Aim *To develop students' existing knowledge of* wish *and explore alternative structures.*

Students will have come across *wish* before but may not be familiar with some of the alternative uses and constructions. This section includes the easier uses (*I wish I was ten years younger, I wish I had brought my umbrella*) but also more complicated uses (*I wish you wouldn't smoke, I wish the weather would improve*). It also focuses on alternative phrases for expressing wishes (*If only ... , It's a pity ... *).

1 Outline the task briefly. Give the students time to work through this on their own before asking them to compare their answers in pairs.

- Go through the answers with the whole class, clarifying as necessary.

- Refer the students to the Language commentary on p.27 for further explanations and examples.

> a regretting something that happened or didn't happen in the past
> b desiring a change in the present situation
> c expressing an impossible fantasy
> d criticizing another person's actions or showing you are annoyed with them
> e hoping for something in the future

2 Ask the students to do this in pairs.

- Monitor and help as necessary. Encourage the students to think of at least three alternatives for each sentence. As you monitor, draw their attention to the different grammatical structures needed with the different phrases.

- Elicit answers from the whole class. Write these up on the board or an OHT so that everyone is quite clear about the correct structures to use. This is time-consuming but picks up on typical mistakes such as **If only I brought my umbrella. *I regret I didn't ...*

Sample answers

a I'm sorry I didn't bring my umbrella.
  If only I'd brought my umbrella.
  Unfortunately I didn't bring my umbrella.
  I regret not bringing my umbrella.
  It's a pity I didn't bring my umbrella.

b I'm sorry it's raining.
  I'd really like it to stop raining.
  If only it wasn't raining. / If only it would stop raining.
  Why won't it stop raining?
  Unfortunately it's raining.
  It's a pity it's raining.

c I'm sorry I'm not ten years younger.
  I'd really like to be ten years younger.
  If only I was / were ten years younger.
  Unfortunately I'm not ten years younger.
  It's a pity I'm not ten years younger.

d I'd really like you not to smoke in here.
  Please don't smoke in here.
  I'd be grateful if you didn't smoke in here.

e I really hope the weather improves.
  I'd really like the weather to improve.
  If only the weather would improve.

Exploitation

1 Ask students to do this in pairs.

• Monitor, drawing attention to the grammatical structure following *wish*.

• Conduct a brief whole-class feedback.

a I wish I could stop smoking.
b I wish you were coming with us. / I wish you would come with us. (This suggests that the other person is able to do so but is choosing not to. 'I *wish* you **could** come with us' suggests that the other person is not able to do so.)
c I wish you would stop telling me what to do.
d I wish I'd brought my camera.
e I wish I was / were young again.

Note

Point out the *was / were* choice. Both are correct nowadays. Some people always use *were* with *I*, and *was* with the other persons (*I wish I were young again. I wish he was here.* Remind students of *If I were you, …*)

2 Outline the task briefly.

• Give the students a few minutes to think quietly about the five areas before putting them into small groups to compare and discuss.

• Monitor, but unobtrusively, joining in the discussions if appropriate but not correcting the grammar.

• Make notes of mistakes made and conduct an error feedback on the board if this seems appropriate or useful.

Personal answers

This stage includes two listenings which contextualize the language of speculating and imagining.

Lead in

Aim *To introduce the topic of time travel.*

Set a time limit for students to discuss the question. If they need prompts, ask them to think of science-fiction films (e.g. *Star Trek*) they know.

Listening

Aim *To build confidence in listening to authentic speech for specific information.*

1 a Ask the students to look at the pictures.

• Spend a few minutes letting the class discuss what / where these places are.

• Outline the listening task and play the recording.

3.2

Speaker 1 First of all, I'd like to go back to around the turn of the century, 1900 I'm thinking – 1899–1900 in England cos I'd really like to see what it was like before the First World War, before things really started to go wrong.

Speaker 2 I'm very curious about the very very early time of the sort of the beginnings of humans when we first came down from the trees, if if that's how we started, so I'd be very curious to see what … how we lived …

Speaker 3 Perhaps the time of the the pharaohs in a in a sort of Egyptian – yes I I quite fancy the idea of being an Egyptian.

Speaker 4 I think I would go back to the time of Jesus, I think – first century Palestine …

Speaker 5 Erm, I dunno, I think the Renaissance would just be absolutely amazing – to go to Florence and sort of walk through those narrow streets and see the workshops, hear hear the noise of people working on these huge canvases and furniture and stuff, I think that would be great.

• Ask students to compare answers in pairs. It probably won't be necessary to do a whole-class feedback as it is quite a straightforward task.

a Speaker 1 Victorian England / England at the turn of the century
  Speaker 2 The time of very primitive humans
  Speaker 3 The time of the Egyptian pharaohs
  Speaker 4 The time of Jesus / first century Palestine
  Speaker 5 Renaissance Florence

b Ask the students to work in pairs and try to remember any reason the speakers gave for their choices. Allow the students some time to think about this – they often remember more than they think they do!

• Play the recording again and let them check together.

b Speaker 1	wants to see what England was like before the First World War / before things started to go wrong	
Speaker 2	wants to see how people lived	
Speaker 3	likes the idea of being an Egyptian	
Speaker 4	no reason given	
Speaker 5	wants to see workshops / hear noises of people working / see huge paintings, furniture, etc.	

2 Check students understand the task, then ask them to do this in pairs.

- Check the answers with the whole class. Clarify / explain meaning and use as necessary.

a	3 e.g. We need to *lay down* the basic structures first.
b	6 e.g. Before we start, let's agree on the *ground rules.*
c	5 e.g. Don't *make* any *bets* – it won't happen.
d	1 e.g. It's a *fly-on-the-wall* documentary about families.
e	4 e.g. The field was covered in cow and sheep *dung.*
f	2 e.g. He finds it difficult to *interact* with children.

Glossary

a fly on the wall – present but invisible

3 Give students a few minutes to look through the questions on their own.

- Ask them to note down any answers they think they know already.

- Play the recording.

3.3

M1 The problem with making choices about time travel is you have to lay down the ground rule of 'Can I change things?' – (Oh) or do you have to leave everything – tell people not to get on the *Titanic* or yeah, ... (Right, yeah) and can I make bets on, you know, can I sell short on Wall Street just before the Crash? If you can't it's not worth bothering to go back ...

W1 Oh no, but I think it'd be interesting to go back and just sort of be a fly on the wall, cos it's one thing to read it, but it's another thing to actually be there and see it and smell it and (Yeah) taste it, you know.

M1 And yeah, you wouldn't realize like if you went back in time in New York and you're so used to New York now that first of all there's going to be horse dung everywhere, you know and multitudes of flies and it must smell and the the noises the sounds you hear are not horns – it's clip-clop, clip-clop. (Right) Things you don't necessarily think of – you just look at photographs and you don't get that sense of like smell and hearing. (Yeah)

W2 Oh that's true and also on a much more personal level, I would love to go back and see my parents as children – see what their lives were like – see how they interacted with their family.

W2 That's a scary thought to me.

M1 No, that's too personal, I wanna go back and look at strangers at a time before anybody I know existed.

M2 I think it might be more fun to project a thousand years into the future.

W1 You would, you'd want to go ahead?

M2 Yeah because we have books and movies to ... you know and now the Internet is like a library in in your home, you know to to explore the past, but er (To go into the future) the absolute unknowable ...

W1 What would it be like to come back? You know to go somewhere and find out – yeah all this stuff to come back – do you think you'd

be able to live in today's world knowing how much it's ... I mean I assume it's going to change a great deal.

M1 Well, if I had no choice – would I want to come back? I don't know till I go into the future.

M2 Yeah, it might be great there. (Yeah)

W1 Or, you know what – it might not exist.

M1 That's the thing that I'd fear, (That's scary) like – or the world ended ten minutes (Yes) before the time I decided to visit.

- Let them think about their answers on their own before checking in pairs.

- Check answers with the whole class.

a	You have to decide whether you are allowed to change things you find in the past. The speaker uses the example of whether someone who travelled back to 1912 would be allowed to advise someone not to travel on the *Titanic*, because the time traveller would know that the ship was going to sink.
b	The transport situation. New York would be full of horses, not cars. There would be horse dung all over the place as well as other accompanying smells and noises.
c	You'd get the smells and noises rather than just knowledge.
d	She'd like to see what her parents were like as children, and how they got on with their own families.
e	We can find out about the past in various ways (films, etc), but the future is unknowable.

React and discuss

Aim *To enable students to discuss and react to what they have heard.*

- Ask the class to do this in small groups.

Exploring natural speech

Aim *To make students aware of contractions (wanna, gonna) in natural speech.*

Native speakers are often unaware, and sometimes unconvinced, that they use these contractions regularly. It will not be surprising if your students feel that such language is 'wrong'. It is not important, or useful, to get into a long debate about the correctness of these contractions, but if the students begin to hear them, then this will help them to understand natural speech.

Note

The words are sometimes written as *dunno, wanna, gotta, gonna, gimme* in informal situations (e-mails, songs, cartoons, etc.).

1 Ask students to discuss this in pairs.

a	dunno
b	wanna
c	gotta; gonna; gimme

2 Ask them to check their answers with the recording, which gives contracted (*dunno, gimme*, etc.) forms as well as uncontracted forms in fast natural speech. The contracted forms are heard first. They (and you) can choose which forms to practise; both are acceptable in normal conversation. (This is not included in the tapescript section of the Student's Book.)

a Erm, I don't know, I think the Renaissance would just be absolutely amazing.

b I want to go back and look at strangers at a time before anybody I know existed.

c A There's a new film at the cinema about time travel – I've just got to see it.

 B Have you decided when you're going to go?

 A No, but if you can give me a lift we could go together.

- Emphasize that practising this pronunciation will also help students to 'hear' the items in context.

▶ There is an extra activity on p.141 which practises colloquial language.

Language focus: speculating and imagining p.23

Aim *To draw students' attention to the different ways of speculating and imagining (would, could, might, Suppose, etc.).*

1 Outline the task briefly. Then ask students to do this individually. Allow them a few minutes to think about it.

- Ask them to check their answers in pairs before they refer to the tapescript on p.141.

a would	c might
b would	d would; might; might

2 Ask the students to do this in pairs.

- Ask them what type of conditional is used in the 'a' sentences (the second conditional: the situation is imaginary). Allow them a few minutes to discuss or argue about the differences before checking with the whole class.

a	*would* – certainty under the condition mentioned – in other words if the other part of the sentence happened (you travelled back in time) then the rest is certain (you *would* discover your family secrets). *might* – possible, not certain even if the condition mentioned happened – in other words even if the travelling back in time were certain, the *might* part (discover your family secrets) is possible but not certain.
b	There is no difference here between *could* and *might*: both are used to express uncertain future possibility.

3 Read through the phrases with the students, pointing out the grammatical features.

- Elicit a few responses to each of the phrases (e.g. *Yeah – it'd be great / I'd hate all that publicity!*). This helps to check that the students really understand how they are used.

- Ask the students to practise these mini-dialogues in pairs. Refer them to the Language commentary on p.27. Monitor and help with the structures as necessary.

Exploitation

Aim *To provide controlled practise of the language of speculation.*

Ask the students to do this individually before checking their answers in pairs. Monitor and help as necessary before conducting a whole-class check.

- You could ask students to practise saying the sentences / phrases to develop their pronunciation. You will need to demonstrate first.

a would	d were; would
b could; would	e would; heard; was going to
c could; had; would	

Speaking

Aim *To develop the students' ability to speak in a semi-formal setting. It is also preparation for the writing task which follows.*

- Divide the class into As and Bs. Ask Students A to look at p.157 and Students B to look at the instructions on this page.

- Put pairs or small groups of As together. Do the same with Bs. Give them time to think through the situation and what they are going to say.

- Now pair up As with Bs (making a group of 3 if you have an odd number) and ask them to conduct the interview.

- Monitor, taking notes if you intend to conduct an error feedback, but don't interrupt.

- You might like to ask one or two pairs to conduct their interview in front of the class.

- Conduct an error feedback if necessary.

Writing

Aim *To give practice in writing a formal letter which needs to make a point.*

1–3 Outline the task. Check that students are clear about the letter writer's motives in writing to the editor of the newspaper. (Their original words have been changed by the unscrupulous journalist.) You might refer to any other situations known to you or the students in which the media has exaggerated or changed the 'facts' of a story.

- Ask the students to discuss and possibly plan their letters in pairs.

- Set the writing activity as a homework task.

- Make sure students refer to the Writing guidelines on p.152 which include a sample formal letter.

This stage includes a rich reading text and has detailed comprehension and discussion work.

Vocabulary

Aim *To stimulate interest in the subject of languages and prepare for the reading.*

- With books closed write up the word *language*.
- Elicit related words from the students and write them up around *language*. Try to elicit the words from the exercise, i.e. *mother tongue, linguist, minority language, native speaker, fluent, dialect, foreign language, second language, accent*.
- Focus students on the exercise and ask them to complete it in pairs.
- Quickly check answers with the whole class.

1	mother tongue	7	classical; dead
2	linguist	8	modern; living
3	minority	9	foreign
4	native	10	second
5	fluent	11	accent
6	dialect		

Reading

Aim *To develop students' ability to read for detail.*

1 Focus students on the questions that precede the text.
- Check that they understand the questions and the task.
- Ask them to read the text. Give the students plenty of quiet time for this. If appropriate to your class, you could set this for homework.
- When most of the class appear to have finished, put them into pairs and give them enough time to discuss their answers before checking briefly with the whole class.

a E	b D	c A	d C	e B

Close up

- Ask the students to do this in pairs. Encourage them to make guesses from context rather than rely on their dictionaries.
- Check answers with the whole class.

1.6	about / approximately
1.15	suicide / homicide / matricide / patricide / infanticide **Note:** insecticide / pesticide / herbicide are words which refer to substances rather than actions, although all are connected with killing.
1.17	inhabit / inhabitant / habitation
1.18	*famine* = severe shortage of food for people often leading to illness or death *drought* = long period when there is little or no rain If there is no rain, crops cannot grow and animals die, so food supply is damaged and famine occurs.
1.43	a *nest* is a warm, protective home in which animals and birds can give birth to and look after their young.
1.50	absolute

2 While you've got the whole class together, ask them question 2. Encourage discussion and debate and ask them to find sections from the text to support their point of view.

> The article is generally positive in outlook (though also realistic, not idealistic). Phrases and sections which show this are:
> **Paragraph C** *But many languages are not in such a serious position.*
> **Paragraph D** *There are some famous cases which illustrate what can be done.*
> *A language can be brought back from the very brink of extinction.*
> *... new government policies brought fresh attitudes and a positive interest in survival.*
> *Several seriously endangered Aboriginal languages of Australia have been maintained and revived.*
> **Paragraph E** *... in some parts of the world* (revived languages) *are attracting ... the range of positive attitudes ... which are the preconditions for language survival.*

3 Ask the students to work in pairs or small groups. Set a realistic time limit and encourage them to provide fairly detailed answers. Monitor and help as necessary.

> a There are only a few speakers of the language left – the language is not being passed on from generation to generation.
> b By destroying small, isolated communities which may be the one remaining place where a particular language is spoken.
> c First of all the community must want to save its language, and funding must be available. There could be courses, teachers, and materials. Linguists could record, analyse, and document the language.
> d Maori – language nests in which young children are intensively exposed to the endangered language, so that they acquire it naturally. They will in turn pass the language on to their children.
> Ainu – Semi-speakers were persuaded to become active speakers again. (Semi-speakers were people who had stopped using Ainu because of the negative attitude of others to their language).
> e In various parts of the world, there are positive attitudes and support for attempts to save languages.

React and discuss   p.25

Aim *To give students an opportunity to discuss the subject more freely, and to round up the topic.*

Students can sometimes find it difficult to discuss an issue with their own ideas; either they may not have any, or they may not be quite ready to express them. In this case it often helps to set up a discussion as an informal debate first.

- Organize the class into Groups A and B. Group A believes that it is essential to save the world's dying languages, Group B thinks it's a waste of time and effort.
- Split the As and Bs into small groups of three or four and give them time to collect some ideas and arguments to support their point of view.
- Reorganize students into groups of around four, with a mix of As and Bs. Give them time to argue / discuss the point. Monitor if you like, but don't interrupt.

- To round up, you can ask them to talk about what they really think, either still in their small groups or, for the more confident classes, as a whole class.

- Alternatively, for classes able to discuss freely, but perhaps wanting slightly different subject matter, you could ask them to think about and discuss the following:

  How would students feel if their language were under threat, for example, from a dominant dialect in their own country, or from a world language like English?

Vocabulary: adjectives and nouns

Aim *To help students remember certain collocations from the text and extend these to other collocations using the same words. This enables students to extend their range of vocabulary without having to learn new words.*

1 Ask students to do this first on their own, then compare with a partner. Once they have had a try, let them look back at the text to find the answers.

> active – speakers
> cultural – assimilation / movements / organizations
> dominant – languages
> fluent – speakers
> isolated – areas
> local – community / organizations
> natural – disasters
> negative – attitudes
> positive – attitudes

2 This is a demanding activity, so it would be best carried out with the whole class. Don't spend too long on it.

> active – community / movements / organizations
> dominant – community / movements / organizations / speakers / attitudes
> isolated – community / organizations / speakers
> local – areas / attitudes / disasters / languages / movements / speakers
> natural – assimilation / community / speakers
> negative – speakers
> positive – organizations / speakers

Role play

Aim *Students extend and develop their oral skills, practising argument and discussion within a semi-formal context.*

- Ask students to keep their books closed as you outline for them the context for the role play.

- Divide the class into four roughly equal groups, As, Bs, Cs, and Ds, and seat them together. The As and Bs look at different information on p.157, Cs look at p.158, and Ds look at p.159. Give the groups time to work out their task together.

- When they are ready, re-organize the students into ABCD groups. Their task now is to describe and discuss the projects together and to decide which two should be supported.

- Monitor, but don't interrupt.

- It's probably a good idea to conduct a whole-class feedback in order to round off the discussions. You could ask each group to nominate a speaker who tells the rest of the class about their decision and the process leading towards it, or you could have a whole-class discussion about this type of project in general, or you could discuss the problems they had in doing the task, i.e. difficulties in reaching decisions / persuading people / finding the right kind of language.

Exploring words p.26

Aim *To extend students' vocabulary using an area that is rich in lexical items.*

1 Either ask students to work through the instructions in the Student's Book, or follow this alternative procedure. With books closed, tell the students that you are going to be looking at the language of crime and punishment.

- Ask them question **a** 'What is the worst crime that you have heard of?' Be prepared to discuss something of your own in case no-one can think of anything. (Usually, someone can after a while, but people often need a bit of thinking time, which your own story can provide them with.)

- Encourage a fairly free discussion and lead in to the second question, **b** 'How should someone who commits this crime be punished?'

- Be prepared for some strong opinions, which may well be conflicting ones. Encourage a fairly free discussion but don't let it go on for too long; this is an introduction to some detailed vocabulary work.

2 a Ask students to draw a table in their notebooks. The heading is *Crimes* and there are three sections: *crime, criminal, verb.*

- Ask them to work in pairs and to do task **a** (deciding what type of crime the various crimes are). Ask them to write the crime in the first column of their tables.

- Check answers with the whole class.

> abduction Pe (taking a person away, unwillingly)
> arson Pr (setting fire to something or somewhere)
> assault Pe (physical attack)
> assisting suicide Pe (helping someone to kill themselves)
> bank robbery Pr
> bigamy Pe (being married to two different people at the same time)
> blackmail Pe (threatening to say or do something unless a condition is met)
> bribery Pe (offering something, usually money, so that another person does something)
> burglary Pr (robbing a house – not a bank, office, etc.)
> drink-driving B (driving with more than a permitted amount of alcohol in your blood)
> drug-dealing Pe (buying and selling drugs)
> forgery Pr (making something look real and pretending that it is – often with paintings, money, etc.)
> fraud B (deliberately trying to mislead people)
> hijacking B (taking a plane / train / bus somewhere else by force)

kidnap Pe (taking a person away by force)
manslaughter Pe (killing a person – without planning it)
mercy-killing Pe (killing someone who is very ill or dying)
mugging B (attacking someone in order to steal a bag or purse)
murder Pe (planning to, and killing someone)
possession of drugs Pe (having illegal drugs on you)
rape Pe (forcefully having unwanted sexual intercourse)
shoplifting Pr (stealing from a shop)
smuggling B (bringing something into a country illegally)
speeding B (driving faster than the speed limit)
stalking Pe (following someone obsessively)
treason B (betraying your country)

b Now ask the students to complete the second column of their tables with the word for the criminal who commits the crime.

- Check answers with the whole class.

b and c

person	verb
abductor	to abduct
arsonist	to set fire to
assailant	to assault
accomplice to suicide	to assist suicide
bank robber	to rob a bank
bigamist	to commit bigamy
blackmailer	to blackmail
someone who offers a bribe	to bribe
burglar	to burgle
drink-driver	to drink and drive
drug-dealer	to deal (in) drugs
forger	to forge
fraudster; someone who commits fraud	to defraud; to commit fraud
hijacker	to hijack
kidnapper	to kidnap
killer	to kill / to commit manslaughter
someone who commits a mercy killing	to commit a mercy killing
mugger	to mug
murderer	to murder
someone who possesses drugs	to possess drugs
rapist	to rape
shoplifter	to shoplift
smuggler	to smuggle
speeder	to speed
stalker	to stalk
traitor	to commit treason

c Ask students to complete the third column in the same way, pointing out that there may not be one verb but a whole phrase to describe the verb.

- Check answers with the whole class.

3 Put students into pairs. You may want to change the pairs that the students have been working in up to now.

- Ask them to do the task (grouping the crimes into major crimes, petty crimes, minor offences) and set a time limit.

- Monitor and help as necessary. Be prepared for some argument amongst the students. Try not to take sides!

The answers may vary according to the country and culture of your students, and also from person to person.

Possible answers

Major Crimes	Petty Crimes	Minor Offences
abduction	assisting suicide	possession of drugs
		speeding
arson	bribery	
assault	burglary	
bank robbery	forgery	
blackmail	fraud	
drink-driving	mercy killing	
hijacking	mugging	
kidnap	shoplifting	
manslaughter	smuggling	
murder	stalking	
rape	bigamy	
smuggling		
treason		

- Now ask the pairs to join another pair to compare their lists. In their fours they must try to agree the three most serious and the three most minor offences. Set a time limit.

- Conduct a brief feedback to see what everyone thought. (Try to avoid a major discussion here though.)

4 a Ask students to work in small groups and to build up a list of punishments. Set a time limit and discourage discussion at this point; they have a chance for this in the next task. Write any new suggestions on the board.

Possible answers
custodial sentence
suspended sentence
'points' added to driving licence
repossession of property

b Ask students to discuss their ideas in small groups. Again, set a time limit.

5 Set the scene for the task with the whole class. Refer them to the picture and give them a few minutes to read through the text.

- Ask them for their first reaction to the facts of this case. Invite comments but do not volunteer an opinion yourself at this stage, or give further information. Don't spend too long on this as there will be plenty of opportunity for further discussion.

- Now ask the students to read the information on p.157. Give them a few minutes to read quietly.

- Ask the class if their opinions have changed. Encourage discussion.

- Now put the class into pairs or small groups and ask them to discuss question c. Set a time limit.

- Then ask the students to turn to p.158 to find out what actually happened.

- Ask the students what they think / feel now. You can ask the whole class, or ask the small groups to finish the discussion together.

Note

The farmer's conviction was reduced, on appeal, in November 2001 to manslaughter.

4 Danger

Theme: people relate stories about dangerous situations

4.1 A near miss

A story about road rage

- **Listening:** gist and specific information
- **Exploring natural speech:** using 'vague' language
- **Vocabulary:** phrases connected with *danger*
- **Speaking:** telling a TV news story

4.2 Anonymous threats

People tell stories about threatening situations

- **Listening:** predicting and specific information
- **Exploring natural speech:** using *sort of*
- **Language focus:** narrative tenses
- **Writing:** a story for a magazine

4.3 Cyber danger

Discussing computer viruses

- **Reading:** jigsaw reading – predicting and interpreting
- **Language focus:** reported speech and reporting verbs

Exploring words

Noun–adjective collocations: fullness and emptiness

Verb–noun collocations: dangers, difficulties, problems

Workbook

- **Language focus:** narrative tenses; reported speech
- **Vocabulary focus:** anger; verb–noun collocations
- **Vocabulary expansion:** travel and transport
- **Listening:** a sense of danger

4.1 A near miss p.28

Stage 1 consists of a listening text which contextualizes past tense use and 'vague' language used in story-telling.

Lead in

Aim *To introduce vocabulary and get the students talking about the theme of the lesson by means of a matching task.*

1 Focus the students on the first picture and elicit as many dangers as they can think of. Then put the students in pairs or small groups to discuss the rest of the photos.

- Elicit their ideas and write them on the board.

> **Possible answers**
> Football match: injury to players / crowd violence
> Rough sea: drowning / ship sinking / flooding
> Rainforest: wild animals / disease / getting lost
> Disco: drugs / alcohol / crime – theft, fights, threatening behaviour
> Traffic: accidents / pollution / road rage
> Kitchen: poisonous substances / electrics / heavy or sharp objects / fire

2 Focus the students on the headlines, and check the meaning of any difficult words.

Glossary

striker – a football player whose main job is to score goals

- Put the students in pairs to match the headlines to the pictures. In the feedback, ask whether they predicted the dangers mentioned in the headlines.

> Twenty arrested in midnight drugs raid – disco
> Striker hit by flying bottle – football match
> Domestic accidents on the increase – kitchen
> Passenger cut free after six-hour ordeal – traffic
> I woke up next to a snake – rainforest
> Helicopter rescues four in off-shore drama – rough sea

- With an imaginative class, an alternative way to do this lead-in is to put students in pairs or small groups, ask them to match photos to headlines, then get them to choose one of the stories and briefly expand on it. You could put these questions on the board to get them thinking:

  Where did it happen?
  Who did it happen to?
  What happened in the end?

- Ask the students to tell their story briefly to the class. This activity previews past tense use and the speaking exercise at the end of Stage 1.

Listening   p.29

Aim *To practise listening for gist in the first part and for more detail in the second part of the listening.*

1 Ask the students to read the extract and discuss the meanings of the words with a partner. If these are new words for your students, a good way to check them is to draw a *junction* and *slip road* on the board and mime the actions of the drivers.

2 Focus the students on the questions and play the recording.

4.1

M1 … late at night on the motorway when I was, erm, I was driving home from London to Oxford, erm about, I don't know, about 11 o'clock at night or something like that on a Saturday night and the motorway was quite deserted – it was a very clear night, very good visibility and I noticed these lights coming up very very fast behind me …

M2 UFO!

M1 Well, it wasn't, it wasn't. I only wish it had been erm and er we were approaching a junction and I thought well this car's coming up very close behind me obviously he's going to go off up the slip road to the junction but he didn't – he came right up behind me and at the last minute swerved out to overtake me, hit the back of my car but not enough to to to send either of us off course, and sped off up the motorway, so I thought well, you know, I'm not having this, so I chased him and flashed him and he pulled over on to the side of the road erm when I caught up with him and I pulled in behind.

M2 Do you think he hadn't noticed or something?

M1 Er well, it's difficult to imagine he couldn't have noticed cos there was a big bang and there was actually quite a lot of damage to both cars when we actually got out and had a look, but I got out of the car erm and of course I could see the car in front in my headlights and both doors opened … (Ah) … and two very large guys in baseball caps and big Puffa jackets got out …

M2 Oh no, big Puffa jackets is fine though, T-shirts would be more dangerous …

M1 … all right well, there were two two big guys in baseball caps and I suddenly realized that I was completely alone on this motorway, it was just me and them and they looked extremely …

• Ask the students to check in pairs before giving the answer.

> He was afraid that the two men in the other car might attack him.

3 Focus the students on the questions and play the recording again. You could get the students to try to answer the questions in pairs before they listen.

4.2

M1 And er I suddenly realized that I was completely alone on this motorway, it was just me and them and they looked extremely intimidating …

M2 Sorry were you still in your car at this stage?

M1 No no, I was out of my car but I was wishing I was back in the car.

M2 No baseball cap I presume?

M1 No baseball cap. No baseball bat – anything like that. Erm, and they they sort of approached me, one from either side of the car erm and there were a couple of minutes when I thought mm yeah this was a bad idea – I really wish I was anywhere but here, erm but in fact they were very apologetic and and said sorry we didn't realize you were going so slowly, erm but it's OK – here's our insurance details and sorry about the damage to your car and everything was fine, but just for those two seconds, you know, …

• Ask the students to check in pairs before giving the answers.

> a Out of his car – he'd got out of his car when the other car stopped in front of him.
> b Terrified / apprehensive / regretting he'd got out of his car
> c They apologized for the damage, said they didn't realize he was going so slowly.
> d Their insurance details.

4 Elicit suggestions from the students.

> **Possible answer**
> Lone driver in late-night motorway scare

• You could do exercise 2 of *Exploring words* (SB p.34) at this stage, as a natural vocabulary extension.

React and discuss

• Encourage a whole-class or group discussion.

• Alternatively, you could do a brief role play at this stage. Imagine the speaker decided to report the accident to the police. Put the students in pairs. Half the pairs are the driver, and half the pairs are a police officer. The drivers work together in pairs to think how they are going to describe the accident. The police officers work in pairs to think of questions to ask about the accident. When they are ready, divide the students into new pairs with one driver and one police officer in each pair. The police officers must ask the drivers questions.

Exploring natural speech

Aim *To introduce students to the use of 'vague' language when telling a story.*

This sort of language, typical in the speech of native English speakers, is used when the speaker cannot or does not want to be precise. This could be because they can't remember exact time or details, because there is no need to be precise as it would distract from the story, or it could be for effect – sometimes being vague can appear 'cool' or laid-back.

It is of course difficult for students to incorporate such items into their own speech. It may seem unnatural and forced. But it is fun to try, and, in trying, students at this level get a feel for telling stories in English in a more natural way, and it improves their ability to follow native speakers when they use a lot of often misleading 'vague' language. If you have a monolingual class, it may be a good idea to get students to think of what sort of vague language they use in their own language.

1 Ask the students to underline any examples of 'vague' language in the two extracts. Ask them why the speaker has used these phrases and what effect this has, (see *Aim* above).

a ... I was driving home from London to Oxford, erm <u>about</u>, I don't know, <u>about</u> 11 o'clock at night <u>something like that</u> on a Saturday night and the motorway was quite deserted ...
Note: *quite* here means *completely* not *fairly* so it is not an example of 'vague' language

b No baseball cap. No baseball bat – <u>anything like that</u>. And they <u>sort of</u> approached me, one from either side of the car erm and there were <u>a couple of minutes</u> when I thought mm yeah this was a bad idea ...

2 Go through the language in the box with the students and check they understand these examples of 'vague' language. Elicit examples of words ending in *-ish*:

Suggested examples
I'll be arriving at eight-ish. / He's got brownish hair. / I'd say she's youngish, not young.

- Before asking students to create sentences for themselves, write one or two sentences on the board and ask students as a class or in pairs to turn them into sentences with 'vague' language, for example:

    I met friends at seven and we went to the cinema.

    The students might suggest:

    I sort of met a couple of / a few / two or three friends at about / just after seven-ish (or) something like that, and we sort of went to the cinema and stuff.

- Put students in pairs to tell each other about what they did yesterday, using 'vague' language. Monitor and correct any misuses of 'vague' language.

Vocabulary: *danger*

Aim *To introduce and practise vocabulary around the key word* danger.

- Without looking at the book, ask the students to give you any phrases they know using the word *danger*. Write them on the board.

- Put the students in pairs to complete the sentences and answer the questions.

    a a danger to himself: he might drive his car and have an accident, or get into a fight
    b on the danger list: in hospital
    c danger money: police officers; deep sea divers
    d out of danger: she will get better
    e hidden dangers: personal answers

Speaking

Aim *To practise speaking from notes.*

1 Check the students understand the headline language.

Glossary
abandoned – left alone
deserted – empty / no people
hostages – people held captive by someone who wants money or has political demands

- Put the students in pairs to choose one of the stories and write brief notes to prepare to tell the story as if it were on a news programme. Monitor and help with ideas.

- If your students need help to get started, you could brainstorm the first story as a class. Ask questions like *Where was it abandoned? Why did it look suspicious? What did the bomb squad do?*

2 Change the pairs, ideally so that the students are with a new partner who has prepared a different story. Monitor the story-telling, and note errors for feedback at the end.

- You could ask one or two students to present their stories to the class.

- You may wish to extend and personalize this speaking stage by getting students to do the following extra activity.

    1 Put the students in groups of four or five, and ask them to think of something dangerous that happened to them which they can tell the group about. Set a time limit for them to prepare.

    2 Students take turns to tell their stories to the rest of the group. (It is a good idea to model the activity by telling a short story of your own first.)
    As they listen to other stories, students write down one or two questions they would like to ask.

    3 When everyone has finished their stories, students ask each other their questions.

4.2 Anonymous threats   p.30

Stage 2 consists of a listening text which contextualizes the use of narrative tenses.

Listening

Aim *To listen for specific information.*

1 **a** Focus students on the pictures and ask them to describe them. *What sort of dangers are there in these situations?*

b Match one or two phrases to the pictures as a class to get the students started. Ask them why they think they match.

- Put the students in pairs to match the phrases to the pictures. One way of approaching this activity is to get the students to match the words and phrases, then to build up predictions about the stories from these words and the pictures.

2 Ask the students to listen to the first story and check their predictions in **1b**. Play the recording.

4.3

W … it was in Italy and I went to erm this er station which was well outside the city and erm the friend that I'd met there took me to the station and I missed the train before last back so I was, I had to catch a very late train back – there were two people on the platform and when I got into the carriage there was only one other person in there and there were about eight stops on the train, erm and halfway through the journey the other person in the train got out so I was on my own in this train late at night …

M With the lights on?

W With the lights on, with the lights on, but I was thinking to myself, well this is all right because when I get to the end when I get to the station it'll be fine because I can just jump out and get into a taxi and I'll be back in the hotel and everything'll be fine. When I got to the end of the, when I got to the station, erm because it was the last train, everybody had gone home there was nobody there, it was virtually deserted erm and I grabbed this person I said 'Where's the taxi rank?' and they pointed over to this sort of clump of trees in the middle of this sort of like very dark patch …

absolutely furious	2
angry gesture	2
clump of trees	1
dark patch	1
eight stops	1
on my own	1
road rage	2
shouted abuse	2
sunroof	2
taxi rank	1

3 Focus the students on the statements in exercise 3 then play recording **4.3** again.

a F one person in train, two on platform
b F *about* eight stops – the speaker didn't count them exactly so it could have been more or less – good example of 'vague language'
c F They were on.
d F It was 'virtually deserted' (although earlier the speaker says 'everyone had gone home, there was nobody there' she then goes on to say she 'grabbed this person'.)
e F It was in a very dark patch.

4 Focus the students on the list of events before they listen to the second story, then play the recording.

4.4

M My only experiences of road rage or potential road rage have been with me on a bicycle and other people in cars which instantly puts you at a fairly large disadvantage erm …

W Have you been knocked off?

M I've never been knocked off, no, no. I made an angry gesture at a car driver once …

W Oh did you?

M Yes, cos I was sort of cycling along as I thought I was in the right as cyclists always are, (Yes, definitely) erm and he didn't think I was in the right and he opened his window and shouted abuse at me, (Yeah) erm so I made an angry gesture as they call it in the newspapers (Uhuh) erm and he actually followed me (Oh) and pulled alongside and stuck his head out of the sunroof while driving along which was slightly odd, stuck his head out of the sunroof and and (He was big

enough to do that) he basically said you know if you do that again I'm going to knock your head off – he was just absolutely furious, so I said I was sorry erm …

W Like you do.

M Like you do, yes, and he drove off and he scowled at me in a very nasty way. But it was quite unsettling.

Correct order of events
1 c he opened his window
2 f and shouted abuse at me
3 b I made an angry gesture
4 e stuck his head out of the sunroof
5 a if you do that again I'm going to knock your head off
6 d I said I was sorry

React and discuss

· Encourage a whole-class discussion.

Exploring natural speech

Aim *To introduce and practise* sort of *as a filler or vague language in spoken English.*

The students have come across *sort of* as an example of vague language in the Exploring natural speech section of Stage 1 of this unit. *Sort of* is often used as a filler which adds no extra meaning. This is similar to *you know* or *I mean*. Sometimes, however, it is a vague language phrase which means *something like*. For example: *He lived in a **sort of** tent*. (i.e. not a conventional tent, but something a bit like a tent). If someone uses it a lot when they are speaking, it can just be a habit, but it could be an indication that the person lacks confidence in what they are saying. Point out the pronunciation, /sɔːtəv/, as it involves two vowel sounds that some students may find difficult to produce accurately.

1 Put students in pairs to discuss the questions.

a Here it is vague language meaning 'it looked a bit / something like …' The speaker is being imprecise.
b Here it is a filler and doesn't have any meaning. The speaker either lacks confidence in what he is saying, or has got into a habit of using this phrase unnecessarily.

2 Ask students to work individually to add *sort of* to the story. Monitor and help.

· When they are ready, ask them to read their story to their partner.

Sort of can be added almost anywhere in spoken English:
He *sort of* glanced at me with a strange *sort of* expression in his eyes and *sort of* told me to *sort of* follow him. I *sort of* smiled and *sort of* did what he said. He *sort of* took me into a *sort of* large room. It was a *sort of* dining room with an enormous *sort of* table *sort of* in the middle. I *sort of* sat down but I felt *sort of* uncomfortable. I *sort of* didn't know what to expect. He *sort of* went out of the room, leaving me *sort of* alone.

Language focus: narrative tenses   p.31

Aim *To revise and practise narrative tenses: Past simple, Past continuous, and Past perfect.*

This is not a new area for students at this level, and the rules of use are fairly straightforward. The emphasis is on practising the tenses in the context of story-telling. The students should be encouraged to try to mix these tenses appropriately when telling or writing stories.

Students should be very familiar with the form and pronunciation. However, you may wish to point out the use of the weak 'schwa' sound in *was* /wəz/ and *were* /wə/. Monitor and correct poor pronunciation when students are doing exercise 2 of the *Exploitation* section.

- You could talk through this section as a class, or get students to discuss questions 1 to 3 in pairs then feedback as a class. A suggested approach is to do number 1 as a class, as it is straightforward revision, then give the students time to discuss 2 and 3 in pairs before feedback. Once the students are clear as to the use of these tenses, put them in pairs or small groups to do exercise 4.

1 Ask the students to read the extract and answer the questions.

> Past simple. It is used to tell a sequence of events in a story.

2–3 Put the students in pairs to discuss these questions. You may wish to refer them to the Language commentary on p.35.

> The Past continuous is used for background description or events in progress, against which the main sequence of events takes place.
> The Past perfect is used to indicate that other actions / events took place before the main sequence of events.
> The difference between the two sentences:
> - everyone went home **before** the speaker arrived at the station
> - everyone went home **the moment / at the time** the speaker arrived

4 Students remain in pairs to make up the next part of the stories. Elicit examples. Make sure the students are using the tenses correctly.

> **Possible answers**
> - I was cycling home last night …
>   … when suddenly it started to rain.
>   … when I had a puncture.
>   The Past continuous action gives the background to an event or action.
> - I cycled home last night …
>   … and got in about 6 o'clock. Then I had a shower, made myself a snack, and called a taxi.
>   The first of a sequence of events.
> - I'd cycled home last night …
>   … That's why I was tired and needed a rest before going to meet my friends.
>   The Past perfect often provides the background to or explanation for a more recent past event or action.

Exploitation

Aim *To practise using narrative tenses in story-telling.*

1 Ask the students to complete the story, then check their answers with a partner.

> | | | | |
> |---|---|---|---|
> | 1 | was walking | 10 | stood |
> | 2 | heard | 11 | looked |
> | 3 | was | 12 | went up |
> | 4 | ran | 13 | grabbed |
> | 5 | had come | 14 | said |
> | 6 | burst | 15 | had never seen |
> | 7 | lay | 16 | did he know |
> | 8 | was | 17 | had murdered |
> | 9 | had been used | | |

- Ask if any students know how the detective knew that the postman was the murderer.

> The lawyer and the accountant were both women. The postman was the only man in the room, and, therefore, the only person called John.

2 a Focus the class on the two photos, and briefly elicit what they show, and what sort of stories they might suggest.

- Put the students in pairs to choose one of the pictures and to prepare a story. Encourage them to write notes so that they can tell their story later, but not to write whole sentences.

b Check that the students understand the interrupting language in the box. Briefly drill the comments and questions for pronunciation.

Note that the words and syllables **in bold** below are stressed:

> I'm not **sure** I under**stand**.
> What a **strange** thing to **do**.
> I'm **sorry**, I didn't **catch** that.
> That's **not** very likely. / That's not very **likely**.
> **Why** did they **do** that? / Why did they do **that**?
> What **happened next**?
> **Where** did this **happen**?

- Rearrange pairs so that they are with students who prepared the other story, then monitor as the pairs take it in turns to tell their stories and be interrupted.

▶ There is an extra chain story-telling activity on p.141.

Writing

Aim *To use narrative tenses in writing a story.*

- Make sure students understand the task and the readers they will be writing for.

- Ask students in pairs to choose a story they have heard or told earlier in the lesson. Ask them to write down as much of the story as they can in note form. Give them a time limit to do this – no more than ten minutes.

- Ask the students to divide the story into three to five paragraphs. Point out that in the first paragraph, they need to set the scene and will probably need to use the Past continuous.

- Set the writing for homework. Refer the students to the Writing guidelines on p.151 where there are notes on story-telling and a model story.

4.3 Cyber danger p.32

In Stage 3 the reading text contextualizes the use of reported speech and reporting verbs.

Reading

Aim *This is a jigsaw reading. The students read to confirm expectations, then share information from the texts in a communicative task.*

Ask the students the questions in the book as a class.

> c It's an appropriate word because in medicine, a virus is a simple organism that spreads quickly to cause infectious disease. Computer viruses spread like diseases and are sometimes difficult to stop or fight.

2 Elicit suggestions from the students. If they don't have any ideas, write a few words on the board and ask them to choose the word they think is appropriate, for example: *shy / outgoing, sociable / anti-social, caring / irresponsible, popular / lonely.*

- Put the students into pairs, and ask Student A to read the text on this page, and Student B to read the text on p.157.

- Briefly feedback the answers to **b**.

3 Ask the students to work through **a–d** with their partner, who has read the other text.

- Feedback answers.

> a **Personal answers. Possibilities:**
> *Melissa:* David Smith admitted the crime / 10 years in prison / $150,000 fine / he did not expect to cause so much damage
> *Johnny:* Johnny's lifestyle / complete dedication to virus writing / his reasons for writing viruses / he is not anti-social / he has not intentionally spread a virus
> b Both men admit to being virus writers / neither man deliberately set out to cause damage
> c Smith does not give a reason, except to deny trying to cause damage
> Johnny said it allowed him to play God / to pretend to be a villain / cyberterrorist / fun to play with
> d **Answers to *Close up* tasks:**
> *Melissa*
> **1.17** loud
> **1.20** insignificant / unimportant / minor consequences
> **1.22** a crime without a victim, e.g. fraud or other crimes involving large organizations rather than individuals
> *Johnny*
> **1.3** done by hand: manual work = physical labour; opposite of *automatic*: cars can be automatic or have manual gears
> **1.8** microscope / microchip / microfilm / microphone / microsurgery / microwave
> **1.12** mathematics / physics / acoustics / economics / statistics / phonetics / politics

React and discuss

- Encourage a short class discussion.

Language focus: reported speech and reporting verbs p.33

Aim *To introduce and practise various reporting verbs, and the reported speech verb patterns that follow them.*

Reported speech is a grammatical area that the students will have come across before. The focus here is on the complex verb patterns that follow reporting verbs.

1 Do the first as an example, then put the students in pairs to change the reported speech to direct speech.

> a 'This is a very dangerous virus.'
> b 'Yes, I entered user groups without authorization.'
> 'I admit I entered / I admit entering user groups without authorization.'
> c 'OK, I deliberately broke into the systems and I knew what I was doing.'
> d 'The virus has paralysed tens of thousands of computer systems.'
> e 'This is (the reason) why I am a virus writer. / Here's why ...'

2 Ask the students to look at the tense of the reporting verb, and the tense of the following clause to help them answer this question. You may wish to refer the students to the Language commentary on p.35, where the basic rules of form are covered in detail.

If the reporting verb is in the present, the tense of the verb in reported speech does not change.
If the reporting verb is in the past, the tense of the verb in reported speech changes from Past simple to Past perfect.
Note also that -ing forms do not change in reported speech.

▶ If the students find this new or difficult, you could copy and set the extra activity on p.141 to give the students accuracy practice.

3 a–b Give the students time to do exercises **a** and **b**, checking their answers in pairs before discussing the answers as a class. Remind students that there are many different reporting verbs in addition to the overused *said*.

verbs from extracts	near synonyms
a states	declare(s)
b admitted	confess(ed)
c acknowledged	concede(d)
d pointed out	observe(d)
e explains	spell(s) out

c Ask the students to discuss the sentences in pairs first.

Sentences 1, 3, 4, 5 are all correct. Only 2 is wrong. *Suggest* cannot be followed by an infinitive construction.

Exploitation

Aim *To practise using reporting verbs and reported speech.*

1 Check that the students understand all the verbs, and are aware that some require a (given) preposition. Point out that after a preposition the students will need to use -ing.
Note that here *maintain* means *claim* or *argue*.

• Ask the students to rewrite the conversation and compare with a partner. Monitor and help.

a Sue accused Nick of using her computer.
b Nick denied that he had used her computer and suggested that she asked Pete.
   Nick denied having used / using her computer.
c Sue asked Pete if / whether he'd been playing games on her computer.
d Pete confessed / admitted that he couldn't even use a computer.
e Sue apologized for accusing him.
f Pete suggested that it was probably Jon.
g Sue asked him how he knew that.
h Pete claimed / maintained that he had seen him sitting at her / Sue's desk the previous afternoon / the afternoon before.
i Sue asked him / Jon if / whether it was true. Had he used her computer? (Had it been him who had used her computer?)
j Jon admitted / confessed that is was him / had been him and apologized.
k Sue told him / Jon not to be sorry. She congratulated him on getting the highest game score ever.

2 Put the students in pairs. Tell Student A to read the e-mail on p.158, and Student B to read the e-mail on p.159.

• When they are ready, students tell their partner about their e-mail, using reported speech. Monitor for errors.

• This is an extended activity to get students to practise reported speech. With slower classes, it is probably better to ask students to read their e-mails carefully two or three times, then close their books and report the key points they remember. If students work through every sentence of the e-mail, it could become boring.

Possible answers
A The director of the English Department said he'd recently received complaints about some of the students in the Advanced class. He said it seemed that a small proportion of students had been enjoying their English lessons. He claimed that this was just a minority who were making it difficult for other students to concentrate.
He maintained that it had even been suggested that some of the teachers had been making their lessons interesting.
He pointed out that this situation could not continue.
He said that in the next few days he would be visiting classes to make sure that there was no unnecessary fun.

B The director of the English Department said he was pleased to tell us that he had just received a letter from the British Government about changes to the English language.
He said that the most important changes would be these.
All verbs would be regular. The verb *drink* would be …
All words would be spelt in the same way as they were pronounced.
All question tags would be replaced by a single …
He pointed out that these changes would come into effect from January 1st.

Exploring words   p.34

Aim *To practise adjective–noun and verb–noun collocations.*

This section is the first of two that looks at collocation. It splits naturally into two parts. Exercises 1, 2, and 3 could be used as an integral vocabulary lesson on collocation. Exercises 4 and 5 could make a reading/vocabulary/speaking lesson. Exercise 2 makes a natural vocabulary extension to the listening in Stage 1. Exercises 2 and 3 could be set as homework.

1 As a lead-in, if you think your students will know what collocations are, elicit some interesting collocations that they often use. Alternatively, write some common (or recently learnt) collocations on the board, and ask students what is special about the way the words go together. For example, *delicious food, handsome man, cosy flat.*

- Let the students choose their definition, before discussing the questions in groups or as a class.

  > **a** The best definition is 2. The others are only partly correct:
  > 1,3: collocation applies to other kinds of words, e.g. verbs and adverbs.
  > 4: collocations can involve more than 3 words and these words are not always used together.
  > **b** It is better to learn words in groups than to learn them separately. The idea of collocation often explains combinations that are otherwise inexplicable.

2 a–b The students work individually to match the adjectives with nouns, then check in pairs.

abandoned	car / village / house
bare	feet / room
busy	house / person / station / street / village
crowded	beach / house / room / station / street / village
deserted	beach / house / station / street / village
empty	beach / bottle / car / house / room
full	bottle / car / house / room
lonely	beach / person

c Put the students in pairs to complete the sentences.

1	abandoned cars	3	beaches / crowded
2	an empty house	4	deserted streets

d Students remain in their pairs to think about the pairs of phrases.

> deserted = no-one is there – it's empty
> abandoned = everyone has left and no-one lives there any more
> busy = a lot of trains and people are leaving and arriving
> crowded = full of people
> empty = there is no furniture in it
> bare = there is furniture, but it is simple and basic

3 a Either do this as a class or in pairs.

beat	an enemy
combat	crime / (a) disease / a fear / a handicap / a problem
come to terms with	(a) difficulty / a handicap / a problem
confront	danger / difficulty / a fear / an enemy / a problem
defeat	an enemy
face	a challenge / a danger / a difficulty / a fear / an enemy / the future / a problem / a risk
fight	crime / (a) disease / an enemy / a (losing) battle / a problem / a war
meet	a challenge
overcome	a challenge / difficulty / a disadvantage / a disease / a fear / an enemy / a handicap / a problem
run	a risk
solve	a crime / a problem

b Put the students in pairs to complete the sentences.

1	overcome / fears
2	combating diseases
3	overcome / problem fighting / losing battle

c Students think of collocations and check them with their partner.

4 Ask the students to look at the title and guess what the text might be about, then ask them to read it quickly to see if they were right.

- Ask the students to underline the collocations and check with their partner.

assess the risks	v–n
daily lives	a–n
everyday situations	a–n
committing suicide	v–n
smokes (40) cigarettes	v–n
exposing himself to (nearly as much) danger	v–n
playing a game	v–n
routine activity	a–n
come into the same category	v–n
accidental fall	a–n
(be) involved in a (driving) accident	a–n
carrying out (household) chores	v–n
household chores	a–n

5 Put the students in pairs to discuss the questions.

Theme: moral and practical dilemmas

5.1 In the workplace

Advice and suggestions about problems in the workplace

- **Listening:** specific information
- **Exploring natural speech:** *I'm afraid*
- **Vocabulary:** three-part phrasal verbs
- **Language focus:** opinions and suggestions

5.2 A quiet Sunday bus ride

Reactions to threatening behaviour in public

- **Reading:** specific information and interpretation
- **Language focus:** inversion

5.3 How far should we go?

Genetic engineering

- **Listening:** general information and specific language
- **Vocabulary:** adjective–noun collocation (*infectious disease*)
- **Speaking:** discussion
- **Writing:** an article for a magazine

Exploring words

Rights, responsibilities, truth, and lies

Workbook

- **Language focus:** opinions and suggestions; inversion after expressions with a negative meaning; other examples of inversion
- **Vocabulary focus:** three-part phrasal verbs; health
- **Vocabulary expansion:** formal style; adjectives and verbs to describe voices; verbs like *shine*
- **Listening:** genetic engineering

5.1 In the workplace p.36

Stage 1 consists of a listening text which introduces the language of opinions and suggestions.

Lead in

Aim *To get students thinking and talking about the kind of dilemmas (problems) that people might encounter at work.*

- Ask students to complete the questionnaire quickly on their own, then put them in pairs or small groups and give them time to discuss their answers. Even if your students do not have experience of work, they should be able to offer an opinion on the issues raised in the questionnaire.
- Conduct a general class feedback to round up the activity and focus on the next task.

Listening

Aim *To practise listening for specific information.*

A pre-listening exercise pre-teaches some of the idiomatic expressions and collocations students will come across in the recording. The recording itself is a radio programme which asks people to give advice on problems e-mailed in. Students have to listen for specific points in the conversations.

1 Give students a few minutes to work through the exercise in pairs.

- Check answers with the whole class.

> **a** Everybody / the general public.
> Property owned by the government or a council, such as roads, parks, etc. The opposite is *private* property.
> **b** **Note:** You can also *spread* gossip.
> **c** Badly: you behave as badly as the other person. *sink = go down*
> **d** If the person had asked you a question about a private matter / a question you are not prepared to answer.
> **e** Quickly.

2 Introduce the listening, i.e. a radio programme giving advice to people who have e-mailed with problems and dilemmas.

- Give students time to read questions **a** and **b**. They may need to take notes in order to answer fully.
- Play the recording.

5.1

P All right. I have another e-mail here. This one's from Jo. Er, let's see what you think of this. She says that somebody she sits near at work is always on the phone – he has a very loud voice and she can hear everything he says. Now she wants to know, does she treat his conversations as public property? You know passing on bits of gossip or even interrupt his conversations – adding her own comments, you know. So, what do you think she should do about that?

W I don't think she has the right, I'm afraid, I just don't think she has the right – she has to put up with it. She's got to concentrate on what she's doing and erm let him get on with it – maybe talk to him about it, but it's absolutely not her right to get involved.

M I completely disagree. I think that erm if he is going to be so rude as to, you know, have conversations like that – at that tone and interfere with her work – there's no way that he can expect her to not take what he's been saying and erm and use it or to to refer to it. I think it's it's the most annoying thing to be in a work environment and have someone shouting down the phone to them so …, you know to to whoever.

W I agree, but why not rise above it? Why sink to their level?

P I would imagine it would be very distracting. What do … when you say rise above it, what do you think she could do to sort that out?

W Possibly try and talk to him about it, but to start gossiping and using his conversations as public property is being absolutely no better than what he's doing – erm I think that would be an appalling way to behave.

M But perhaps by doing that he would stop, he would get the hint. He'd start maybe being a little more considerate with his conversations.

W But why not simply talk to him in an adult manner?

M Yeah, you're probably right. That's probably the first thing that she should do, but erm I think that she should definitely confront it, either by speaking to him or by just making it completely obvious that she's heard everything he's said.

P Well, Jo, hopefully you're listening and hopefully that can be of some help.

- Ask students to compare their answers in pairs.

> a Colleague has loud telephone conversations. The speaker doesn't know whether to regard the information she hears as private and confidential or public property to be passed on to other colleagues.
> b Female adviser says she has no right to pass on what she hears. The male adviser disagrees. He thinks the loud telephone caller is giving up the right to privacy by speaking so loudly.
> Both advisers agree how annoying it is to have to put up with someone shouting down the phone when you are trying to work, but they disagree about what should be done about it.

3 Students look at questions a and b.
- Play the recording.

5.2

P Well, let's move on to our next e-mail from someone in London. They don't give us their name and we don't know if they're a man or a woman, so we'll call them Sam. Let's hear what Sam says. 'My boss has asked me to book him a double room at a hotel for a conference. The thing is he's not taking his wife with him. I feel like protesting – but I know that if I do he'll just tell me to mind my own business.' So, do we have any advice for Sam?

M Well Sam, erm, I think this might be a case of jumping to conclusions because erm …

- Students check their answers together.

> a Boss has asked someone to book a double room for him at a conference he is going to, but they know boss is not taking his wife.
> b They want to protest, but know they will be told to mind their own business.

React and discuss

Aim *To provide a free speaking practice activity which gives students the chance to express their own opinions.*

- If you are short of time, you could omit this section because students have the opportunity for free speaking later in the *Exploitation*.

- Ask students to compare their ideas in pairs. If you want to extend the activity, you can then ask pairs to team up so that they discuss answers in fours.

- You could then conduct a whole-class feedback and discussion.

Exploring natural speech   p.37

Aim *To focus students' attention on the way the phrase* I'm afraid *is used in natural spoken English in order to express disagreement or criticism.*

1 Read the sentence aloud to the students as they follow in their books.

- Ask them what the phrase *I'm afraid* means and why it is there. Make sure they realize it does not mean *I'm frightened*.

2 Ask students to work on these in pairs.

- Check answers as a class. Note that *I'm afraid* can go in various positions, but tends to be used at the beginning or end of a sentence.

> 1 Your work is not good enough. You'll have to do a lot better, **I'm afraid**.
> (**I'm afraid** your work is not good enough. You'll have to do a lot better.)
> (Your work is not good enough, **I'm afraid**. You'll have to do a lot better.)
> 2 **I'm afraid** the business is doing very badly. We can't afford to keep you.
> (The business is doing very badly, **I'm afraid**. We can't afford to keep you.)
> (The business is doing very badly. **I'm afraid** we can't afford to keep you.)
> 3 Your behaviour at work is completely unacceptable, **I'm afraid**.
> (**I'm afraid** your behaviour at work is completely unacceptable.)
> 4 **I'm afraid** the office was broken into last night.
> (The office was broken into last night, **I'm afraid**.)

3 Play the recording and get students to check their answers. (This is not included in the tapescript section of the Student's Book.)

5.3

a Your work is not good enough. You'll have to do a lot better, I'm afraid.

b I'm afraid the business is doing very badly. We can't afford to keep you.

c Your behaviour at work is completely unacceptable, I'm afraid.

d I'm afraid the office was broken into last night.

- Give students time to practise saying the sentences in pairs. Monitor and help, especially with pronunciation. Demonstrate yourself if necessary.

Vocabulary: three-part phrasal verbs

Aim *To draw students' attention to the fact that the majority of three-part verbs are not separable and to recognize and practise a number of these.*

As with all phrasal verbs, it is better to practise a few at a time rather than a lot all at once.

1 Ask students to look at this on their own. Give them a few moments to think, then elicit answers from the whole class.

• Do not get drawn into a long explanation of all the different kinds of phrasal verb and whether or not they are separable. This exercise is simply intended to draw attention to the useful generalization that most three-part verbs are inseparable.

> The majority of three-part phrasal verbs are not separable – the three parts always stay together.
> In sentences a–c, the object of the verbs follows the verb.
> In sentences d–e, the pronoun object *it* separates the two parts of the phrasal verbs.

2 Ask students to do this on their own first, then compare answers with a partner.

• Check answers with the whole class.

• Faster students could be asked to write their own example sentences.

> **Possible answers**
> a He's (not) **looking forward to** it.
> b No, he **got away with** it.
> c Yes, but we've nearly **run out of** it. / No, I'm afraid we've **run out of** it.
> d They used to **look down on** them.
> e No, I'm afraid she **went back on** it.
> f You'll have to **send off for** it. / You could try **sending off for** it.

Language focus: opinions and suggestions

Aim *To extend students' repertoire of language for offering opinions and making suggestions.*

Students will probably tend to use only a limited range of language, for example *I think* and *I suggest*, to express opinions and make suggestions. This gives them an opportunity to develop more sophisticated language, e.g. *It might be an idea to … I'd advise him to …*

1 Ask students to do this on their own first, then compare answers in pairs. Allow them enough time to try and remember or work these out before moving on to 2.

2 Play the recording and get students to check their answers. (This is not included in the tapescript of the Student's Book.)

5.4

> a I completely disagree. I think that erm if he is going to be so rude as to …
>
> b … there's no way that he can expect her to to not take what he's been saying …

c I agree, but why not rise above it? Why sink to their level?

d Possibly try and talk to him about it, but to start gossiping …

e Yeah, you're probably right. That's probably the first thing she should do …

f I think that she should definitely confront it …

• Play the recording again if necessary.

> a I **completely** disagree. I think if he is going to be so rude …
> b … there's **no way** that he can expect her to not take what he's been saying
> c I agree, but **why not** rise above it? **Why** sink to their level?
> d **Possibly** try and talk to him about it, but to start gossiping …
> e Yeah, you're **right**. That's probably the first thing she should do
> f **I think** she should **definitely** confront it …

Note
___
Students will already know the normal ways of expressing opinions and making suggestions. This activity draws attention to some of the more subtle ways.

b *there's no way* – in my opinion this is impossible. This is a colloquial expression.

c *Why not / why* – is a short way of saying *Wouldn't it be a good idea to* and *What's the point of …*

d *Possibly* is used to make the suggestion sound more tentative, less dogmatic.

3 You could either do this in pairs or small groups, or you could do it as a whole-class activity. Whichever you do, don't spend too long on it or you might lose the focus of the lesson. There are more examples in the Language commentary on p.43.

> **Possible answers**
> If you ask me … (he shouldn't have done it)   for opinions
> I'm inclined to think …
> Have you / he / she (ever) thought of …?   for suggestions

Exploitation

1 You might want to play the recording again to remind the students of the context.

• Split the class into three roughly equal groups: Presenters, Adviser 1s, and Adviser 2s and give the groups a few minutes to prepare their ideas together.

• Regroup so that you have a Presenter, an Adviser 1, and an Adviser 2 in each group (extra students can work in pairs or join threes to make fours).

• Ask the students to discuss the dilemma. Set a time limit. Monitor but don't interrupt.

• Conduct a class feedback to find out what most people thought.

2 Organize the class into small groups of three or four. Remind them of the three 'dilemmas' from the *Lead in*, or you could use your own or those of the students. Here are some more examples:

1 Your best friend cheated in the last test / exam. You know he / she has been under a lot of pressure at home recently. What should you do?

2 You saw someone / a friend / the parent of a friend shoplifting. It was only a small item. Should you do / say anything to anyone?

3 You know that people have been talking about a friend of yours, saying that he / she is likely to lose his / her job / be expelled from school. Your friend seems to be oblivious to such dangers. Should you say anything?

4 You saw your friend's boyfriend / girlfriend / husband / wife in a restaurant with someone else last weekend. What should you do?

- Monitor but don't interrupt. If you have time and it's appropriate, write up some examples that you heard of language which could be made more sophisticated (for example, using other phrases to replace *I think*).

5.2 A quiet Sunday bus ride p.38

This stage includes a reading text which contextualizes the use of inversion in writing.

Reading

Aim *To develop students' ability to read for general meaning and to extend their vocabulary.*

1 a With books closed, write up the words from the Student's Book on the board or an OHT. Tell the students that these words all appear in the article they are going to read. What do they think the article will be about?

- Listen, but don't say whether they are right or wrong at this stage. Explain that they are going to look at this vocabulary in greater depth before going on to the reading.

- Write up the column headings from the Student's Book table and ask students to copy these into their notebooks.

- Ask them to group the words on the board under these headings. They can do this in pairs or small groups.

People	Bad language	Violent behaviour	Parts of the body
children	abuse	fight	brains
grown-up	swear	punch-up	fist
kids		scrap	knuckles
opponent		smack	lip
victim		spit	
yob			
a youth			

Note

Children are often referred to as **kids**.
Smack generally refers to a light, open-palmed hit, (*If you don't put it back, I'll give you a smack*) but in the language of the young, and in this article, *smack* simply means *hit*.

b–e Students can do these in small groups or you can do them as a whole-class activity.

b	children / kids
c	children (kids) / grown-up
d	fight / punch-up / scrap
e	hand: fist / knuckles
	head: brains / lip

2 Ask students to read the questions.

- Set them a realistic time limit for reading the article.

- Ask them to compare their answers in pairs.

| a | He asked the yobs to stop using bad language in front of his young children. |
| b | They were amazed that anyone had dared to criticize them. Then they became abusive. |

Note

Asterisks (****) are often used in newspaper reports to avoid printing offensive language.
A **yob** is a colloquial word for a young person (late teens or early twenties), usually a boy / man who behaves badly.
Road rage refers to the kind of crime committed on the roads because those involved are extremely angry, in a rage. '*There was another case of road rage on the M11 yesterday when the driver of a Landrover attacked a woman he claimed had come out of the slip road too fast*'. People also refer to 'air rage' to describe attacks or aggressive behaviour on aeroplanes.

Close up

- Ask students to do this in pairs. Encourage them to make guesses from context rather than rely on their dictionaries.

- Check answers with the whole class.

1.6	continuous / unstoppable
1.39	*A close shave* is less serious. It means you just manage to avoid a bad situation. *let alone* means *and certainly not*. It is used after a negative statement to emphasize how unlikely a situation is because something even more likely has never happened. *I can't afford a week's holiday in Britain, let alone a month in the Caribbean.*
1.47	a ban on expressing yourself
1.70	to cause an increase in a quality. *trendify* = to make more trendy / *simplify* = make more simple, etc.
1.71	violent anger caused by the stress and frustration of driving a car or, in this case, travelling on a bus.
1.78	*making eye contact* means looking someone directly in the eye.

React and discuss

Aim *To provide an opportunity for free speaking and also act as a comprehension check for the article.*

1 You might want to do this as a whole-class discussion.

2 You could start by telling the students about one of your own personal experiences. Students often like this, and find it easier to talk themselves afterwards. Then organize the students into small groups and ask them to recount their own experiences. You could omit this stage if short of time.

3 In addition to being a speaking exercise this is a check on students' understanding of the text as they need to have understood the reading text in order to do the task.

- Organize the class so that the As work together and the Bs work together first. Give them time to reread the article.

- Then pair the As and Bs to conduct the interview. If you have uneven numbers it doesn't matter; you can have two journalists and one interviewee, or vice versa.

- You might want to demonstrate with one of the more confident and able students first.

- Monitor but don't interrupt. Write up some of the mistakes you've noticed and ask students to correct them.

Language focus: inversion p.39

Aim *To familiarize students with the use of some of these phrases and to make them aware of how powerful they can be.*

Students often quite enjoy practising inversion because it makes their language sound much grander. However, they are often unaware of the extent to which it is used. This is quite an informally-written article in many ways, and yet it uses inversion a lot to emphasize the drama / seriousness of the situation, and the author's shock.

1 Set this up for students to do individually or in pairs, or with weaker classes, as a whole-class exercise.

- Check answers.

> Each sentence starts with a negative or restrictive word or phrase. This causes the subject and verb to be inverted. In each case it is the auxiliary verb that precedes the subject and the main verb follows it.
> **a** Never ... did I have ...
> **b** Nor could we trendify ...
> **c** Not only did the boys swear ...
> **d** At no time did any of the other passengers support me.
> **e** Hardly had the bus moved off ...

2 Ask students to do this in pairs, then check answers with the whole class.

> The negative words and phrases at the beginning make these sentences sound more dramatic or more serious.

3 It is probably a good idea to do the first one or two with the whole class, to make sure they understand.

- Ask students to complete the rest individually or in pairs, then check answers with the whole class.

- Refer them to the Language commentary on p.43.

> **Possible answers**
> **a** Not until three weeks later / Only three weeks later did I find out the names ...
> **b** Not once did I think of ...
> **c** Hardly ever / Seldom have I felt as frightened ...
> **d** No sooner had I got on the bus than the driver drove off.
> **e** On no account / Under no circumstances / No way will I take my children ...
> **f** Under no circumstances / On no account are bus drivers allowed ...
> **g** Nothing / Not a thing did he hear from the police ...
> **h** Never before have I been involved in ...

Exploitation

Aim *To give the students the opportunity to plan a story together which includes inversion.*

1 With books closed, tell the students they are going to write a story.

- Put them into small groups of three or four and ask them to read the instructions.

- Check that they have understood what they have to do.

2 Now ask them to brainstorm what happened. Set a time limit. Monitor and help with ideas as necessary but don't be too intrusive.

3 Go through the instructions with them. Make sure they understand that the phrases can go anywhere in the story. Set a time limit.

- They don't need to write the whole story out but they will need to make notes. Even at advanced level, students need guidance in making notes. Suggest that they list the main events of the story and the phrases that use inversion.

4 Each group tells or reads their story to the others. Make sure that the groups that are listening are not busily trying to finish or amend their own stories.

- These stories could be written up neatly for homework.

5.3 How far should we go? p.40

This stage includes a listening text which introduces a speaking and writing topic.

Listening

Aim *To develop the skills of listening for general and specific information and to stimulate interest in the topic in general.*

1 With books closed, write the phrase 'genetic engineering' on the board.

- Check what students understand by this and ask what they think and feel about the issue. Avoid a lengthy discussion; just let them get interested.

- Then ask students to look at the questions. Focus students on the questions. You can cover tasks **a**, **b**, and **c** in an informal whole-class discussion or you could ask the students to discuss them together in small groups. Don't spend too long on this – there will be later opportunities for discussion.

2 Focus students on the questions.

• Play the recording.

5.5

M Have you read about the progress they're making with the whole mapping of the of the genes for for for humans?

W No, I mean a little bit about that it could help them solve some er diseases and things like that or understand them …

M Right, that's the good part …

W … which I think is great yeah.

M Sure, I mean I guess probably like most people I have incredible ambivalence about this, because you know we we, no matter what your religious faith is, you know, we move into sort of playing God if we can actually pinpoint, you know what gene in the body does what in effect …

W Definitely, and then if we start to choose 'Well we want this or we want that', it's I think you're right, I think the whole issue of God and erm creation really comes into play and I think it's actually a scary area, I think as as far as, you know, helping the medical field, I think that's wonderful, (Sure) but when we get into actually changing things (Right) – that's a little scary to me.

M Right – well I'm a Star Trek fan (yeah) and that's always amazing when one of the crew people, you know, are are sent to the erm, you know, the doctor and they just do a (*Noise*) you know …

W Right right and they're all better right.

M Right, and they're they've been scanned and you know and somehow they're they're better within seconds usually, you know. (Right) So in terms of eradicating disease, you know, that's that's a wonderful thing, although I guess if we all lived to two hundred years old because so many natural cause diseases, if you will, have been eradicated (Right) – that cause a natural death is what I'm trying to say (Right), then then we have economic issues to deal with, you know.

W Well, right and I guess what, what scares me is where does it all end? (Sure) You know where does it stop and how do we control it (Right) and I really don't know how we do. Who in the end says 'OK, enough,' or you know, what can actually happen in these labs? What what can they create?

M Right, right and er the expense of all of it is just astronomical and er it it could be very exciting to finally find cures for cancer and to and to be able to pluck out those genes or modify them so so that people don't have these horrible diseases …

W Right, but I think choosing whether your child has blue eyes or brown eyes, whether it's male or female I, I really, I don't agree with that personally. I think you know, I think that should be left up to God.

M I agree.

• Let students check their answers in pairs.

> **a** Personal answer
> **b** They have mixed feelings / they are ambivalent. They can see the potential advantages, but are also worried about the speed of developments.

3 Give students time to look at the sentences carefully. Check that they understand them.

• Play the recording.

• Give students time to complete their answers individually, then play the recording again.

• When they have all finished, ask them to compare their answers in pairs.

> **3 Possible answers**
> **a** … eradicate disease.
> **b** … play God.
> **c** … to 200 (years old) / … to a much older age.
> **d** … consequences / … results / … repercussions.
> **e** … choose their children's gender or eye colouring / … decide on their children's appearance.

Vocabulary: adjective–noun collocations p.41

Aim *To extend students' vocabulary by drawing their attention to collocations often used in the context of health and illness.*

1 Check that students know the adjectives and nouns before they do the task individually or in pairs.

• Check answers with the whole class.

drastic	cure / treatment
effective	cure / operation / recovery / treatment
gradual	recovery
infectious	disease
instant	cure / recovery
old-fashioned	cure / treatment
painful	cure / disease / treatment
serious	disease / operation
successful	cure / operation / recovery / treatment

Glossary

drastic – severe, serious
infectious – passed from one person to another through the air
operation – usually happens in hospital. The word *surgery* is used either to refer to the place where doctors see you, or to the process of having an operation.
Your knee will require surgery.
The surgery is open from Monday to Friday.

2 Make sure students understand they have to use ten different adjective–noun combinations.

• Ask them to do the task individually or in pairs, then check answers with the whole class.

> **a** infectious disease   **d** effective treatment
> **b** serious operation   **e** old-fashioned cure
> **c** successful recovery

Speaking

Aim *To give students the chance to discuss the subject presented in the listening text. They also develop the skills of arguing for and against a particular point of view, which is preparation for the writing task.*

1 Organize the students into pairs or small groups and check that they understand the statements.

• Ask them to choose two or three of the statements, or allocate the statements to the different groups. If you prefer, get students to look at only one or two statements, so that they discuss them in more detail.

- Ask them to discuss their statements, using as much detail and complexity of thought as possible. Faster groups can be asked to move on to some of the other statements as long as they have discussed their first one in depth.

2 Check that students understand the task, especially that they have to include the moral, practical, and economic issues involved.

- Ask them to work in the same groups as before so that the focus is on writing the lists of pros and cons rather than on discussing the issues again. Set a time limit.

- Monitor and help as necessary. Encourage the students to consider the issues in as much depth as possible.

Writing

Aim *To give students practice in writing an article about a serious issue.*

This activity follows on directly from the speaking activity.

1–2 Briefly outline the task. Check that the students understand what kind of magazine their article would appear in. Refer to a relevant title in their country, if possible.

- Let the students stay in the same pairs or small groups as they were in for the speaking exercise. Give them time to work through the planning stages and refer them to the Writing guidelines on p.154.

- Monitor and help as necessary. Make sure the students have understood the kind of style that is required here: informal, light, and personal.

3 Set this as a homework task.

Exploring words   p.42

Aim *To extend students' vocabulary in the context of ethical issues.*

1 a You may need to help them get started by pointing out some of the rights you feel you have, e.g. to live in a reasonable place (what does 'reasonable' mean?), to express a point of view, to have access (free?) to health, education, etc.

b Ask students to try this on their own first before comparing answers with a partner.

- Check answers with the whole class.

1 for	**2** of	**3** in	**4** on	**5** of	**6** on
7 in; about	**8** to				

c Students can do this in pairs or individually.

- Check answers with the whole class.

1	in two minds about
2	in the public interest
3	blowing the whistle on
4	sit on the fence
5	be laying myself open to
6	lesser of two evils
7	discussed the rights and wrongs of
8	responsible for their own actions

d If you are short of time, you could leave this out. You may already have discussed dilemmas earlier on in the unit.

2 a Outline the task. Make sure they understand that the task at the moment is simply to make two lists: people they would trust / believe and people they wouldn't trust / believe.

- When you have checked the list, go through the vocabulary.

These people are trustworthy: Mike, Dave, Sue, Liz, Matt, Kate.
These people are not: Jo, the President, Helen, Jeff.

Glossary

above board – honest and open
two-faced – hypocritical, dishonest, has two different 'faces'
as good as his word – honest, no need for formal contract, the word is the contract
came clean – confessed to something she'd done wrong
cover-up – an attempt to hide what really happened
made up – invented
sticks to the facts – only says what is definitely true; doesn't exaggerate or guess
straightforward – honest, direct, no fabrication
telling tall stories – telling untruths, lies
tells it like it is – frank, honest

b You could do this as a whole-group discussion, or ask students to work together in small groups.

3 a–c This article provides another example of a moral dilemma. As it is providing further practice and free speaking on the topic of the section, it could be omitted if you are short of time.

- Outline the pre-reading question, **a**. You might also want to explain that a 'first-class honours degree' is the top category of degree and that Cambridge University, along with Oxford University, is considered by many to be the best university in England.

- Ask the students to read the text, then to discuss the answers to **3a** and **b** in pairs before reading the end of the story on p.158.

d Ask students to consider this in small groups. You may want to give them a few minutes of thinking time first, in order for them to come up with some ideas.

6 Natural assets

Theme: talents, gifts, and abilities

6.1 Personal gifts

People talk about their talents

- **Listening:** interpretation, specific information, and summary
- **Exploring natural speech:** interaction within conversation
- **Language focus:** *should, ought to, must, have to, need to*

6.2 Survivors

Why crocodiles have existed successfully for so long

- **Reading:** checking ideas and interpretation
- **Language focus:** determiners
- **Speaking:** interview

Exploring words

Words and their roots

Workbook

- **Language focus:** modal verbs *should, ought to, must, have to, need to,* and other expressions of obligation; *didn't need to / needn't have*; determiners *some, any, every, no, all, few, a few, little, a little*
- **Vocabulary focus:** words and their roots
- **Vocabulary expansion:** nouns with *take*; nouns and expressions with *turn*
- **Listening:** talented children

6.1 Personal gifts   p.44

Two listenings contextualize the *Language focus* (*should*, etc.) and introduce the theme.

Lead in

Aim *To introduce a useful vocabulary set to be used with the theme.*

1–2 Either ask students to work through the instructions in the book, or follow this alternative procedure.

- Start the lesson with books closed and the students' attention focused on you and the board.
- Write up the expressions from the list and elicit any others that the students might know (*have a head for figures, be a gifted artist*).
- Quickly make sure that the students know how to use these, by showing them which words in the phrases can be substituted:
  a born *teacher / musician / artist / athlete*
  a talented *singer / footballer / musician*
  an aptitude for *languages / numbers / figures / words*
  a gift for *making people laugh / writing clearly / understanding other people*
  a(n) *musical / artistic / incredible* talent
- Now get the students talking about people they know who fall into these categories. You may want to describe someone yourself first, then ask the students to discuss in pairs or small groups.
- Conduct a whole-class feedback or go straight on to the preparation for listening.

Listening

Aim *To practise picking out specific information from natural conversation.*

1 Before you set up the listening task, check the vocabulary quickly. You can either do this from the book, or ask the students quick questions ('*What do you call someone who has a high opinion of themselves?*' '*Big-headed.*' '*How do you describe the way you feel when you've done something really silly?*' '*Embarrassed.*')
- Outline the task briefly and play the recording.

6.1

Speaker 1 Yes, wordgames, I'm quite good at, I'm quite quick about words and visually, I'm good at crosswords and I can spot an anagram very very quickly – and I always impress the children with these quiz games on the television where you have a couple of letters and you have to think of the word or the phrase and I always get it straight away and they, they're open-mouthed in amazement and tell me I ought to go on the telly.

Speaker 2 A natural asset I have which I didn't realize I had until relatively recently is incredibly good eyesight. Erm, I haven't had my eyes tested for about 20 years, probably more, erm but I was driving along with a friend one day, who's got particularly bad eyesight and we were doing the kind of classic driving-test test, where you have to read somebody's number plate from, I dunno, X metres behind you and erm I could see, sort of four or five cars in front on the motorway and this friend of mine was completely astonished and then she was testing me all the rest of the weekend as to what I could see and what I couldn't see.

Speaker 3 Yes, bizarrely enough, I do have this ability to remember things like phone numbers and birthdays and dates of all kinds – erm I've no idea where the ability comes from – er it's not something I cultivate consciously erm but I don't actually need to carry people's phone numbers around with me – I've got them in my head.

Speaker 4 Erm I've always been, I've always been fiendishly fiendishly good at mental arithmetic erm, which goes back an awfully long way, erm I mean even when I was at at primary school at the age of eight I used to come erm sort of top in the mental arithmetic tests, which were probably, just things like you know eight plus seven and you'd have a roomful of seven-year-olds scratching their heads and I would get 15 straight away.

- Let students check answers together in pairs.

- Compare answers with the whole class. There may be some discussion here as there are no specifically right or wrong answers; it's a question of interpretation.

> **Possible answers**
> 1 matter-of-fact = not showing any emotion
> 2 amused / mystified
> 3 mystified
> 4 mystified / amused / big-headed

2 Allow students a few minutes to try and complete the chart on their own before comparing with a partner. Give them enough time to attempt this before playing the recording again. Students often remember more than they think they do, especially when they talk to someone else about it.

- Play recording **6.1** again and let students check their answers together.

> **a** Speaker's talent
> S1: word games, crosswords; S2: good eyesight; S3 memory; S4: mental arithmetic
> **b** Example given by speaker
> S1: TV quiz games; S2: reading car number plates; S3: telephone numbers, dates, birthdays; S4: came first in class at primary school
> **c** Other people's reactions
> S1: children amazed; S2: friend astonished; S3: no answer; S4: no answer

3–4 This speaking activity can take as much or as little time as you want it to; the important thing is to decide beforehand how much or little speaking you want at this stage of the lesson and organize the class accordingly.

- Ask the students to work in small groups to discuss the questions in 3 and the beginning of 4 and set a time limit. Monitor, but don't interrupt.

4 a Check that students know what the phrases mean and ask them to predict what might be said.

Glossary

an affinity for something – a liking and an understanding for something
inclination – tendency, aptitude
environment /ɪnˈvaɪərənmənt/ – note the spelling and pronunciation
influence – the speaker uses unusual stress: inˈfluence, rather than the standard stress ˈinfluence.

b Play the recording and let students check their ideas.

6.2

W1 Oh gosh there are all kind of gifts that people can be born with – you know mental gifts, intelligence, physical attributes – beauty – strength

W2 Definitely, yeah. Talent …

W1 Talent absolutely, musical inclination.

W2 And I definitely believe that people are born with certain talents – I think that they can can also, er you know they can grow depending on the environment that they're in, but …

W1 Yeah, but I think you either have an affinity for something or you don't.

W2 Definitely.

W1 Two children take piano lessons – one's going to be amazing and the other …

W2 … the other is just OK, I agree and I …

W1 Do you think it comes from the parents?

W2 I think, you know, maybe partly, like I said, I think that it can influence a talent, but I think I think some people are born with certain talents and some people aren't.

W1 And the people that are born with it, is it because their parents, like were their parents musically gifted so they have an inclination?

W2 I think so, yeah …

c Ask students to summarize the main ideas orally with a partner and check their answers together.

> **Main ideas**
> People are born with talents. Talents are from parents. They can be affected by environment.

React and discuss

Aim *To give students the opportunity to develop their free-speaking skills.*

- Ask students to work in pairs or small groups. Monitor but don't interrupt.

- Conduct a whole-class feedback to round up the activity.

Exploring natural speech
p.45

One of the features of natural speech is the way in which people interrupt each other, finish off sentences or thoughts for each other, or simply punctuate the conversation with apparently meaningless phrases (*Yeah*; *Definitely*).

Although it is extremely difficult for non-native speakers to interact in this way themselves, it is important that they can recognize the way conversation proceeds because it helps them to follow the flow of natural speech. This section draws their attention to some of these conversational devices so that they can develop their listening skills.

- Talk to the students briefly about the way people connect with each other in conversation. In a monolingual class, you could discuss the words and phrases used in the students' own language.

- Ask the students to look at the transcript of **6.2** and follow it as they listen. Don't worry about the task just yet.

- Play the recording.

- Now focus the students' attention on the task. Make sure they understand what they have to do and that some answers are used more than once.

- Play the recording again.

- Ask students to check their answers together, then check with the whole class.

1	B	shows agreement
2	B/A	shows agreement and adds to an idea
3	E	shows slight disagreement
4	B	shows agreement
5	C	finishes an idea
6	D	replies to a question
7	A	adds to an idea
8	D	replies to a question

Language focus: *should, ought to, must, have to, need to*

Aim *To focus students' attention on the sometimes subtle distinctions between expressions of obligation (I have to do a test / I must do a test) and encourage them to use them more accurately and confidently.*

Students will have come across all the structures dealt with here (*should, ought to, must, have to, need to*) but are still likely to have some difficulty in using them appropriately.

- You could start this section with the books closed. Write up the word *obligation* on the board and see which words the students come up with.

- Accept any verbs and phrases that the students offer but only write up the ones that will be dealt with here: *should, ought to, must, have to, need to* and elicit meaning and use as you deal with each one. Ask students to refer to the Language commentary on p.49 if they are having specific difficulties.

Note

Pronunciation and spelling of *ought to* /ˈɔːt tə, ˈɔːtə/ can cause problems. Note too the 'f' in *have to* /ˈhæftə/

1 It will probably be a good idea to do the first one or two together with the whole class. Then ask the students to work individually or in pairs. Give them enough time to work through all the extracts.

- Monitor and help as necessary, but be careful not to give too much help too quickly. It is useful for students to have to think about language and articulate their reasons for using a particular word.

- Check the answers with the whole class.

a	ought to / should
b	have to
c	need to / have to
d	should / ought to
e	should have / ought to have
f	don't have to / needn't / don't need to
g	needn't / don't need to
h	must

2 Check that students understand what is required here, and do the first one with the whole class.

- Ask the students to continue in pairs, then check the answers with the whole class.

a	advice / recommendation
b	rule
c	necessity (in this case absence of necessity)
d	duty / responsibility / advice
e	advice / recommendation about the past
f	rule or law
g	necessity (in this case absence of necessity)
h	advice or order that the speaker gives to themselves.

3 *Had better* is likely to be more familiar to students than the expressions *supposed to* and *meant to*, though in natural English all three phrases are heavily used. *Had better* sometimes causes problems because of the contracted *'d: I'd better do it now* which is sometimes dropped altogether in spoken English so that what you hear is *I better do it now*.

- Look at the example with the students, then ask them to do the exercise in pairs. Monitor and help as necessary but, as before, give them time to work it out before offering help.

- Check answers with the whole class and get them to practise saying the sentences in order to improve pronunciation.

Possible answers
a You're not supposed to / meant to park here without a permit.
  You're supposed to / meant to have a permit to park here.
  You'd better not park here without a permit.
b You're not supposed to / meant to travel without a ticket.
  You're supposed to / meant to have a ticket if you want to travel.
  You'd better buy a ticket if you want to travel.
c You'd better not tell him you've seen me.

4 Ask students to do this together in pairs. Monitor and help. Some students may not be aware of any difference at all between the sentences. Without telling them the answer, you can ask them to think about who has decided on the action in each sentence; the person themselves or an outsider? (What is sometimes referred to as an *internal* or *external* agent.)

- Check answers with the whole class. Note the stress in the sentences and get the students to practise saying them.

> **a** 1 *I have to* means the obligation is external – my manager has told me to work. **Note:** /ˈhæftə/
> 2 *I must* means the obligation is internal – I personally feel the need to work. **Note:** *must* is stressed.
> **b** 1 *You don't have to* means you are not obliged to / you needn't (if you don't want to).
> **Note:** *needn't* tends to sound more formal.
> 2 *You mustn't* is a prohibition – you are not allowed to.
> **Note:** /ˈmʌsnt/, i.e. *'t'* at end of *must* is dropped.
> **c** 1 *I needn't have* means I wore a suit but it wasn't necessary. **Note:** /ˈniːdəntəv/ may need some drilling to make it sound like one word.
> 2 *I didn't need to* means it wasn't necessary, so I didn't wear a suit. **Note:** *'t'* at end of *didn't* tends to be dropped.

Exploitation

Aim *To give students the opportunity to practise using some of these expressions in short, functional contexts.*

1 The students may find it difficult to come up with appropriate, natural-sounding language straight away, but given time and encouragement, they should be able to produce something that sounds realistic.

- Give them a few minutes to read through the situations. Check any unknown language, e.g. *day off*.
- Go through the first situation with them. Ask for suggestions and ideas, and refine or elaborate as necessary.
- Ask the students to do the rest in pairs. Monitor and help as necessary.
- Ask students to read out their sentences, using appropriate intonation.
- If you want to extend the exercise, you can ask students to develop them into mini-dialogues:

> A *You shouldn't have taken my car without asking.*
> B *I know, I'm sorry. The thing is, it was an emergency and you weren't around and I just had to go.*
> A *What do you mean emergency? What kind of emergency? …*

> **Possible answers**
> **a** You shouldn't have borrowed my car without asking.
> You should have asked before borrowing my car.
> **b** You needn't have bought me a present. / You didn't need to buy me a present.
> You shouldn't have …
> **c** I don't have to go to work tomorrow. / I don't need to …
> **d** I didn't have to go to the meeting. / I was supposed to / meant to go to the meeting but it was cancelled.

2 Here the students are given the opportunity to talk quite freely about relatively serious issues. Because of the nature of the task, students will need to use some of the modals and related expressions presented.

- Put the students in pairs or small groups and ask them to choose two or three of the topics. Tell them to make notes about these, paying particular attention to needs, obligations, and responsibilities. Set a time limit.

- Now ask the students to take it in turns to talk to each other about their topics. Again, set a time limit. Monitor, but don't interrupt. Make notes about any mistakes made, particularly those to do with the target language.
- Write up the errors that you hear and ask the students to correct them.

▶ There is an extra discussion activity on p.142 which leads in to a letter-writing exercise – both practising the use of these structures.

6.2 Survivors · p.46

This stage continues the theme of natural talents, in this case survival, to provide a context for reading comprehension and the *Language focus*, determiners.

Lead in

Aim *To prepare students for the text by getting them to think about crocodiles and make their own questions for the text.*

This is a useful way of preparing for reading texts, particularly factual ones; it arouses interest by making students focus on the text in a way that is personal to them.

- Write up the word *crocodile*.
- Put students in groups to note down all they know, or think they know, about crocodiles under the two headings.
- Ask the class what they know about crocodiles.
- Write up any facts and ideas they come up with, whether or not you know them to be true.
> *they live in Africa; they live for a long time; they are bigger than alligators; they have different names in different parts of the world*, etc.

Reading

1 Ask students to read the text to check their answers. (Not all their ideas will necessarily be confirmed by the text.)

- Now let them answer the question about the survival of crocodiles. They should find four or five main reasons.

> Basic design / have adapted to environment / tough and robust / effective immune system / adapt to changes / learn quickly / intelligent (according to some people)

Close up

- Put the students in pairs to do the exercise. Encourage them to make guesses from context rather than rely on their dictionaries.

1.28 frogs, toads, salamanders

1.32 only *enough* – check the pronunciation of the other words with them: though /ðəʊ/; through /θruː/; thorough /ˈθʌrə/; cough /kɒf/

1.40 in captivity (*in zoos* and *in a cage* are correct, but the phrase used is *in captivity*)

1.78 emerge from an egg; birds *hatch*

2 Again, suggest that students work together on these. Set a time limit, but allow the students time to grapple with the answers. Monitor and help as necessary, but avoid giving answers too quickly.

> **a** Human beings represent the greatest threat there has ever been to crocodiles and other wild animals.
> **b** Modern day crocodiles are very similar to fossils of crocodiles that lived in the past.
> **c** The reason appears to be that crocodiles learn very quickly to avoid dangerous situations and have adapted to the devastating effect of humans on their environment.
> **d** This is an interpretation question to which there is no right or wrong answer. Dr Ross probably associates the word intelligence with humans rather than animals; he may feel that intelligence is multi-faceted whereas the rapid learning referred to is only to do with learning to adapt to the environment.

Language focus: determiners   p.47

Aim *To introduce students to more sophisticated and subtle use of determiners.*

Students will be very familiar with the determiners *some*, *any*, *every*, and can probably use them accurately and fluently. However, in this section more sophisticated and subtle uses are introduced, some of which may appear to contradict what the students have already learned (as is often the case when students get to an advanced level).

For example, students will have learnt that *some* is used in affirmative sentences, whilst *any* is used in the negative and interrogative. Here, however, they will be shown *any* used in the affirmative, *I like **any** wildlife programmes.*

Differences of emphasis are also illustrated: *There isn't any food in the house* and *There is no food in the house*; *There were a few people at the party* and *There were few people at the party.*

Remind students to refer to the Language commentary on p.49.

1 Go through these different meanings with the whole class to make sure that everyone understands. The distinction between *a proportion* and *a quantity* is small, but not difficult to use.

> *a proportion of* = *part of a whole*, like a percentage
> *a quantity of* = *a number of*.

- *Some* with the meaning of *approximately* may well be new. You can drill students in it quite quickly by giving them other numbers (always large, always round) which they rephrase using *some*, e.g.

about 150 million people = *some 150 million people*
approximately 10,000 dollars
around 500 visitors
about 25,000 years ago
approximately 50 kilometres wide
around 60 million inhabitants

> **a** approximately
> **b** a proportion (not all) of
> **c** a quantity of

2 Ask students to discuss and do the exercise in pairs, then check answers with the whole class.

> **a** *some programmes* = not all / a proportion
> *any programme* = all / it doesn't matter which
> **b** *some money* = the speaker assumes the person has some money to lend
> *any money* = the speaker isn't sure whether the person has money or not
> **c** *Every 18-year-old* = All 18-year-olds
> *Any 18-year-old* = No 18-year-old is banned from going to university. The implication is that they have to meet certain criteria; the sentence could well continue with *provided that they ... .*

3 Ask students to do this together, then check the answers with the whole class.

- Ask students to practise saying the sentences with the correct intonation.

> **a** The sentences with **no** sound more negative and therefore more emphatic.
> **b** Uncountable nouns like *food*; plural countable nouns like *friends*; singular countable nouns like *passport*: in other words, all types.

4 It's probably a good idea to do this with the whole class. This is one of those exercises where students either know or don't know the answer, and discussing it in pairs or groups does not really help.

- Ask the students if they know the answers. If they do, write them up. If not, tell them and explain the difference to the whole class.

> *a few* and *a little* sound more positive or optimistic.

Note

few and *little* are formal and are mainly used in written English. In speech people more often say *not much* and *not many*, which sound more obviously negative or pessimistic.

Exploitation

Aim *To give the students some controlled and semi-controlled practice in using determiners.*

1 You may want to do the first question with the whole class and then get students to work on their own or in pairs.

- Give them time to check their answers with a partner before checking with the whole class.

> **a** any   **b** no   **c** some   **d** any   **e** No   **f** Some

2 Check that the students understand the task, i.e. that they only have to write down the second part of the sentence.

- Ask them to do this individually.

- Now put them in small groups. Students take it in turns to read out their endings, while the others in their group try to guess which beginning phrase they go with.

- You may want to conduct a whole-class feedback of some of the more amusing / the best sentences.

- You could vary this activity by asking students to work in small groups throughout. Do the first sentence with the whole class, eliciting and demonstrating various possibilities: *live in Igloos*; *have worked with crocodiles and still have four limbs*; *do not lie*.

- Now ask the students in their groups to produce the best sentences they can. Set a time limit. Monitor and help as necessary.

- At the end of the activity, ask for some examples from the groups. You may want to write up an example for each phrase so that the students can copy them.

> Personal answers

Speaking: interview

Aim *To give students freer speaking practice around the theme of the unit.*

- Outline the task. Explain that it's a radio / TV interview about the ability of humans to survive in the world.

- Divide the class into two halves: journalists and media pundits. (If the class is uneven it is easier to have more pundits.)

- Then put the class into pairs, journalists together and pundits together. Give them time to prepare their part of the interview. Monitor and help as necessary. You may need to encourage them to be more adventurous, more expansive, more 'advanced' in their ideas.

- Now split the class into groups of four, two journalists and two pundits. One of the journalists conducts an interview with one of the media pundits. The others are, for the moment, the audience. You probably won't need to set a time limit, but will need to encourage the students to keep going, to extend a line of questioning, to probe further, to stop the interview dying. You could demonstrate this with one of the more able students first.

- When the interview is finished, the pairs swap over and the former audience members conduct their interview.

- You may want to round up the activity by asking one of the pairs to demonstrate their interview while the rest of the class is the audience.

- Students could write up the interview for homework as a magazine article. Refer them to the Writing guidelines on p.154.

Exploring words p.48

Aim *To give students practice in recognizing and forming words from their roots, and also to highlight potential pitfalls in over-generalizing the basic rules.*

It is extremely useful for students both to be able to try and work out the meaning of an unknown word by looking at how it's made up, and to be able to make new words from a known base.

1 a Ask students to draw a table in their notebooks with the headings *Adjective, Adverb, Noun, Verb*.

- Do the first one or two words with the whole class, just to get them started, then ask the students to work in pairs or small groups. Monitor and help as necessary.

- Check the words with the whole class. (If you have access to an overhead projector, a transparency with the complete table will save time in writing up the answers.)

- As you check the words, pay attention to pronunciation and word stress. It's a good idea to get students into the habit of marking the stress on words as they write them down; very often if you get the stress in the right place, the rest of the pronunciation follows and the word will sound right.

> **a Adjectives:** a'stonished / 'beautiful / 'dangerous / 'fearsome / im'pressive / 'musical / 'natural / prehi'storic / 'scratching
> **Note:** *fearsome* is not a very common adjective, *'frightening* is more usual.
> **Adverbs:** suc'cessfully
> **Nouns:** a'bility / a'mazement / bi'ologist / ex'tinction / incli'nation / 'modesty / musical / re'searcher / sur'vivor / 'toughness
> **Verbs:** a'risen / a'stonished / 'scratching

b Again, it is probably best to start students off as a whole class, so that they're clear what to look for, then allow them time to work together in pairs. Monitor and help as necessary.

- Check with the whole class, but don't worry about everyone writing everything down. It's more important that they get the general idea of what we look for, rather than getting stuck on the differences between *-ible* and *-able* endings, for example.

> **Adjectives:** -ed / -ful / -ous / -some / -ive / -al / -ic / -ing
> PLUS -able / -ible / -less / -ly / -ish / -y
> **Adverbs:** -ly (some are adjectives)
> **Nouns:** -ity / -ment / -ist / -tion / -ation / -y / -er / -or / -ness
> PLUS -ee / -ism / -hood / -ship / -th
> **Verbs:** -en (past participle) / -ed / -ing
> PLUS -ize or -ise / -ify / -en

c You could ask students to do this individually, for a change of focus, and then compare answers with a partner, or simply conduct a whole-class check.

> 1 *smaller* is a comparative adjective (the others are nouns for people / occupations).
> 2 *roomful* is a noun (the others are adjectives).
> 3 *critic* is a noun (the others are adjectives).
> 4 *table* is a noun (the others are adjectives).
> 5 *outlive* is a verb (the others are adjectives).

2 a Outline the task briefly, then do the first one or two with the whole class. Make sure they realize just how many words they can make, by including opposites and negatives: *disagree, disagreement, disagreeable* as well as *agree, agreement, agreeable.*

- You could ask students to do this individually or in pairs, but let them compare answers in pairs. Monitor and help as necessary.
- Check answers with the whole class. Make sure the students are able to pronounce the words correctly.

	Noun	Verb	Adjective
a	adaptability, adaptation, adapter	adapt	adaptable
b	agreement, disagreement	agree, disagree	agreeable disagreeable
c	amusement	amuse	amusing, unamusing
d	art	x	artistic, unartistic
e	base	base	basic
f	danger	endanger	dangerous
g	description	describe	descriptive, nondescript
h	injury	injure	injured, uninjured
i	reliability, unreliability	rely	reliable, unreliable
j	truth, untruth	x	true, untrue

b It may be best to do this as a whole-class activity in order to make it more focused. Students either know some collocations or they don't; unlike many other activities, they don't get better at it by discussing it with a partner.

- What is important here is that they get a few words to use with each adjective, so don't spend too much time on whether or not certain words collocate.

> **Possible answers**
> a **adaptable** person / piece of furniture / position
> b **(dis)agreeable** person / food / disposition: both words tend to sound rather old-fashioned.
> c **(un)amusing** person / story / situation
> d **(un)artistic** person / film / culture
> e **basic** instinct / truth / life
> f **dangerous** water / person / cliffs / situation
> g **nondescript** story / paragraph / person
> **descriptive** story / paragraph / film
> **Note:** *descriptive* and *nondescript* are used rather differently; *nondescript* means something so ordinary and uninteresting that there is nothing about it worth describing, and so cannot be used merely as the opposite of *descriptive.*
> h **(un)injured** player / footballer; **injured** (but not *uninjured*) lover
> i **(un)reliable** witness / source / person
> j **true** (but not *untrue*) identity / love / life; **(un)true** story

3 Quickly check that the students know the root words and understand the task (i.e. that they may need to use derivatives of these words to complete the paragraph, not just the words themselves).

- Ask them to complete exercise 3 individually. Monitor and help as necessary.
- Put students into pairs to check their answers, then check quickly with the whole class.

> | 1 | seriously | 6 | faultless |
> |---|---|---|---|
> | 2 | predictions | 7 | impossible |
> | 3 | accompanying | 8 | difference |
> | 4 | distinctive | 9 | entertainment |
> | 5 | symmetrical | 10 | perfectly |

4 This activity provides free speaking practice so it's up to you how much time you want to spend on this.

- Brainstorm some personal qualities / personal descriptions onto the board, e.g. *beautiful, intelligent, conscientious, hard-working, punctual, ethical, moral, sensible, sensitive,* etc. Get as many as you can, but do this activity quite quickly.
- Split the class into at least four groups or pairs. Give each group a different subject a, b, c, or d. Tell them what letter they are.
- Ask them to discuss and decide on the qualities needed to be successful in that particular profession. Set a time limit, but encourage students to discuss the issue properly, e.g. *I think you'd have to be really patient to be a teacher – it must get so frustrating when people don't learn or do their homework …* rather than simply to list different qualities.
- Monitor and join in the discussions as appropriate, but don't interrupt or correct. This is a free-speaking activity, not a grammar or vocabulary exercise.
- Just before the groups appear to be running out of steam, stop the activity and regroup. Make new groups of four, each with an a, b, c, and d in them.
- Now ask the students to talk to each other about the qualities they felt their profession needed. Encourage them to ask and answer questions, to agree and disagree as much as possible.
- Again monitor by going around the groups and joining in where appropriate. Stop the activity before students start to lose interest.
- You can conduct a whole-class feedback if you feel the activity needs to be rounded off.

7 Senses

Theme: the senses, intuition, and common sense

7.1 Gut feelings

A discussion about intuition and a survey of beliefs

- **Listening:** gist and developing interpretation skills
- **Exploring natural speech:** incomplete sentences
- **Language focus:** degrees of agreement
- **Speaking:** conducting a survey
- **Writing:** reporting a survey

7.2 Don't stare – it's rude!

A scientific study of how people know when they are being stared at

- **Vocabulary:** verbs of seeing
- **Reading:** gist and specific information
- **Language focus:** Present perfect

7.3 Common sense

Common sense in business management

- **Reading:** intensively to complete a questionnaire
- **Vocabulary:** verb–noun collocations
- **Language focus:** making generalizations
- **Speaking:** talking about the best way of learning English

Exploring words

Colloquial words and expressions

Workbook

- **Language focus:** Present perfect; making generalizations
- **Vocabulary focus:** senses – sight and sounds; noun–verb collocations
- **Vocabulary expansion:** idioms with *keep*; compound adjectives
- **Listening:** déjà-vu

7.1 Gut feelings   p.50

Stage 1 consists of a listening text which contextualizes phrases used when expressing agreement and disagreement.

Lead in

Aim *To introduce vocabulary and get the students talking about the theme of the lesson.*

1 Put the students in pairs to ask the questions and complete the table.

- Feed back to a table on the board, or prepare an OHT with the answers.

a Senses	b Parts of body	c Sensitive to	d Adjectives
hearing	ears	noises; sounds	audible; aural
sight	eyes	movement; light	visible; visual
touch	skin; fingers; all body	texture; temperature	tactile; tangible
taste	tongue (taste buds)	tastes: sweet; sour; bitter; salt	tasty
smell	nose	smells; odours; scents	smelly; odorous; scented

2 In pairs, or as a class, check the vocabulary and discuss the questions.

> **Possible answers**
> *sixth sense* = an awareness of something you can't see or hear
> *gut feelings* = feelings based on instinct rather than thought (*gut* = stomach)
> *intuition* = ability to know or understand something without the need to think, learn, or reason
> *déjà-vu* = the feeling that you've been somewhere or done something before even though you 'know' you haven't.
> **Other possibilities:** second sight / telepathy / mind reading / being clairvoyant or psychic

- You could personalize the lead-in at this stage. Ask the students in small groups to discuss the following questions.
  Which is the most important of our senses and why?
  Do you believe in a sixth sense or in déjà-vu?
  Have you ever had a psychic experience?

Listening

Aim *To listen for gist and develop interpretation skills.*

1 Focus the students on the questions and play the recording.

7.1

M1 Well now, you see, the thing, what I think is, is the reason that the five senses are called senses is because they are in effect tangible in that there's something that we can either agree on or disagree on – if you start talking about erm intuition or instinct as a sense, you're into a vaguer area, you know – your instincts – your both your instincts are different to mine, whereas if I say 'Do you think this feels like cat's fur' or whatever, then there's a point that we can agree on – we can use our tangible senses, but I I don't think instinct and intuition is something that's – I think some people have more intuition than …

W I was going to say – there does seem to be, which is is peculiar, I mean why that should be.

M2 There's a heck of lot we don't know about the human mind though, isn't there, (Yeah) when you you go into the situation where you think 'I've been here before, I know I've been and I know what's going to happen next.' How can you explain that?

M1 Well exactly – it's a vague area. I mean it's the way I always feel about, you know, psychology and therapy and psychiatry because, you know, you're supposed to be dealing with something that is tangible or recognizable, but there's nothing to go on and I think instinct and intuition is much the same thing – it's different for all of us, you know.

W Would you agree that there is such a thing as female intuition?

M2 We know there is.

M1 Well if I do, I could only take that, I could only accept it as a female point of view, so we could, yeah, we could debate that all night. I mean, yes, I'm prepared … Convince me.

W Well, I have to say I feel that there is, but erm I might just be just a little bit biased.

> **a** instinct, intuition, déjà-vu, female intuition
> **b** Yes

2 The students listen again and answer the questions. Let them check in pairs before checking with the whole class.

> **a** They are concrete / provable / definite / undisputed / everyone experiences the same.
> **b** They are unprovable / people experience them differently and to differing degrees / some people think they don't exist.
> **c** As an example of something *tangible* – everyone can feel it.
> **d** Persuade him of the existence of female intuition.
> **e** Because she is a woman. She may feel she is more likely to believe in female intuition than a man would.

Exploring natural speech
p.51

Aim *To expose students to unfinished lines of natural conversation and to get them to make guesses about the missing words.*

In natural speech, people often fail to finish what they intend to say. This might either be because it's obvious to the listener what they are about to say next, or they can't think of the right word, or because they choose to rephrase what they are going to say. The aim of this exercise is to expose students to this feature of speech, and get them to make guesses about the missing words. It is an exercise in guessing vocabulary from context, but it should also improve the students' ability to follow natural speech.

• Put the students in pairs to compare their guesses. Play the extract from the recording. (This is not included in the tapescript section of the Student's Book.)

7.2

M1 … Whereas if I say 'Do you think this feels like cat's fur' or whatever, then there's a point that we can agree on – we can use our tangible senses, but I I don't think instinct and intuition is something that's (?) – I think some people have more intuition than (?)…

M1 Well if I do, I could only take that, I could only accept it as a female point of view, so we could, yeah, we could debate that all night. I mean, yes, I'm prepared (?)… Convince me.

> **Possible answers**
> • so definable / measurable / definite / concrete
> • others
> • to be convinced / persuaded

Language focus: degrees of agreement

Aim *To introduce and practise phrases used to express different degrees of agreement and disagreement.*

1 Discuss **1a** as a class, then put the students in pairs to discuss **b–d**.

• As a strongly-stressed pronunciation is important to express the strength of feeling with these phrases, you may wish to drill them briefly before moving on to exercise **2**.

> **a** I agree
> **b** Agreement phrases: *Absolutely / Indeed / Of course / Quite / Sure / You're right*
> The others are expressions of disagreement: *I don't know / I'm not so sure / Nonsense*
> **c** *Absolutely / Indeed / Quite* are stronger than *Of course / Sure / You're right*, although it can depend on how strongly you say these expressions. *Nonsense* is stronger than *I don't know*, which is stronger than *I'm not so sure*.

2 Model the activity with a quick student – they read out the first sentence, and you agree using one or two strongly-stressed expressions.

• In pairs students take it in turns to practise. Monitor and correct as necessary.

Speaking

Aim *To practise expressing agreement and disagreement by doing a class survey on the theme of the lesson.*

1 Write: *Female intuition, The significance of dreams, The special relationship between twins,* and *Déjà-vu* on the board. Ask the students which of these they believe in, or have experience of, and encourage one or two to briefly share their views.

- Put the students in pairs or small groups to discuss the statements about the beliefs listed.
- Have a brief feedback.

2 Ask students, in their pairs or groups, to prepare questions to ask other students in the class about two of the ideas. Focus the students on the examples, and elicit one or two more from them to get them started.

3 When the students are ready, get them to circulate and ask their questions. They should ask as many students as they can, and should note their answers. Set a time limit: five to ten minutes.

4 Put the students back in their original groups to discuss the results of their survey. Ask them to select a spokesperson to present their findings.

- You could put some language on the board to help them present their findings statistically, for example:

  We found that …
  Our research has shown that …
  …% of the class … whereas …
  Most of the class …
  The majority of the class …
  Some of the class …
  A few members of the class …
  A small minority …

- An alternative way to do this is to divide the students into four groups, depending on which belief they were most interested in at the lead-in stage above. Ask each group to prepare a questionnaire about their belief to ask other students in the class. Then conduct the survey as above.

Writing

Aim *To write a report summarizing the class survey above.*

1–3 Let the students work in the same groups they prepared the survey in.

- Read through the information with the students, refer them to the Writing guidelines on p.155 of their books, and monitor and help as they write the report. Make sure they think about the audience they are writing for.
- You could do the preparation in class, and let the students write the report for homework.

7.2 Don't stare – it's rude! p.52

Stage 2 consists of a reading text which contextualizes uses of the Present perfect.

Vocabulary

Aim *To introduce and practise verbs of seeing.*

- If you prefer a more teacher-focused start to a lesson, write *look* on the board and try to elicit synonyms for *look* from the students. You could mime some of the words, and see if the students can tell you which words you're miming. Or ask: *What do you call it when you look quickly / in an angry way / for a long time / because you're in love*, etc.
- Put the students in pairs or small groups to work through questions a–f.

  a They are all to do with looking.
  b *watch* = look at something for a length of time, especially something changing or moving
     watch a TV programme / a football match / someone's every movement
     look at = to point your eyes in a direction to see something
     look at a clock / a book / newspaper headlines
  c Probably embarrassed or uncomfortable.
  d *gaze* = look at someone or something for a long time (e.g. because they are beautiful or interesting) often without realizing – *gazing* is not deliberate.
     gaze at someone you love / the stars / the sky
     stare = deliberately look at someone or something for a long time without moving your eyes (e.g. because you are angry or interested)
     stare at someone you dislike / a road accident
  e *glare* = stare angrily at someone for a long time, often to intimidate them
  f *glance* = look at something very briefly

Reading

Aim *To read for gist and specific information. The text also contextualizes uses of the Present perfect.*

1 As a lead-in, ask the students whether they can tell if they are being watched or stared at. Have they ever been in a situation where they felt someone was watching them, even though they couldn't see them? Alternatively, you could do the experiment described in the text as a lead-in.

- Focus students on the questions and ask them to read the text.

  a He is trying to show that some people have an instinctive awareness of when they are being stared at. (In other words he wants to prove the possible existence of some kind of sixth sense.)
  b She thinks that the people who do experiments only submit positive results and that in these cases some kind of cheating may be going on.

Close up

- Put the students in pairs to do the exercise. Encourage them to make guesses from the context rather than rely on their dictionaries.

> 1.2 *so-called* is used to introduce a word or phrase that the readers may not be familiar with. It draws attention to the name. It can also cast doubt on a fact.
> 1.25 The children would have an equal chance of being wrong or right. / There's an equal chance that the children could be wrong or right.
> 1.35 Such a high success rate
> 1.47 roughly / approximately / about / more or less
> 1.61 sceptical

2 Let the students remain in pairs to answer the questions. These questions require them to read the text closely and interpret the implied meaning of words and phrases, so encourage them to spend time discussing the answers, and be prepared for different answers in the feedback.

> **a** In wartime conditions pilots would be under great stress and might imagine all kinds of strange things.
> **b** To prove that his first set of experiments were valid. / To counter accusations of fraud. / To tighten up the conditions of the tests – to make sure children were not picking up sounds.
> **c** To make sure no sound got through.
> **d** That children are very skilled at cheating and had in fact cheated in the first set of experiments.

- At this stage, you could do the following extra activity to practise the variety of ways used by the writer to convey doubt about the study. These include:
  - referring to Dr Blackmore as a *controversial biologist*, and introducing a sceptic to counter his view.
  - referring to the theory as *so-called*, and mentioning accusations of fraud.
  - using 'casting doubt' phrases: *claim(ing) / (even) claimed / seems to be / According to Dr Sheldrake / he believes / His own theory*

- Write these sentences on the board. Do the first as an example, then put the students in pairs to rephrase the rest in a way which implies doubt.
  1. A flying saucer landed in New York last night.
  2. Half of Europe will be under water by the year 2100.
  3. Eating three apples a day will help you live to the age of 100.
  4. Smoking is good for you.
  5. Exercise kills more people than it helps.

> **Possible answers**
> 1. It is claimed that a flying saucer …
> 2. According to one controversial scientist …
> 3. Dr … seems to believe that …
> 4. …'s own theory seems to be that …
> 5. This so-called expert claims that …

React and discuss

- Put the students in small groups to discuss the question. Students might like to try out the experiment described in Paragraph 2 of the article with other students in the class. It's not necessary to use blindfolds unless the students want to.

Language focus: Present perfect p.53

Aim *To revise and check various uses of the Present perfect and Present perfect continuous.*

Although students will have come across this tense many times before, they are still likely to have problems. This is because the concept of the Present perfect – a tense that in some way links past to present – is probably not easily translated into the student's language. In many languages the form of the Present perfect in English is the same as the form used to refer to the past. This leads to errors such as: *I have worked in London last year*. At this level, it is worth looking at 'perfect' in terms of aspect – what connects all the uses of the Present perfect and Present perfect continuous discussed is that they happened or started in the past and lead up to or have some sort of result now.

1 Elicit the answer to the first question as an example. Ask the students: *Are the stories still circulating now, or are they finished?* Check that the students are aware of this basic idea that the Present perfect is connected to the present, before doing the rest of the exercise.

- Put the students in pairs to choose the correct forms, and then to check in the article.

a	have circulated	(Clue: *for years* is often used with the Present perfect – although you could use it with the past)
b	has completed	(Clue: Now)
c	sat	(Clue: In the experiments – completed past events)
d	I've never seen	(Clue: never)
e	organized	No clue in the sentence itself.

2 Put the students in pairs to look at the examples and answer the questions. You may wish to refer the students to the Language commentary on p.57.

> The Present perfect always connects the present in some way with the past.
> The Past simple refers to completed past actions which we have no interest in linking with the present.

3 Put the students in pairs to match the time expressions with the correct tense.

yesterday	PS	recently	PS / PP
since 1997	PP	just	PP
in 1999	PS	already	PP
for 22 years	PS / PP	several times	PS / PP
when I was 15	PS	It's the first time …	PP

4 Put the students in pairs to discuss the forms.

> **a** I've done three experiments – these are completed experiments. Emphasis on achievement / product / quantity
> I've been doing experiments – the experiments may not yet be complete. Emphasis on process / activity
> **b** I've been carrying out experiments – repeated action in time leading up to the present
> He's been staring at me – continuous action in time leading up to the present

5 Ask the students to discuss the sentences in pairs.

> **Possible answers**
> **a** I know both sides of the argument. / Now I can make up my own mind about the theory.
> **b** So I don't know what it feels like to be in the dark.
> **c** And now I am qualified. / So I know what I am talking about.

Exploitation

- Put the students in pairs to complete the article with the correct tenses. Do the first as an example.

> **1**
> 1 has won
> 2 did
> 3 have done / have been doing
> 4 have spent
> 5 have won
> **2**
> 6 has dropped
> 7 fell
> 8 told
> 9 have ever had
> 10 have been looking forward
> 11 joined
> **3**
> 12 left
> 13 rang
> 14 have now passed
> 15 saw
> 16 I have been telephoning
> 17 I've contacted
> 18 has seen
> 19 (has) heard
> 20 has just disappeared

- To give the students some fluency speaking practice at this stage you could do the following extra activity.

  1 Students work in groups of three to think of three interesting events that have occurred in class this week. For example, a student has done their homework, or the fire alarm has gone off.

  2 Explain that students are going to read the news. They should prepare to read out the three short news stories by adding a few details, and be careful about using the Present perfect or Past simple.

  3 Students choose one person from their group to read the news to the rest of the class.

Stage 3 consists of a reading text which contextualizes the language used when making generalizations.

Lead in

> **Aim** *To introduce the theme of the lesson and get students talking.*

1 Check that students have understood *common sense*. You could check by asking questions like:

If you always forget your key, what would be a *common sense* solution?
– putting it in something that you never forget, like your wallet or purse
– not doing anything
– sticking it to your forehead

2 Ask the students to discuss the problems in pairs.

> **Possible answers**
> There are many possible answers here. A couple of possibilities for the first are that you should stay at home and try not to spend too much, or that you should try to get a part-time job. For the second, you should try to share cars to work with other colleagues, or introduce a scheme where you allocate parking spaces on the basis of who has furthest to travel or needs their car most for their job, etc.

Reading

> **Aim** *To read intensively to complete a questionnaire.*

1 Ask students to discuss the questions in pairs. The words in italics are from the text. This is a way of checking in advance that students are familiar with their meaning.

> **Possible answers**
> **a / b** Personal answers. *Challenging* often collocates with *job* or *career* and means difficult and hard work, but in an interesting and stimulating way. Here, *goal* means ambition.
> **c** Working conditions / pay / attitude of management / whether the company is growing or shrinking / staff relations. *Morale* means the state of confidence and enthusiasm felt by a person or group of people.
> **d** Between employees or unions and management over, for example, working hours / pay and conditions / job descriptions. *Negotiations* means discussions aimed at coming to an agreement.
> **e** This depends on the kind of job. By sales figures / exam results / productivity. Your *performance* is how well you do the job.
> **f** Soldiers are *reprimanded* by officers.
> Drivers are *reprimanded* by police officers.
> Prisoners are *reprimanded* by prison officers.
> *Reprimand* means tell off / criticize.

2 a Ask the students to read and tick True or False.

   b Students compare in pairs then listen and check.

Number 1 is false. Paying someone to do something they already like to do will not lead them to enjoy the task more.

Number 2 is false, too. The majority of employees prefer non-challenging jobs that allow them to socialize.

Number 3. Again, this is false. Most people get upset about inequity in pay rather than their own low pay. People can be happy with low pay when everyone in the company is the same.

Number 4. False again. It is better to start with the most extreme position you can take. Most negotiations end up in the middle of where the two parties started. The more extreme your starting point the more likely you are to end up with the better side of the bargain.

Number 5. This is true. The essence of leadership is sticking to a position despite appearances. By changing their position too often, leaders create confusion in the organization.

Number 6. True again. Groups do not bring out the best in people unless they are well-structured and individual contributions are clear. Most people, it seems, need to be held accountable.

Number 7. False. The data does not support the idea that happy workers are necessarily better, more productive workers. Unfortunately, while angry workers may be unproductive, satisfied workers are not necessarily productive.

Number 8. Once more, this is false. Employees do better when they are told what is expected.

Number 9. False again. All the data shows that groups can make more extreme and less accurate decisions than individuals.

Number 10. This one's true. Give your feedback immediately. Don't wait. This has been shown on mice and men alike. Tell them what's wrong right away.

> 1, 2, 3, 4, 7, 8, 9 are False
> 5, 6, 10 are True

React and discuss

1–2 Put the students in pairs or small groups to do this exercise. If your students have a business background, encourage them to talk about their personal experiences in the feedback.

Vocabulary   p.55

Aim *To check verb–noun collocations around the topic.*

1 Ask the students to work in pairs to match verbs with nouns. They could refer back to the reading text where some of the collocations are contextualized.

express	an idea
give	a decision / feedback
make	a decision / an effort
put in	an effort
stick to	a decision / an idea
take	a decision

2 Ask the students to complete the sentences on their own.

• Check the answers as a class, then put the students in small groups to ask each other the questions. Feed back some of the interesting comments as a class.

a	making / taking	**c**	express
b	give	**d**	made / taken; stick to

Language focus: making generalizations

Aim *To introduce language used in making generalizations.*

This section looks at generalization expressions such as *on the whole* and *broadly speaking*; the use of the zero and first conditional to express general truths; and the use of the Present simple with frequency words and expressions when generalizing.

1 Start by eliciting from the students as many generalization expressions as they can think of. Write them up on the board.

• Ask the students to look back at the questionnaire and underline or highlight any other expressions. Let them check in pairs before feedback. You may wish to refer the students to the Language commentary on p.57.

If you pay someone ..., they will ...	Statement 1
If you have to reprimand ..., it is better ...	Statement 10
Most people ...	Statement 2,3
(it is) usually (best)	Statement 4
In most cases	Statement 5
they tend to	Statement 6
almost always (improves)	Statement 7
often	Statement 8
In general	Statement 9

2 Ask the students the question.

The Present simple

Exploitation

• Do the first subject together on the board to check that the students can manipulate the various forms. Elicit sentences from students and write them up on the board. Correct any errors as a class.

• Put the students in pairs or small groups to make generalizations. One way of doing this is to ask students to write generalizations for **b** and **c** while you monitor and check. Then ask them to do **d**, **e**, and **f** as a speaking activity. This way you combine some controlled accuracy work with some more creative fluency work.

Speaking

Aim *To practise using generalizing language.*

1 Either ask students to work through the instructions in the book, or follow this alternative procedure.

• Ask the students to work individually or in pairs to brainstorm their own list. You could start them off by eliciting from the class three or four ideas for the first category, *Learning new words and phrases*, and writing them on the board. Monitor and prompt ideas.

2 Put the students in groups of four to agree on a 'Top 10' list.

3 Ask the students to think about how they are going to present their ideas using generalization language. Give them some time to prepare, then ask a spokesperson from each group to present their 'Top 10' tips.

Exploring words

p.56

Aim *To introduce and practise colloquial words and expressions.*

Students usually enjoy learning informal expressions and slang – and pick them up quickly. Make sure they note the degrees of informality and pay particular attention to expressions that should only be used if they are sure the people they are talking to will accept their use of them.

1 Put the students in pairs to match the words with the pictures.

clockwise from top left:

ciggie	cigarette
pickie	picture (photograph)
cardy	cardigan
woolly	pullover (woollen garment)
zapper	TV remote control
sarny	sandwich
wellies	Wellington boots
telly	television
hanky	handkerchief
specs	spectacles / glasses

2 a Put the students in pairs to decide whether the expressions mean *a lot* or *a little*.

c, d, e, and g mean *a lot*
a, b, and f mean *a little*

3 a Ask the students to match the two parts of the questions then check their answers in pairs.

1 c *boiling* = very hot
2 d *parched* = very thirsty
3 e *peckish* = a bit hungry
4 a *shattered* = very tired
5 f *gutted* = very disappointed
6 b *sozzled* = drunk

b Play the recording so that the students can check their answers. (This is not included in the tapescript section of the Student's Book.)

7.4

1
A It's boiling in here.
B Take your coat off, then.

2
A I'm parched.
B Do you want some of my Coke?

3
A I'm feeling a bit peckish.
B We'll be having lunch soon.

4
A It's been a hard day – I'm shattered.
B Have an early night, then.

5
A I failed the exam and I'm gutted.
B Don't worry. You can take it again.

6
A He can't walk. He's completely sozzled.
B Hardly surprising – he's been drinking all night.

c Put the students in pairs to answer the questions.

Personal answers

4 a Do the first with the whole class as an example, then put the students in pairs to guess the answers to the rest.

1 person; any man's name
2 thing; the name of any object (probably with an unusual name); corkscrew / stapler / battery charger
3 thing; like **2**
4 person; a man
5 thing; like **2**
6 person; any woman's name
Note: These are all words we use when we can't remember a word or a name.

b–c Put the students in pairs to think about the pronunciation, then listen, check, and repeat. (This is not included in the tapescript section of the Student's Book.)

7.5

1 Where's what's-his-name?
2 Pass me that thingummyjig, please.
3 There's a blue and red whatchamacallit in my case.
4 There's this bloke in our street …
5 I can't find that little doodah.
6 I saw thingy the other day.

d Put students in groups. Give them a short time to think of their description, then take turns to describe their people and things, while the rest of the group guesses.

8 Control

Theme: family pressures on children to succeed, gun control, and waste control

8.1 Family pressures

How far parents push their children to succeed early in life

- **Reading:** prediction, specific information, and interpretation
- **Vocabulary:** *take up*
- **Language focus:** reference words (1)

8.2 Gun control

A report on gun control in the USA

- **Listening:** prediction and note-taking
- **Exploring natural speech:** consonant linking
- **Language focus:** *what* and *it* clauses for emphasizing
- **Speaking:** a discussion on gun control

8.3 Waste control!

The damage that plastic waste can do to the environment

- **Reading:** gist and summarizing
- **Language focus:** talking about the future
- **Writing:** a magazine article about the future

Exploring words

Countable and uncountable nouns

Workbook

- **Language focus:** *what* and *it* clauses; similar constructions; the future
- **Vocabulary focus:** crime
- **Vocabulary expansion:** the prefix *anti-*; Latin phrases
- **Listening:** parental control

8.1 Family pressures   p.58

Stage 1 consists of a reading text about family pressures which contextualizes reference words like *they* and *those*.

Lead in

Aim *To get the students talking about the theme of the lesson.*

- Focus the students on the picture and ask them what they know about the Williams sisters. Do they think it's a good thing that their father planned their career from an early age?

Note

Richard Williams, the father of Venus and Serena, planned his daughters' tennis careers from an early age. He consulted psychologists and coaching videos, and the girls lived and breathed tennis. The girls are both ranked in the top ten in the world. Venus Williams has won both the US Open and Wimbledon titles twice and is currently ranked number one.

- Put the students in small groups to discuss the questions. Encourage students to express their views or even experiences in feedback.

Reading

Aim *To give practice in prediction, reading for specific information, and interpretation.*

1 Read the introduction as a class, then put the students in pairs to do the task. This pre-reading activity is designed to pre-teach some of the key words and phrases from the article. Encourage the students to guess the meanings of words before using dictionaries.

- Elicit one or two predicted stories before doing the reading.

Glossary

young prodigies – young people with exceptional intelligence or abilities
accelerated learning – learning more intensively than in mainstream education
insular family – a family that tends not to meet other people
The other difficult words are dealt with later in the *Close up* section.

2 Ask students to read the article and check their ideas.

> Sufiah's father says she has been led astray by 'nasty socialists and boyfriends' and has been brainwashed. He says this was against her will.
> Sufiah's own explanation is that she has finally succeeded in escaping from a stifling home environment in which she suffered from physical and emotional abuse.

Close up

- Put the students in pairs to do the exercise. Encourage them to make guesses from the context rather than rely on their dictionaries.

> **1.17** *naive* is pronounced /naɪˈiːv/. The noun is *naivety*.
> **1.19** has it ever *occurred to you …*
> **1.29, 31** spies / espionage / war
> **1.46** choose / select
> **1.46** If you want to push your children

3 Ask the students to answer the questions in pairs. They will need to refer back to the text.

> **a** That the learning process in children can be accelerated.
> **b 1** Sufiah talking about her parents having chosen to publicize her disappearance.
> **2** Sufiah talking about why she disappeared.
> **3** Sufiah comparing her experiences at Oxford with her brother's fate as a competitive tennis player.
> **4** Mr Yusof expressing his pessimism about the future of the family's relationship with Sufiah.
> **c** She supports Sufiah's rebellion and does not approve of how her parents treated her.

4 Ask the students to look at the descriptions, and discuss with a partner which fit(s) Sufiah. Note that *parent-bashing* means constantly criticizing or shouting at her parents.

- Discuss as a class in feedback.

React and discuss   p.59

1–2 Put the students in small groups to discuss these questions, then do a brief class feedback.

Language focus: reference words (1)

Aim *To revise and practise the use of reference words in written English.*

This section looks at the use of reference words in written English. In particular, it looks at subject pronouns like *he, she, they,* and object pronouns like *him, her, them,* which refer to and replace a noun, and it looks at definite (or demonstrative) pronouns like *this, that, those* which refer to a clause.

In the practice section, it checks the use of *one* as a reference or substitute word. The use of *one* is quite difficult to get right. In the example here it is used to replace or avoid repeating the noun. But the following basic rules are worth noting:

You can only use *one* to replace countable, not uncountable nouns.

Compare, for example:
> *I enjoy films, especially the* **one** *on last night.*
> *I enjoy dancing, especially the* **dancing** *we did last night.*

You can use articles before *one*, but you can only use *a / an* if there is an adjective.

Compare, for example:
> *I like that shirt. Could you get me* **one**?
> *a blue* **one**?
> *the* **one** *over there?*

1 Put the students in pairs to consider the extracts briefly, then discuss the answers as a class.

> **a** *the same* = passed A level maths at grade A at the age of 13
> **b** *All this* = the effort Mr Yusof has made to speed up his children's education
> **c** *They* = Sufiah's parents
> **d** *those* = the things that Sufiah said about her family in her e-mail

2 Let the students complete this individually then check their answers with a partner. Do the first as an example.

- In the feedback, ask the students to say why they have chosen each reference word. In particular, check the rules for using *one*, discussed in the Aim section above. Check that the students understand that *then* refers here to the time when Venus and Serena were born.

> **1** him   **2** them   **3** then   **4** one   **5** all this
> **6** The man   **7** they   **8** that

Vocabulary

Aim *To check and practise the different meanings of the multi-word verb* take up.

1 Put the students in pairs to match meanings with examples.

> **a** accept   **b** start   **c** adopt   **d** continue
> **e** occupying   **f** moved into

2 a–c Put the students in small groups to discuss the questions.

8.2 Gun control   p.60

Stage 1 consists of a listening text about gun control which contextualizes *what* and *it* clauses for emphasizing.

Lead in

Aim *To get the students talking about the theme of the lesson.*

1 If you have a class of students from the same country, do this as a class discussion. If the students come from different countries, put them in small groups to talk about the differences before discussing briefly as a class.

2 This activity introduces the students to the subject of the listening to follow. Read through the extract and discuss the questions as a class. Note that *bear* means *carry*, and here *to infringe* means *to interfere with* or *restrict.*

> **a** Carry guns for self defence
> **b** There are too many guns around. They can easily get into the wrong hands. One of the results is an increase in the number of deaths from guns – especially massacres in schools and other public places.

Listening

Aim *To give practice in prediction and note-taking.*

1 Ask students to work in pairs to guess the answers. Elicit a few thoughts, but don't give the answers yet.

2 Play the first part of the report so that the students can check their guesses.

8.1

Presenter   Gun control is a subject which concerns most people in the United States – whether they want to defend their right to own and use weapons – or whether they see them as the curse of modern America. And it's easy to see why it's such an emotive issue when you study the statistics. Each year half a million gun-related crimes are committed in the US – including thirteen thousand murders. And with nearly two hundred and fifty million firearms in circulation it's clearly not an easy task to keep track of who has a gun and why they want to keep it.

> a B – 500,000 (half a million)
> b C – 13,000
> c C – 250 million

3 a Make sure the students know whether they are A or B, and what they are listening for, then play the recording – the complete report.

8.2

Presenter   Gun control is a subject which concerns most people in the United States – whether they want to defend their right to own and use weapons – or whether they see them as the curse of modern America. And it's easy to see why it's such an emotive issue when you study the statistics. Each year half a million gun-related crimes are committed in the US – including thirteen thousand murders. And with nearly two hundred and fifty million firearms in circulation it's clearly not an easy task to keep track of who has a gun and why they want to keep it.

[**Radio extract** The Million Mom March flooded the national mall today with a call for tougher gun control. 'I was eight years old when my father …']

Presenter   The Million Mothers' March, when tens of thousands of people converged on Washington to call for tighter gun laws, was an example of how strongly many campaigners feel about the issue. But while tragedies like Colombine – when two teenagers shot dead twelve of their classmates and a teacher – have heightened public concern about guns, many people want to keep their right to own one. Trish Gregory is a member of the NRA – the National Rifle Association.

Trish Gregory   I am a law-abiding American – I've never broken a law. I'm a single woman who lives alone and I feel like I have a right to defend myself. For instance if someone was stalking me or I was fearful about myself or my family, I have a right to own a firearm.

Presenter   The gun lobby argues that the second amendment gives everyone the right to carry a firearm. But as with most things to do with the gun debate, it's not that simple. The amendment is open to a variety of interpretations – as Yan Vernick, the Assistant Director of the Centre for Gun Control in Baltimore, explains.

Yan Vernick   One of the primary controversies is whether the second amendment protects an individual right to own a gun, or whether, instead, the second amendment protects only some kind of collective right, that's closely related to the old-fashioned idea of state militias – groups of citizens who collectively were there to help to keep the peace.

Presenter   And while campaigners on both sides of the argument will continue to put as much pressure on politicians as possible the battle is increasingly being fought in the courts. Not only are people testing out what the second amendment actually means, but more than thirty cities and states are trying to sue gun manufacturers for medical costs that stem from the misuse of firearms. Barbara Holt of the group New Yorkers against Gun Violence explains the basis of the cases being brought.

Barbara Holt   When you are making and distributing a product that is particularly dangerous, you have a duty as a manufacturer to take particular care in how you distribute it – whose hands it gets into. And **what they're arguing is that the gun manufacturers have not taken care**.

Presenter   While similar law suits have been successful against other industries, it's far from clear what the results of the ones against the gun manufacturers will be. **What is certain is that the process is being watched closely by campaigners** and politicians alike, to see what it will mean for the future of gun law in America.

b   Students exchange information from their notes in pairs.

> **Student A**
> • The NRA supports citizens' right to own guns (*a firearm*). The association also teaches people how to use guns safely and responsibly.
> • NYAGV believes that the gun manufacturers have direct responsibility for how the guns they produce are used or misused.
>
> **Student B**
> • The Million Mothers' March called for tighter gun control laws.
> • The gun lobby thinks the 2nd amendment gives individual citizens the right to carry a gun.

c Put the students in small groups to discuss.

Exploring natural speech

Aim *To get students to recognize and practise the way words run into each other in natural speech.*

This section looks **specifically** at the linking that takes place when a consonant sound at the end of one word merges with a consonant sound which starts the next word.

1 If your students haven't done this sort of activity before, write the first line on the board, read it out, and ask the students where they hear examples of linking.

> Gun control is a subject which concerns most people in the United States.

- Point out the example of the loss of the /t/ sound in *most*.
- Ask the students to work in pairs to mark where they think there are similar merged consonants.

2 Play the recording and ask the students to check where they have marked the merges. You may need to play and pause to let the students hear these merges (This recording is the same as **8.1** but is recorded again for convenience.)

- Check as a class. If you have access to an OHP, write the answers below on a transparency.

> Gun control is a subject which concerns most people in the United States – whether they want to defend their right to own and use weapons – or whether they see them as the curse of modern America. And it's easy to see why it's such an emotive issue when you study the statistics. Each year half a million gun-related crimes are committed in the US – including thirteen thousand murders. And with nearly two hundred and fifty million firearms in circulation it's clearly not an easy task to keep track of who has a gun and why they want to keep it.

- Put the students in pairs or threes to take turns reading out the passage with the correct linking.
- Monitor and correct.

Language focus: *what* and *it* clauses p.61

Aim *To introduce and practise* what *and* it *clauses.*

As discussed in the Language commentary on p.65, these structures, sometimes referred to as cleft sentences, are used to add emphasis to the speaker's key information by effectively giving prominence to that information. It's important that the students are aware that this is very much a feature of spoken English. Manipulating the complex form of the structures is difficult, so spend time checking this when doing the transformation exercises in the Exploitation section. You may also need to introduce some drilling work so that the students have an opportunity to practise putting the stress in the right place.

1 Do this as a class. Elicit answers from the students, and write the correct answers on the board. Point out that in **a**, *What* is replacing the object, whereas in **b** it replaces *it*, the subject.

> a What they're arguing is that the gun manufacturers have not taken care.
> b What is certain is that the process is being watched closely by campaigners.

2 Read through the examples and explanations with the students.
- Put the students in pairs to change the sentences.

> a What the gun lobby argues is that people have the right to carry guns.
> b What their opponents say is that so many guns on the streets lead to serious crime.

3–4 Read through the examples and explanations with the students.

5 Ask the students to do this in pairs, then check the answers with the whole class.

> a her father, not her mother, her friends or anyone else.
> b the increase in crimes of violence, not crime in general, theft or fraud, etc.
> c the Columbine High School killings, not any of the previous shooting incidents, or the general level of shootings.
> d the Million Mothers' March, not what politicians or any other individuals or groups said.

Exploitation

Aim *To practise* what *and* it *clauses for adding emphasis.*

1 You could do this orally. Elicit a few suggestions from the class for the first sentence stem, then give the students a few minutes to think of ideas for the others. Put the students in small groups to share their ideas.
- Alternatively, you could ask the students to write sentences, then ask them to read out a few.

> **Possible answers**
> a the warm weather / holidays / eating outside / having time off work
> b having to get there so early / my boss / getting home so late / the low pay
> c resign / reduce taxes / put up taxes / improve the health service

- Before the students read out their sentences, or talk in groups, it is a good idea to drill the structure for pronunciation. Point out that the main stress in these sentences is on *best*, *most*, *really*, and *should*, and on the key information word that follows. Model it, and ask the students to repeat:

What I like best about summer is the holidays.

- Check that the students try to get the pronunciation correct as they speak.

2 Ask students to think of sentences then compare them with a partner.
- Monitor and correct the key stress.

3 Do the first as an example, then ask students to complete this exercise in pairs.

> b It was in 1980, not 1990, that John Lennon was shot.
> d It was his wife, not his sister, who was with him when he was shot.
> e It was a single gunman, not a group of three gunmen, who killed John Lennon.
> f It was Mark Chapman, not John Chapman, who shot John Lennon.
> **Note:** In each of these sentences, the *not* phrases can be put at the end.
> a It was in 1980 that John Lennon was shot, not 1990.
> b It was his wife who was with him when he was shot, not his sister.
> etc.

Speaking

Aim *To practise speaking fluently by encouraging a discussion on the theme of the lesson.*

1 You will need to decide whether this is a relevant subject for students in your country. If not, or if you have a mix of nationalities in your class, you could get them to discuss the United States.

• Divide the students into groups of three or four to discuss the topic for a few minutes. Ask them to draw up a five-point action plan – five things that should be done to improve the situation.

2 Ask one person from each group to present their five-point plan. You could encourage the use of *what* and *it* clauses for emphasizing by writing on the board some language for the students to use to organize their presentations:

What we should do is …
The first thing we should do is …
It is vital/imperative that we …

• The following extra activity could be set for homework.

• Students write a magazine article putting forward their own ideas about the causes of violence in modern societies and what could be done to reduce it in the future. Refer them to Writing guidelines p.154.

8.3 Waste control! p.62

Stage 3 consists of a reading text about the damage that plastic can do to the environment. It contextualizes future forms.

Lead in

Aim *To get the students talking about the theme of the lesson, to practise listening for specific information, and to prepare the students for the reading to follow.*

1–2 You could do this as an open class discussion. Alternatively, let the students do the survey by themselves, then put them in pairs or small groups to compare answers.

3 Play the recording. The students listen and note answers to the questions in 1.

8.4

Speaker 1 The rubbish in my house consists of food, packaging, paper, cardboard, plastic, newspapers, bottles, that kind of thing. Erm, I don't really sort into different types, I'm afraid. I'm not a very green person – I try to put the bottles in the bottle bank er when I've got the energy and I do put the newspapers into a a collection box that we have for newspapers, but apart from that I don't sort the rubbish. Erm I use about one large plastic bag a week, not very much, because I live by myself, and the local council takes the rubbish away. I don't know where it goes. I presume it goes to a local rubbish dump. Erm, I presume that when it gets there – I hope they sort the newspapers and the bottles and things like they say they do, but I'm not convinced and I think the rest of the rubbish just goes to erm fill in the land.

Speaker 2 Rubbish that we regularly get rid of in our household, erm is normally paper, erm paper packaging and plastic packaging for food, cardboard, newspapers, bottles, tins, and we do sort them into different types. Erm we sort out the bottles and the paper which we leave out for recycling and that's collected once a week. We probably use about three to five bags a week, I should say, for getting rid of actual rubbish, er but that obviously depends – over Christmas we certainly got rid of a lot more. The rubbish is taken away by the local council refuse collectors or dustmen, whatever you like to call them, and the recycling is also taken away on a weekly basis by the same council. I would imagine that the rubbish goes to landfill sites and is buried there and the bottles and the paper are taken away and recycled into some other form.

Speaker 1	Speaker 2
• food, packaging, paper, cardboard, plastic, newspapers, bottles	paper, packaging, plastic, cardboard, newspapers, bottles, tins
• She says 'Not really,' but she does sort bottles and newspapers	Yes: bottles and newspapers.
• Yes: 1 large bag	Yes: 3–5 bags
• Local council	Local council: refuse collectors, dustmen
• Rubbish dump Sorted, then rest goes into landfill site.	Landfill site Some sorted and recycled, the rest buried.

Reading

Aim *To practise reading for gist and summarizing.*

1 Put the students in pairs to answer the questions. In the feedback, make sure they understand these more technical words.

a landfill site **b** biodegrade **c** recycle **d** fossil fuel
e disposable

2 Focus the students on the headline and the picture, and ask the class to predict two or three examples of damage that plastic waste can do to the sea and to animals.

• Ask the students to read the passage and answer the questions.

a litters sea bed and coasts in ever-increasing quantities
b can get inside animals like turtles and seabirds

Close up

• Put the students in pairs to do this exercise. Encourage them to make guesses from the context rather than rely on their dictionaries.

1.32 make
1.49 *ingest* = to take food into stomach
     digest = to process food in the stomach
1.59 negative. It means the negative side.
1.63 *refuse* here is a verb /rɪˈfjuːz/. The noun *refuse* /ˈrefjuːs/ means rubbish.

3 Ask the students to read the text again and match the summaries to the paragraphs, then check in their pairs.

a D	b E	c A	d C	e B

- An alternative way of doing this activity, if it is new and difficult for your students, is to get the students to work in pairs to try to remember or guess answers to the summarizing questions (a–e) first, before reading the text again. This way they create a prediction task, so that when they read to match the paragraphs with the summaries, they will be reading for the key information they have predicted.

React and discuss p.63

- Encourage a whole-class discussion.

Language focus: the future

Aim *To revise and practise future forms.*

Learners at this level often still have problems with accurate use of different future forms. The aim of this revision section is to get students to match form to use, and to discuss the difference between use of one form and use of another. The most important and difficult confusion is between *will* and *going to*, and it is worth taking time to check that the students grasp the differences checked in **3a** and **b**, and **5a** and **b**. The rules of use are covered in the Language commentary on p.65.

If you have a monolingual class, you could approach this lesson by thinking about how their own language is different from English, and by asking students to translate example sentences. It is also worth pointing out that uses often overlap, and that understanding the basic rules and then developing some sort of 'feel' for which one to use is all the students need worry about.

1–2 Ask the students as a class or in pairs to label the tenses and match their uses.

a Future simple (or *will* future)	future fact or certainty
b Future continuous	prediction or expectation
c Future passive	prediction or expectation

3 Ask the students to discuss in pairs, then feedback as a class.

- **a** This prediction, using *going to*, is based on observable present evidence.
- **b** There is no concrete evidence for this prediction. It is simply an expectation.

4 Ask the students to discuss in pairs, then feedback as a class.

- **a** At some point in time before 2020 we will stop using plastic bags. *By* means **at** or **at sometime before** this time. This sentence uses the Future perfect.
- **b** We will stop using plastic bags in, **but not before**, the year 2020.

5 Ask the students to do the matching task in pairs.

- Be prepared to discuss the answers as a class, and deal with students' queries here. You may wish to refer the students to the Language commentary on p.65. The important point to make is that the choice of tense depends on the point of view of the speaker. Consequently, you could use *going to meet* in **c**, for example, but then you would be stressing your personal intention, rather than the more neutral fact that this is all pre-arranged. Similarly, you could say *will retire* in **d**, but then you would be stressing a prediction, your personal point of view, rather than the fact that this is a general social trend.

a an intention (or plan)	d a future trend
b an offer	e a scheduled event
c an arrangement	

Exploitation

Aim *To raise awareness of common errors in future forms, and to improve the students' accuracy.*

1 Do the first as an example, then put the students in pairs to correct the sentences.

- **a** I'll send you a postcard. (a promise)
- **b** I'm going to give up smoking … (an intention)
- **c** ✔
- **d** My sister is going to have a baby. (a prediction based on evidence now)
- **e** I'll pay. (an offer)
- **f** I'm having lunch … (an arrangement)

- You might like to write on the board (or on a handout) five or six typical errors with future forms that your students have made recently, or errors that speakers of your students' first language typically make. Then ask the students to correct in pairs. This will focus on the problems your particular students are most likely to have.

2 Model the activity with two quick students.

- Divide the students into groups of three, and allocate their roles if they can't agree.

- Monitor and note errors that the students make. They should mostly be using the Future simple and continuous.

- With a quiet class, it is better to set this up more thoroughly – it usually results in more and more accurate language production. First of all, divide the students into roughly equal groups of optimists, pessimists, and realists, with three students to each group. Ask them to write as many predictions as they can for each subject in five or six minutes. Insist on a strict time limit, but monitor and help with ideas. Finally, re-divide the groups so that there is an optimist, a pessimist, and a realist in each group. Then instruct the discussion as above.

Writing

Aim *To write a magazine article.*

- Discuss this task in class, before setting the actual writing for homework. Here is a suggested way of approaching it:

- Put the students in pairs, an optimist with an optimist, a pessimist with a pessimist, etc.

- Ask the students to note down five or six views that they expressed in the discussion, then to put them in a suitable order for an article. You might suggest that they put their most strongly-held or interesting point first or last.

- Ask them to decide on a headline for the article, and to decide on the tone. How are they going to start the article? Contemplatively, perhaps: *What will life really be like a hundred years from now?*

- Refer them to the Writing guidelines on p.154.

Exploring words   p.64

Aim *To introduce and practise countable and uncountable nouns.*

1 Write on the board: *Where would you normally find piped music or muzak? Do you think it is a good thing or bad thing? Why?* Encourage a brief class discussion. This introduces the text and creates a prediction task.

- Ask the students to read the article and underline nouns that can be *both* countable and uncountable.

- The students should work with a partner to discuss **1b**, and think of sentences to illustrate different meanings.

- Put the pairs together to share their ideas, then write up some of the best sentences in the feedback.

Nouns that can be countable (C) and uncountable (U):

organization
Pipedown is an *organization* which fights against muzak. (C)
He's good at *organization*. (U)
life
Cats have nine *lives*. (C)
My granddad's 85 but he's still got a lot of *life* in him. (U)
sound
Who's making those funny squeaking *sounds*? (C)
Sound travels more slowly than light. (U)
noise
Stop the car. There a rattling *noise* coming from the engine. (C)
Modern cities are full of *noise*, even at night. (U)
conversation
That was one of the most interesting *conversations* I've ever had. (C)
To be successful at *conversation*, you've got to be a good listener. (U)

---

2 Do one as an example, then ask the students to complete the exercise in pairs.

a Crime; crimes; violence
b means; traffic; places; cars
c rubbish; food; paper; packaging; newspapers; card; bottles; facilities; metal; plastic
d people; control; information; Internet
e parents; abuse
f music; form; pollution

always countable: places; cars; bottles; facilities; people; parents
always uncountable: violence; traffic; rubbish; packaging; information; music; pollution; Internet
can be countable or uncountable: crime; food; paper; newspaper; card; metal; plastic; control; abuse; form
singular words ending in -s: means
plural words which do not end in -s: people

3 Put the students in small groups to discuss the subjects.

- Give them a few minutes to decide which subjects they wish to talk about, and what they are going to say. Then start the activity, making sure that they take it in turns to speak. Ask one student in each group to time the speaker carefully. Having to speak for two minutes makes it more demanding.

- Monitor and note errors, especially with the use of the nouns, for feedback.

- An alternative is to play *The 60 seconds game*. See explanation of the rules on p.103. To make it even tougher, you could allow challenges if speakers make grammar mistakes, or misuse a noun.

9 Music matters

9.1 My music   p.66

This stage includes a listening which contextualizes adverbs of degree.

Lead in

Aim *To get students thinking about music as an introduction to the theme of the unit.*

It will probably make a change for the students to listen to music in class. Because this is a completely different area from language learning, you may find that the dynamics of your class change quite dramatically. Previously quiet students may have a lot to say, they may be passionately interested in an obscure music type, while previously articulate students may have little to say. Be prepared!

- Before playing the music, write the word *music* on the board and elicit from the students all the different types of music they know. Make sure you have the ones listed in the Student's Book (*ballroom dance, Celtic, choral, classical, country, disco, folk, heavy metal, latin, jazz, opera, pop, reggae, rock 'n' roll, soul, traditional jazz (trad jazz), world music*). Don't spend too long on this though, and try to avoid at this stage any drawn-out discussions. The point is to demonstrate how wide the variety of musical styles is.

- Now tell the students they are going to listen to some snippets of music. Tell them there will be 17 quick bursts of music, each lasting about 20 seconds, and get them to write down numbers 1–17 in their notebooks before they listen. You don't have to play them all, just as many as you or your class want to do. The whole 17 take just under five minutes.

- Play the recording and ask students to identify the types of music.

  9.1

  Snippets of different kinds of music

- Ask them to compare answers with a partner, then play the recording again so that the students can check.

- Go through the answers with the whole class, playing the recording again, pausing after each section and checking that they all know which type of music it is.

1	Rock 'n' roll	7	Ballroom dance	13	Soul
2	Traditional jazz	8	Jazz	14	Pop
3	Classical	9	Choral	15	Disco
4	Opera	10	Reggae	16	World music
5	Celtic	11	Country 'n' western	17	Heavy metal
6	Latin	12	Folk		

Listening

Aim *To pick out specific information from a conversation between a group of speakers.*

1–4 Ask students to read questions 1–4. Check that they understand how many speakers there are (four) and that there may be more than one answer to each question.

- Check the pronunciation of the names in **2** (Mozart /ˈməʊtsaːt/, Bach /baːk/, Ella Fitzgerald /ˈelə fɪtsˈdʒerəld/, Michael Jackson /ˈmaɪkəl ˈdʒæksən/), otherwise they might not 'hear' the names.

- Play the recording.

9.2

Speaker 1   I have quite specific music tastes. If I'm working, I have to listen to classical music because … anything with words I start singing along and then I can't work. So I like Fauré's Requiem and Mozart's Requiem and depressing things like that – a bit of Debussy. Er, otherwise I like acoustic rock, as everybody laughs at me. I like acoustic guitars and Jeff Buckley and Tom Waites because it's fairly depressing but very soothing kind of music. I like Radiohead, makes me quite mellow cos otherwise I am quite an intense person. So my music calms me down.

Speaker 2   I've always loved Michael Jackson music and sort of really poppy stuff – everything that's in the charts. I know that it's cheesy but it's erm, I don't know, it's fun to dance to and it's catchy – you you hear it once and I dunno next time you hear it, you sort of know know the lyrics and you want to sing along. And then when you go to night clubs or wherever, it's fun to dance to. Erm, but more serious stuff, I, I really like Ella Fitzgerald and jazzy stuff but yeah, that's about it.

Speaker 3   Well I'm actually a bit of a classical music buff myself and I like all the Classic FM Standards by sort of Mozart and Elgar, and people like that. The really sort of clichéd ones. I think my favourite piece of music is probably Bach's Brandenburg Concertos. Erm, I like listening to that and it helps me unwind and relax at the end of a day, something like that. Erm, I also quite like erm, erm classical music when it's adapted in films, I particularly like the way someone like Stanley Kubrick uses it sort of in an undermining way, sort of, in *A Clockwork Orange* – the Beethoven scenes in that, I think that there … that's very clever and very moving and erm, yeah.

Speaker 4   Erm, my favourite music is kind of older music. The sort of erm, the sort of standards, I think they're called – jazz standards, which are sung by people like Ella Fitzgerald and er people like that. I like it because erm, I like singing it myself. Erm, I used to sing in a band where we did a lot of stuff like that. Erm, I find it very relaxing, erm and it's just very calming music. It's something that you can just sort of lie down and listen to. Erm I like having it on in the car cos I sing in the car a lot which is quite embarrassing at traffic lights because it's quite obvious that I'm singing very loudly. Erm and er it's just nice – it's nice music to go to sleep to, it's nice music to sort of just relax to, it's nice music to drive to, erm and they're just they're they're classic pieces, they're sort of classic melodies.

- Give students a few seconds to complete writing their answers, if necessary, then ask them to check with a partner.

- If there are any doubts or queries, play the recording again.

- If necessary, check the answers with the whole class once they have checked with their partners.

		Speaker(s)
1	Classical	1; 3
	Pop	2
	Jazz	2; 4
	Dance	2
	Film music	3
2	Mozart	1; 3
	Ella Fitzgerald	2; 4
	Michael Jackson	2
	Bach	3
3	1; 4	
4	4	

Exploring natural speech

Aim *To draw the students' attention to the form of certain adjectives in informal English,* (poppy, cheesy, catchy).

It is quite easy, and useful, for students to create their own adjectives in this way (*papery, leathery*), and can really help to develop informal speaking skills.

1–3 Ask students to read the transcript briefly.

- Play the recording and give the students time to complete the blanks. (This does not appear in the tapescript section of the Student's Book.)

9.3

I've always loved Michael Jackson music and sort of really poppy stuff – everything that's in the charts. I know that it's cheesy but it's erm, I don't know, it's fun to dance to and it's catchy – you you hear it once and I dunno next time you hear it, you sort of know know the lyrics and you want to sing along. And then when you go to night clubs or wherever, it's fun to dance to. Erm, but more serious stuff, I, I really like Ella Fitzgerald and jazzy stuff but yeah, that's about it.

- Ask them to compare answers with a partner.

- Now ask them to do **2** and **3** together.

- Briefly check the answers.

1	All the adjectives end in *-y*. The suffix *-y* means *like*. (Similar to *-ish*.)
2	*poppy* root = noun *pop* + *-py* *catchy* root = verb *catch* + *-y* *cheesy* root = noun *cheese -é̸* + *-y* *jazzy* root = noun *jazz* + *-y*
3	**a** poppy (like pop), jazzy (like jazz) **b** catchy **c** cheesy

4 You may want to do the first one quickly with the students. Then set the other three for them to do in pairs.

- Check the answers. You may want to extend the activity and add some other adjectives, e.g.

  like rubbish   rubbishy
  (tastes) like wood   (tastes) woody

a	This meat tastes rubbery.
b	I hate chewing gum that tastes fruity.
c	He's worked as a builder all his life – that's why his hands are leathery.
d	I don't like that camera. It looks plasticky.

React and discuss

Aim *To allow the students to talk about the music they like.*

It's up to you how much time you spend on this, but it is likely that all students will want to spend at least a few minutes talking fairly freely about their music.

1–2 If you think the students may find it difficult to get started, it sometimes helps to do the activity yourself, in front of the whole class. Talk to them quite freely, naturally, and fully about your favourite kinds of music, why they're your favourite, how they make you feel, when you tend to play them, where, and whether you play or have played music yourself. Let the students ask you questions if you like and then put them into small groups to do the same themselves.

- Monitor by listening and contributing, if appropriate, but don't interrupt or correct.

Language focus: adverbs of degree   p.67

Aim *To raise awareness of and practise using adverbs of degree.*

Students will be very familiar with most of the adverbs illustrated (*quite, really, fairly, rather, slightly*) but may not realize the extent to which they are used in natural speech and will probably not be able to use them fluently and naturally themselves. In this section students practise putting adverbs in the correct place in a sentence and using them in a freer speaking activity.

1 Outline the task briefly, then do the first one or two sentences with the whole class.

- Now ask the students to do the rest in pairs.
- Check the answers with the whole class.
- Refer students to the Language commentary on p.73.

a quite		**f** a lot; quite; quite; very
b really		**g** fairly
c quite		**h** slightly
d particularly		**i** rather; absolutely
e very (x 2)		

2 It's probably best to do this with the whole class, since it's a single question.

> **Meaning 1** *quite em'barrassing* = fairly, but not very – *quite* is not stressed.
> **Meaning 2** *'quite 'obvious* = completely / absolutely – here the word *quite* and the following word have equal stress.

- For pronunciation practice, it would be useful to ask students to go back to exercise 1 and practise saying the sentences aloud. Although there is often no right or wrong way of saying a sentence – the words we choose to stress depend on our point of view, or our mood at the time of speaking – students often find it difficult to read or say a longer sentence with a certain degree of fluency. It is useful to give them opportunities to practise.
- Ask them to work together in pairs. Encourage them to read the sentences with fluency, stressing the adverb or not, as

they see fit. Demonstrate these examples yourself, or write them on the board.

> I am **quite** an intense person. (very)
> I am quite an **intense** person. (fairly)
> I **really** like Ella Fitzgerald. (extra emphasis)
> I **really like** Ella Fitzgerald. (maybe other people don't)

3 Ask students to do this in pairs. Make sure they realize that there may be more than one answer.

- Monitor but don't do the work for them.
- Check the answers with the whole class.

> **a** quite; really; particularly; very; fairly; slightly; rather
> **b** as for a
> **c** quite; really; particularly; rather
> **d** quite; rather
> **e** really; particularly; very; fairly; slightly; rather

4 Outline the task. Ask students to copy the table headings into their books, then work in pairs to do the task.

- Monitor, but again, don't do the work for them. Struggling slightly to work out the answers will make the language more memorable.
- Check the answers with the whole class.

> **Note:** Full degree adverbs are used with non-gradable adjectives.
>
> | Full degree | High degree | Medium degree | Small degree |
> |---|---|---|---|
> | particularly | really | fairly | slightly |
> | quite (#2) | very | quite (#1) | a little |
> | absolutely | | rather | |
> | OTHERS | OTHERS | OTHERS | OTHERS |
> | totally | awfully | somewhat | a bit |
> | entirely | terribly | | |
> | | dreadfully | | |
> | | rather | | |

Exploitation

Aim *To give fairly controlled speaking practice which gives the students the chance to personalize the language.*

This can also be extended into a freer speaking activity if you feel that this would be useful for your students.

1 Briefly check the meaning of any words you think the students might not know.

Glossary

impulsive – doing things on impulse, without considering / thinking about them first
inquisitive – curious, or wanting to know everything
moody – describes someone whose mood changes, easily gets in a bad mood

- Now ask the students to make up sentences about themselves, using an adverb of degree with each adjective.
- Students can then compare with a partner, or in a small group, or you could elicit a few examples from the whole class.

- If you want to extend the activity you can ask the students to prepare to talk about two or three of the qualities, giving examples to explain their choice of adverb. You could start by talking yourself, e.g.

  I'm extremely stubborn; when I've set my mind on something, I stick to it and I don't let anyone or anything change my mind. There was one occasion when … .

- Now ask the students to do the same, in small groups of three or four.

2 Put students into small groups and ask them to discuss two or three things from the list.

- Monitor and encourage – particularly encourage the use of the adverbs.

Speaking

Aim *To round up the section by asking students to discuss, explain, and defend their choice of music.*

1 Set the listening task briefly by asking students to read the questions.

Glossary

trip-hop – a style of music, usually slow, that combines other styles – hip hop, reggae, and ambient sounds.

- Play the recording.

9.4

W1 Right, well. I've got to have my boys – my Backstreet Boys.

M Oh no.

W2 Oh Ellie.

W1 We've got to have some pop in the car to sing along with.

M OK, but just short bursts of that, please.

W1 Oh all right. Well what do you want?

W2 Well, I like to sing in the car …

W1 Exactly!

W2 So, I think some sort of, I dunno, girl with a guitar, some Joni Mitchell, Suzanne Vega.

W1 Yeah but nobody knows them.

W2 I know it.

W1 God, Mum and Dad'll probably know that more than you.

W2 Shut up. It's better than Backstreet Boys.

M I definitely want … I want some quite chilled-out stuff, some instrumentally kind of trip-hoppy stuff, so when we've got the nice vistas, the nice things to look at through the window …

W1/2 All right. OK

M … we can all feel very relaxed.

W1 Well Backstreet Boys do a really chilled-out one on their album.

W2 No.

M Leave the Backstreet Boys, honestly.

W1 OK.

W2 You wanna bring Kylie as well, don't you?

W1 No.

W2 You did last time.

W1 That was last year.

M Do we want any rock?

W2 Yeah.

W1 Really?

M So we can rock out …

W2 Yeah, maybe some classics.

W1 Yeah maybe a bit of Queen classics. What else?

W2 How about some classical stuff?

M / W1 Hmm.

W2 OK. Write that off. That says it all.

M Not too sure. Maybe.

W1 Erm.

W2 How about some songs from the musicals? Come on we all love that …

W1/M No, No.

W2 … we can all sing …

W1 No we don't want …

W2 Pleeese.

M1 We should have some Motown.

W1 Yeah, definitely.

W2 Some Diana Ross, some Stevie Wonder, …

M Stevie Wonder, yeah stuff like that.

W1 Jackson Five, we'll have some of the old …

M Ah, (I) like (the) Jackson Five, very good.

W1 Yeah, definitely.

M That'll keep us awake.

W1 Sing along with that.

W2 Yeah, sing along with Stevie, that would be good …

W1 … show off your musical voice.

W2 It passes the time, doesn't it?

W1 All right, OK what else, what have we got here?

W2 Eminem?

W1 Could have a bit of that.

W2 Yeah, we like that.

W1 Yeah.

W2 You don't like that, do you?

M Well, no, it's all right. I don't mind.

W1 You'll just start getting all political, and contro …, d'you know what I mean?

M I'll bite my tongue.

W1 Controversial.

M It's fine.

W2 So, so far we've got Joni Mitchell, the Backstreet Boys …

M Yeah.

W1 All right.

W2 Some chill-out stuff,

M Yeah.

W2 Some Queen …

M Some Queen, some Motown …

- Ask students to compare their answers.
- Play again if necessary.
- Check answers with the whole class if you think it's necessary.

> **a** They are choosing music to take with them on holiday.
> **b** Personal answer

2 Outline the task carefully and check that students understand the scenario.

- Now put them into groups of three or four and give them time to speak.
- Monitor and join in if appropriate, but don't interrupt. Take notes of mistakes made.
- Write the mistakes up (don't say who made them!) and ask the students to correct them themselves.
- You might like to ask each group to choose someone to present their group choice of albums to the rest of the class.

9.2 The player and the listener
p.68

The extract from a piece of literature demonstrates the use of a formal written style.

Vocabulary

Aim *To prepare the students for the text that follows.*

- Outline the task briefly. Don't let students quiz you about the meaning of the words yet – that's what they are going to work out themselves.
- Ask them to do the task individually or in pairs.
- Let them compare answers in pairs before checking with the whole class.

Note

Pronunciation of *discerning* /dɪˈsɜːnɪŋ/ and *insatiable* /ɪnˈseɪʃəbl/

> **a** **People:** absorbed; discerning; engrossed; insatiable; longing
> **Music:** harmony; melody; rhythm
> **b** absorbed; engrossed
> **c** insatiable
> **d** discerning
> **e** rhythm; melody; harmony
> **f** longing

Reading

Aim *To practise intensive reading of a literary text.*

This is a dense, richly descriptive text which immerses the reader in the heavily-charged atmosphere of the scene. You will need to prepare your students for this, not only in terms of language, but in terms of the atmosphere and emotion that the text creates.

1 Set the scene briefly first. You could either ask if anyone has seen the film / video of *The Piano* or heard the music and discuss what they thought about it, or you could ask the students to look at the pictures. What impressions do they evoke? What kind of film / book do you think it is?

- Now ask the students to read questions a–c.
- Give them quiet time to read Part 1, then ask them to answer the questions and compare in pairs.
- Check with the whole class if necessary. Don't worry about individual vocabulary questions at this stage – remind students that there will be a *Close up* stage later on when their questions will be answered.

> **a** To give him piano lessons.
> **b** She played with George's dog, Flynn.
> **c** To play the piano for her own pleasure.

2–3 Repeat the same procedure for Parts 2 and 3.

> **2**
> **a** It was completely different.
> **b** It awakened emotions in him. He could listen to her forever. He enjoyed watching her and listening to the music.
> **3**
> **a** She couldn't understand why he was satisfied by just listening and not playing.
> **b** **Possible answers:** to concentrate on the music / to see images created in his mind by the music.
> **c** She wasn't sure about his motives / what he really wanted.

Close up

- Put students in pairs to do the exercise. Encourage them to make guesses from context rather than rely on their dictionaries.
- Check the answers with the whole class. If there are other questions or queries about language, this is the time to deal with them.

> **1.12** a stick
> **1.28** and not
> *not refined and not discerning* (either)
> **1.38** piano keys
> Other meanings: *key* for a door / *key* to a puzzle or a problem
> **1.40** bow /baʊ/ noun = front end of a ship
> bow /bəʊ/ noun = 1 weapon that shoots arrows;
> 2 loop: tie your shoelaces with *bows* / *bow* tie
> bow /bəʊ/ adjective = rounded: *bow*-window / *bow*-legged
> **1.55** further
> **1.61** so / therefore / consequently

Part 1
mongrel – a dog without a pedigree, a dog of mixed parentage
torment – tease / bother
complied, comply – agreed to, agree
whereupon literary or old-fashioned – meaning when this happens / happened
at once – at the same time (not *immediately* here)

Part 2
ports – harbours
whirled, whirl – turn fast
counter rhythm – a rhythm that beats against the first rhythm
cessation – stopping
parlor – a sitting room
jig – a kind of dance

Part 3
presently – soon
shifted, shift – moved, move
supple – flexible
tapered – slim, narrowing to a point
suffused – filled

Language focus: formal and informal style p.69

Aim *To use the formality of the text the students have just read to highlight some of the many differences between formal and informal text.*

Students will have already seen many differences between formal and informal text. However, this section will introduce them to some quite sophisticated differences, some of which are likely to be quite challenging even for advanced students. Make sure they refer to the Language commentary on p.73.

1 Outline the task. You may want to talk briefly about general differences between formal and informal styles.

• Ask students to work together to complete the task then check the answers with the whole class.

> a 2 long sentences
> b 4 participle clauses to link
> c 5 formal grammar (*whom* is rarely used in spoken English nowadays, but is still quite common in written English.)
> d 1 precise vocabulary
> e 3 uncontracted verb forms

2 Set the task briefly. It is probably a good idea to do the first one or two examples with the class to start them off. Remind them that they are finding further examples from the text.

• The task requires intensive reading and understanding of the text. Allow students enough time to complete it. Monitor and help as necessary.

• A general feedback stage may be too time-consuming, so you may want to ask students to hand in their answers, or if you have a small enough class, make sure that you have seen everyone's work as you monitor. Alternatively, if you have access to an OHP, prepare the answers on a transparency.

More examples of formal features from the extract

1 precise rather than everyday vocabulary
torment (tease); *complied* (went along with); *taking refuge* (hiding); *weapon* (stick); *dropped all efforts* (stopped trying); *whirled* (went round and round); *observed* (watched); *cessation* (pausing / stopping); *presently* (soon); *conscious* (aware); *suffused with* (full of / filled with); *longing* (desire)

2 long sentences with several clauses
1.15 *Inside, George Baines … insistent.*
1.17 *She had dropped all efforts … beneath his gaze.*
1.21 *Baines had heard …whirled gaily.*
1.40 *Baines kept his head … eyes to watch.*
1.53 *She became engrossed … closer to the keys.*
1.60 *From this position … emotion on her face.*

3 uncontracted verb forms
All verb forms are uncontracted.

4 use of participle clauses to link ideas
1.11 *Flora tried to force him out into the driving rain by pushing her weapon through a hole in the veranda floor, her excited leaping and shouting **keeping tempo** with her mother's rhythmic melodies.*
1.17 *She had dropped all efforts to teach Baines, and now played for her own pleasure, **stealing time** for herself from beneath his gaze.*
1.42 *He sat at a far corner of the room, **enjoying** the whole vision of this woman at her piano.*
1.57 *Again Baines shifted his chair, **carrying** it round the back and to the other side of the piano.*

5 formal rather than conversational grammar
whereupon 1.11; *thus* 1.61

Exploitation

Aim *To provide some semi-controlled practice in rewriting formal and informal texts.*

1 Outline the task briefly. This is often an enjoyable task for students as it gives them a real sense of being able to manipulate quite difficult language.

• Ask students to do this individually or in pairs. Monitor and help as necessary, but give students the space and time to try to work something out for themselves.

• Elicit possible answers from the whole class. You might want to give them a possible answer to copy out.

> **Suggested rewriting**
> Baines kept a friendly mongrel dog (that) he called Flynn, and Flora loved to tease Flynn with a stick. The dog went along with her games passively. He hid under the hut when she got too enthusiastic / excited. When he did this Flora tried to force him out into the pouring rain by pushing her stick through a hole in the veranda floor. As she did this she jumped and shouted with excitement in time with her mother's piano playing / rhythm on the piano.

2 a You may want to ask students to complete the writing tasks with a partner before going on to part **b**, so make up pairs of As and pairs of Bs and outline the task.

• Direct the As to p.158 and the Bs to p.159. It is essential that everyone writes out the text, not just one person in each pair. Set a time limit, and monitor and help as necessary.

• Now ask students to form AB pairs.

b They compare their written texts – and should find they've written each other's starting text! Look back at pp.158–9 and check.

c Let students discuss the differences in their pairs, then feedback briefly with the whole class on what they found difficult / easy.

- If you want to give the students further writing practice of this kind, you could set up this similar writing task.

  1 Give different students different topics, e.g.

  A great night out
  The worst day of my life
  A good friend
  My first English lesson
  The first CD I ever bought

  and give them a few minutes to think about the topic, without writing anything.

  2 Now ask them to work individually to write, informally and quickly. Set a short time limit, e.g. five minutes, after which time they exchange their pieces of writing with a partner.

  3 Give the students a minute or two to read each other's writing, to clarify handwriting, etc.

  4 Now ask them to rewrite the piece using formal language. Again, set a time limit – a little longer for this one, e.g. seven minutes.

  5 When time is up, students return the formal piece to the student who wrote the original informal piece.

9.3 The good and the bad p.70

This section extends the theme of music and looks at the language and style of music reviews.

Lead in

Aim *To extend students' music vocabulary and prepare them for the recording they are about to hear.*

1 You could ask students to do this in their books, working in pairs, or alternatively you could do it as a whole class working from the board. Either way, you will need to do the first one or two with the whole class to set them off.

- If you are working from the board, you could set this out as a spidergram / bubble map, writing the word *music* in a central bubble, with the other categories, *music people, instruments, musical features, types of music* and *types of recording* written in smaller bubbles radiating from it.

- You then elicit words from the students and write them on the board, radiating out from the appropriate bubble.

- Check the pronunciation of the words as you write them, marking the word stress as you do so. Some words are often

referred to in their abbreviated form e.g. *sax*, while *cello* is hardly ever referred to by its full name *violoncello*.

> **Possible answers**
> - **Music people:** band; group; orchestra; musician; instrumentalist; violinist; pianist; guitarist; drummer; singer; vocalist; choir
> - **Instruments:** drum; guitar; trumpet; clarinet; flute; piano; violin; accordion; cello; double bass; synthesizer; keyboard; sax(ophone); trombone; percussion
> - **Musical features:** tune; note; rhythm; harmony; melody; chord; major; minor; arrangement; key
> - **Types of music:** rock; heavy metal; folk; classical; choral; country
> - **Types of recording:** album; CD; vinyl record; single; tape; cassette; minidisk; MP3

2 Outline the task briefly and play the recording.

9.5

Speaker 1 (A) piece of music that I was actually given, not a piece of music that I bought recently erm was a CD by someone called Badly Drawn Boy, which I'd heard of but I assumed that I wouldn't like and in fact it's one of the best CDs that I've heard in a very long time – and the reason why I like it is that it's got some excellent tunes and some very sensible and meaningful lyrics which I think is quite a rarity nowadays and since we were given it at Christmas we've played it non-stop, so we obviously like it very much.

Speaker 2 I went to this concert in Oxford a couple of months ago. It was Elgar's the Dream of Gerontius, which is a choral piece and I'm not a big fan of choral music but it surprised me. It was fantastic. It had some really really surprising stuff in it that I didn't expect – it sounded like erm a movie soundtrack …

Speaker 3 I went to a concert last year which I thought was really fantastic, erm it was a violinist who I'm quite keen on in any case and it was just really good to see him perform. He was conducting the orchestra as well so as well as seeing him perform I can't remember what piece he did, erm as well as seeing him perform that, we were able to get an idea of how he felt erm music should be interpreted. The atmosphere was really nice erm it was at the Albert Hall which is, er, an interesting place to go to a concert – although the acoustics aren't that good the actual atmosphere in the audience is is excellent.

- Ask students to compare their answers in pairs. You may need to play the recording again.

- Check the answers with the whole class.

> **a** Speaker 1   a CD by Badly Drawn Boy
> Speaker 2   choral music (Elgar's *The Dream of Gerontius*)
> Speaker 3   orchestral music with a violinist
> **b** Speaker 1   excellent tunes; sensible and meaningful lyrics (words)
> Speaker 2   sounded like film music
> Speaker 3   violinist who also conducted; interpretation of the music
> atmosphere in the concert hall; acoustics (not very good)

3 Read through the questions with the students before listening to the recording again.

- Let students check answers with a partner.

> **a** She has played it non-stop since being given it as a present.
> **b** Because he is not usually a fan of choral music.
> **c** Because the violinist, who was also conducting, was someone she already knew she liked.

Reading

Aim *To familiarize students with the language and style of reviews and practise reading for gist.*

Reviews have a very particular style and for some reviewers the cleverness of the review becomes more important than the subject they are reviewing. It can be quite difficult to read through the sophisticated language to extract the basic sense of what the reviewer is trying to say. But with encouragement, students often enjoy reading reviews and are quite motivated to try to produce their own.

1 Focus students on the questions. Read quickly and check there are no problems of meaning.

- Ask students to discuss the questions in small groups. Set a time limit. Monitor but don't interrupt.

- Conduct whole-class feedback if you feel it's appropriate to round the discussion off.

2 Outline the tasks. Check that the star system in **b** is clearly understood (unmissable = it is excellent, so good that you shouldn't miss it; mediocre = it's nothing special, neither good nor bad, unexceptional)

- You may want to pre-teach some of the vocabulary that comes up in the reviews, if you feel that it will seriously detract from their understanding of the text. At this stage though, only provide one or two items of vocabulary per text and do not let yourself get drawn into discussions or questions about meaning. The students will probably be able to work out quite a lot of the meanings from the contexts.

Glossary

Genesis text
I'd trailed down to Earl's Court – I'd gone down to Earl's Court. *Trail* suggests a long, not very pleasant journey. Earl's Court is an area of London, and in this case, a very large hall used for international trade fairs, concerts, etc.
thrilling – exciting
provocative – arousing anger / sexually exciting
lighting pods – pods are what peas and beans grow in, a lighting pod is therefore a section of lights, in a pod-like structure.
a trip down ... memory lane – commonly-used expression meaning to remember, as if going down a lane (small road) to your memories.
aversion – extreme dislike
plonk – an unmusical noise, hitting keys without any skill or musicality
aimlessly – without direction
huff and bluster – make huffing sounds, as when you are trying to defend yourself but can't think of the right words to say.
blue in the face – from lack of oxygen. Usually used about a pointless activity: *You can argue until you're blue in the face. The answer is still no.*

El Hadj N'Diaye text
has created quite a stir – has caused a lot of interest
elsewhere – in other places (only used in written texts, quite literary)
little known elsewhere – note the use of *little* (cf. Unit 6 *little* vs. *a little*)
suffused – filled (literary / poetic language)
stirring voice – a voice which stirs the emotions
Besides – as well as (Beware confusion with *beside*, meaning *next to*)
outstanding – stands out from the rest, i.e. well above average
intriguing – mysteriously interesting
gripping – grips / holds your attention
haunting – mysterious
utterly – completely, very
compelling – forces you to pay attention, irresistible

- Ask half the class to read the Genesis text, half the El Hadj N'Diaye text. Give them time to read quietly. Try not to answer any questions at this stage, but reassure them that there will be a time when you will deal with any words they still don't understand.

- When most of the class has finished, pair them up with someone else who has read the same text. You may need to make up some threes.

- Ask the students to compare their answers to 2a and **b**. Encourage them to underline or highlight all the words or phrases that gave them their answers.

- Monitor and help as necessary.

- You can deal with any unknown vocabulary now, and you could incorporate task 4 here (adding the words to the columns or bubble map of the *Lead in* exercise) or after the next, paired discussion activity.

a	**Genesis**	
	Likes	production: lighting; animation; the group computer graphics; video
	Dislikes	the music itself
	El Hadj N'Diaye	
	Likes	music: emotional intensity; arrangements; N'Diaye's voice; musician; lyricist; love songs
	Dislikes	nothing
b	**Suggested rating**	
	Genesis	1–2 stars
	El Hadj N'Diaye CD	4–5 stars

3 When the students have discussed their texts sufficiently, ask them to re-pair / regroup in AB pairs.

- Now ask the students to do tasks **a** and **b**.

4 This can be done now, incorporating all the other unknown vocabulary, if you haven't already done so.

Writing p.71

Aim *To give students practice in writing a review.*

Having read the reviews and discussed them quite fully, the students should feel well prepared for this task.

1 a Outline the task. It is important to give the students a few moments of quiet time to *think* about what they are going to review.

b Now put the students into pairs or small groups to talk about what they are going to review. This is a very important stage in preparing for the writing. For a lot of people, talking about something helps them gather their thoughts and ideas, as well as check them out with a colleague before committing them to paper.

2 Ask the students to work on their own again now as they make their paragraph plan. Refer them to the Writing guidelines on p.156).

• You could ask the students to show their paragraph plans to each other, and to talk their partner through their intended review.

3 Set the activity to be done as homework, or in class if you have the time.

• It's a nice idea to ask the students to follow up the paired work they did earlier by showing each other the final version, either before or after you have marked it. But check with the students first; some people are very sensitive about their written work becoming more public.

Exploring words p.72

Aim *To extend students' active and passive vocabulary connected with music, focusing particularly on adjective–noun collocations.*

1 a Check the words with the whole class, paying attention to word stress and thereby pronunciation (Note too the silent 'l' in *calming*).

• Ask them to complete the task in pairs or small groups, then check the answers with the whole class.

> **These are the most likely collocations – others may be possible but would be less common.**
> **calming** influence
> **catchy** slogan / title / tune
> **cheerful** book / film / person / smile / story
> **depressing** look / comments / film / influence / person / story
> **lively** book / film / influence / meeting / person / tune
> **loud** person / tune / comments
> **moving** book / film / story
> **relaxing** holiday / swim / shower
> **romantic** book / film / holiday / person / smile / story / title / tune
> **soothing** influence / shower

b Ask students to complete the task in pairs, then check the answers with the whole class.

> **1** depressing meeting **4** relaxing shower
> **2** catchy tune **5** calming influence
> **3** moving story

c Outline the task. You may want to do the first one for them to get them going. Try to think of a *depressing* and a *moving* film yourself first!

• Make sure you give students a couple of minutes to collect their thoughts, then set them up to complete the task in pairs or small groups.

2 Ask all the students to look at the first pair of sentences. Elicit answers and check / confirm with the whole class.

• Now ask the students to do the rest of the task in pairs or individually, then check answers with the whole class.

Note

Even native speakers confuse these two adjectival forms, e.g. comic = intended to be funny / comical = funny because it is silly, strange, etc.

> **a 1** classical **2** classic
> **b 1** economic **2** economical
> **c 1** historical **2** historic
> **d 1** comical **2** comic

3 Ask students to complete the task individually or in pairs, then to compare their answers together.

• Check with the whole class whether there are any problems. If not, you can move on to the next activity.

> **1** gripping **2** intriguing **3** thrilling **4** poignant
> **5** remarkable **6** haunting **7** impressive

4 This is a free-speaking activity and students will need time, and may need some extra stimulus to begin.

• Focus students on the subjects and give them a few moments to read through them.

• Start by talking about one of the subjects to the whole class yourself (live listening). Speak freely and naturally giving plenty of detail, whether central or incidental, thereby showing students the kind of thing they might do themselves. Let the students comment or ask questions as they wish.

• Now ask them to work in pairs or small groups to choose one of the subjects and talk about it to the group. The others listen, ask questions, and comment.

10 From place to place

Theme: travel – adventure holidays and first impressions of a place

10.1 Travel

The increasing popularity of adventure holidays

- **Listening:** specific information
- **Exploring natural speech:** *just*
- **Vocabulary:** vague language used to refer to people's ages
- **Language focus:** *as* and *like*
- **Speaking:** planning an adventure holiday

10.2 First impressions

First impressions of the South Pole

- **Reading:** gist, interpretation of tone, specific information
- **Language focus:** historic present in story-telling
- **Writing:** an account of a first visit to a town or city

Exploring words

Compound nouns

Workbook

- **Language focus:** *as* and *like*; story-telling – the Historic present; performative verbs
- **Vocabulary focus:** compound nouns
- **Vocabulary expansion:** similes; adjectives ending in *-ous*
- **Listening:** travel impressions

10.1 Travel   p.74

Stage 1 consists of a listening text about adventure holidays which contextualizes uses of *as* and *like*.

Lead in

Aim *To get the students talking about the theme of the lesson.*

1 You could do this in small groups, or, if your class is not too big and if space allows, as a mingle.

- Check the students understand *remote,* (far away and difficult to get to), and *landmark* (an easily recognized building, often symbolic of a place – e.g. the Eiffel Tower in Paris, or the Taj Mahal in India).
- Ask students to think about which of the places in the list they have been to.

2 Ask the students to stand up, walk round and talk to as many people as possible about where they have been. Set a short time limit – five or six minutes. Monitor or join in yourself.

- Do a brief feedback, and find out who has been to the most interesting place.

Listening

Aim *To listen for specific information.*

1 Put the students in pairs to discuss the questions, then do a brief whole-class feedback.

- Alternatively, before doing the discussion and instead of exercise **1a**, you could build some vocabulary on the theme of extreme sports and activities.
- Elicit and teach some vocabulary around the theme. Either bring in some pictures of extreme sports and activities, or brainstorm as many as the students can think of to the board. Suggested vocabulary should include words mentioned in the report, i.e. trekking and camel-riding. Other suggested activities include: *white-water rafting; scuba-* or *deep sea-diving; climbing; bungee jumping; canoeing; rally driving; windsurfing; waterskiing; potholing* (climbing into underground caves); *abseiling* (jumping down a mountain, pushing against the sides, in a special harness).

2 Play the recording. The students listen and check their answers to the questions in **1**.

10.1

Presenter You work hard all year and your few weeks of holiday are precious – so surely the last thing you'd want to do during them would be to give up your creature comforts. But in fact that's exactly what a growing number of people are choosing to do. Travel companies which specialize in anything from deep-sea diving or trekking to camel-riding are reporting a year on year growth in customers. Michelle Cook, who's worked as a tour leader with an adventure holiday firm for more than ten years, says the interest doesn't just come from students or twenty-somethings.

Michelle Cook We actually take people from fourteen to seventy-nine years old. In the past I've led tours with people in their eighties and they've been the life and soul of the group. And the people that travel with us are people that have the right attitude, a sense of adventure, a sense of humour – they're people that want to go on holiday, have some fun, but they also want to learn about the country they're travelling in. They really are all different types of people, from different backgrounds, different nationalities, all ages.

Presenter Michelle's company regularly holds information evenings for people who want to find out more about their holidays. Some of the potential clients explained why they were interested in trying out something different.

Woman 1 I think because I want to be a traveller rather than a tourist – or I want to believe that I am and I want to understand a bit about the culture and where I'm going to – and lying on a beach is kind of boring by comparison.

Woman 2 I'm just really interested in getting to know exactly what's going on in the country and really seeing the place rather than going out and just having a relaxing time. I just think this gives a more comprehensive look at a country rather than just going to relax really.

Man You're not staying in a you know always a British or in an American mentality, I mean anyone can be a tourist – see all the pictures you know when you get home, but to really experience the food, and the experience and and the way they dress and how they treat one another …

Woman 3 Cos life's too safe at times. I mean I'm not going to be doing anything very adventurous but I think riding a donkey is going to be adventurous for me and for the donkey so um I think it's a challenge cos, yeah, we live very safe lives, and it keeps you lively if you try something new.

Presenter And as tour leader Peter Crane points out, this trend towards adventurous holidays is likely to continue. As people's disposable incomes increase, more are encouraged to experiment with their holidays – just as with the first foreign holidays a generation ago.

Peter Crane The beach holiday in itself is a relatively new phenomenon – it began in the nineteen sixties with the advent of air travel. It may be the case that after a generation of beach holidays people are just finally getting a little bit bored with lying on beaches. It's not as fulfilling and as exciting as erm as many people want their holidays to be. They want to know what happens away from the tourist hotels, how the local people live their lives, where the children go to school – really just understanding the real country as opposed to the tourist version of it.

Presenter So it looks as if the quest for challenge and excitement and the desire to be a traveller rather than a tourist, will continue to shape the kind of holiday many people decide to take.

b 14–79; people in their eighties; all different types of people
c discover other cultures; get to know a place properly; get away from the 'safe life'; experience more than what they already know; keeps people lively
d boredom; people want to find out about how other nationalities live their real lives
Deep-sea diving, trekking, and camel-riding are all mentioned.

React and discuss

1–2 Do this in small groups or as a class discussion.

- Note that a *traveller* is someone who likes to make their own way from place to place around a country, often carrying a backpack and seeking out more remote places, whereas a *tourist* pre-books a holiday, stays in hotels, goes on organized excursions. There is also a difference in attitude: the traveller enjoys the challenges of the difficulties such as the language barrier, or public transport, whereas tourists expect to have everything arranged for them.

Exploring natural speech   p.75

Aim *To introduce and practise the use of* just *in natural speech.*

1–2 Read through the explanation of the use of *just* with the students, then play the recording so that they can hear the pronunciation. (This is not included in the tapescript section of the Student's Book.)

10.2

I'm just really interested in getting to know exactly what's going on in the country and really seeing the place rather than going out and just having a relaxing time. I just think this gives a more comprehensive look at a country rather than just going to relax really.

***Just** is almost always pronounced /dʒʌs/ before a consonant.*

- Play the recording again so that the students can listen and repeat.

- If you would like to give your students further practice using *just*, ask them to think of three or four things they expect from a holiday. Put them in pairs, and ask them to tell their partner about them. Encourage them to include the word *just* several times, for example: *I just like to get away from – just relax, you know, just have fun.*

Vocabulary

Aim *To introduce and practise vague language expressions used when referring to ages. For example,* mid-twenties, late teens, *etc.*

1 Put the students in pairs to find and underline the expressions in the extract.

- Alternatively, you could try to elicit expressions from the students. Write *25* on the board, and ask students to think of as many ways as they can of expressing that age. Or put one or two photos of people on the board and ask students to predict their ages. Ask questions like, *How old do you think she is? Are you sure?*

> twenty-somethings / from fourteen to seventy-nine years old / people in their eighties

2 Students remain in pairs to discuss which expressions use vague language.

> All the expressions in the list are vague except the first *Pete is twenty-five.*

3 Students work in pairs or small groups to talk about people in their family.

Language focus: *as* and *like*

Aim *To revise and practise* as *and* like.

Students often confuse the use of *as* and *like*. In this section, the subtle differences in meaning between the two words are contrasted, and the informal use of *like* as an alternative to *as* or *as if* is focused on. The rules are discussed in detail in the Language commentary on p79. Basically, though, the rules are as follows:

as means *in the role/function of.* For example, *He works as a secretary.*
It is often used as a conjunction followed by a clause, meaning *in the same way as, because,* or *while.*

like means *similar to* or *in the same way as.* For example, *He looks like his father.*
It is a preposition and therefore followed by a noun or pronoun.
In informal English, *like* can be used as a conjunction, and as an alternative to *as* or *as if.*

1 Put the students in pairs to discuss the paired sentences.

> **a 1** Michelle was a tour leader.
> **2** Michelle worked in the same way as a tour leader.
> **b 1** My function / purpose when I travel is to see …
> **2** I am not a traveller, but in a similar way to a traveller, I like to see …

2 Put the students in pairs to decide in which sentences *like* can be used.

> *Like* could be used instead of *as if* in **b**.
> In everyday informal language some people might also use *like* instead of *as* in **c** and *as if* in **d**.

Exploitation

- Elicit the first answer as an example, then put the students in pairs to complete the news story.

> **1** as
> **2** As
> **3** like (We can also say *unlike anything he had ever done before.*)
> **4** as if (like)
> **5** Like
> **6** As
> **7** as (= because)

Speaking

Aim *To develop spoken fluency in a group work activity based on the theme of the lesson.*

1–2 Put the students in pairs or small groups to discuss the points and plan the holiday. Monitor and help with ideas and vocabulary.

- Ask one of the students from each group to present their holiday plan to the whole class. You could ask students to vote on which holiday they think is best.

- If you wish, you can do this alternative to the speaking activity above.

1 Put students in groups of four and ask them to imagine they work for an adventure holiday firm. Ask them to discuss the sort of holiday their firm is selling, using the questions in *Speaking* 1.

2 Give them a sheet of A3 paper and coloured pens, and ask them to design a poster to illustrate their holiday. The poster should have a heading to attract attention, a picture to illustrate the holiday, and features listed in bullet points.

3 When they have completed their poster, ask them to pin it to the wall behind them. Two of the four students stay with the poster to describe it, while the other two students walk around the class, 'visiting' the other holiday firms. Encourage the 'visiting' students to ask questions about the holiday in each poster they visit.

4 At the end, ask the students to say which adventure holiday was best and why.

10.2 First impressions p.76

Stage 2 consists of an extract from a book which uses and contextualizes the Historic present.

Lead in

Aim *To get the students talking about the theme of the extract.*

1–2 Put the students in pairs or small groups to discuss the questions. You could start by asking them to describe the photos in the book. Alternatively, ask what they know about the Poles and ask them to share information with the class.

Reading

Aim *To read for gist, interpretation of tone, and specific information.*

1 Put the students in pairs to do this exercise. The aim here is to focus on some key vocabulary, so allow the students to use their dictionaries. You may not want to tell students the answers before they read the article; ask them to check their predictions as they read for the first time.

> *scudding to a halt* describes the plane as it lands on the snow runway.
> *scud* means to move quickly and smoothly.
> *in a dream* describes the writer as he is walking from the plane to the base camp.
> *brightly-lit* describes the canteen at the base at the South Pole.
> *almost paralyzing* the low temperature
> *numb-faced* the effect of the low temperature
> *short of breath* the effect of the low temperature
> *anoraked figures* people walking about at the South Pole wearing anoraks to keep warm

2 Focus students on the questions, then ask them to read the extract. Let them check in pairs before going through the answers. You could also check their vocabulary predictions from 1 at this stage.

> **a** He feels as if he's in a dream; walking makes him feel tired; he feels confused (*'I've completely forgotten why we are here.'*); he's very cold.
> **b** **Factual:** he describes the site, the Pole.
> **Impressionistic and personal:** he describes the effect of the place on him: *after what seems like a lifetime, … we trudge …, … we all stand together at the bottom of the world. Or the top.*
> **Impersonal:** no examples

Close up

Put the students in pairs to do this exercise. Encourage them to make guesses from context rather than rely on their dictionaries.

> **1.26** a collection of things which are left behind, no longer useful
> **1.43** *proffer* is similar to and sounds like *offer*. Literally it means to hold something out for someone. It is also used with these collocations: *to proffer advice, help, opinions, your resignation.*
> **1.44** walk slowly and with heavy steps because you are tired or depressed
> **1.67** *crunch* normally describes a sound. Here it refers to the sound of footsteps on the snow.
> **1.86** This can have two meanings: either, literally, it depends whether you look at it from above or below, or, it depends on your point of view.

3 Read through the questions with the students, then ask them to read the text again and find the answers. Let them check in pairs before doing a whole-class feedback.

> **a** The US Government is not prepared to take responsibility for the safety of everyone who arrives at the South Pole. The air traffic controller is telling the pilot that he must take this responsibility; both of them know that the plane intends to land.
> **b** Because of the weather conditions (cold, wind) and maybe because the visitors have to walk through deep snow.
> **c** It has to be thick and therefore heavy to keep out the cold and to keep in the warmth.
> **d** He has become so involved in the routines of their arrival that he has forgotten the main purpose of the trip, which is to see the South Pole.
> **f** He can cross all the lines of longitude by walking in a small circle around the small bronze post which marks the South Pole.

React and discuss

1–2 Put the students in small groups to discuss the questions.

Language focus: story-telling

Aim *To introduce and practise the Historic present.*

When telling stories set in the past, the Present simple, Present continuous, and Present perfect can be used. Using present tenses has the effect of making the listener (or reader) feel as though they are witnessing the events of the story as if they are happening now. It makes the story more immediate and dynamic. Using present tenses to tell stories is more common in spoken English, when telling anecdotes and jokes, for example. However, it is also used in writing, as here, for dramatic effect, to involve the reader and give the writing a sense of immediacy. It is not a difficult area for students to grasp – you use the Present simple instead of the Past simple, the Present continuous instead of the Past continuous. Effectively, the present tenses are used in the same way as narrative past tenses. There are some examples in the Language commentary on p.79.

1 Put the students in pairs to underline the main verbs in the extracts.

> Present simple: **a** wait / shake; **c** realize / are; **d** it's / set out
> Present perfect: **c** I have completely forgotten
> Present continuous: **b** is piling

2–4 Discuss these questions as a class.

> **2** Past tenses: simple, perfect, continuous.
> **3** The use of the present tense makes the sentence more immediate. The intended effect is to make readers feel that this is happening now. The past tense emphasizes the fact that the event took place in the past and is over.
> **4** You can use past tenses to tell any story that happened in the past. Present tenses are usually used when you want to make a story conversational, dynamic, and immediate, so you can use it in anecdotes and jokes, but also in novels, short stories, and personal letters.

Exploitation

1 Do this as spoken practice. Put the students in pairs to prepare the story. Ask them to underline all the past verbs, but not to change them. Then tell them to take it in turns to tell the story to each other, changing the tenses as they go.

> It's Tuesday and I'm driving to work when my mobile phone rings. The traffic's very busy and by the time I pick up the phone to answer it, it's stopped ringing. It's my girlfriend's number, so I call her back. While I'm waiting for her to answer, a police car overtakes me and flags me down. I stop the car and open my window. The police officer points out that it's an offence to use a mobile phone while driving and fines me £40 on the spot. As soon as I get to work, I ring my girlfriend to find out why she was calling. I ask her why she's phoned. She says she's missing me and wants to check I'm OK.

- When telling an anecdote, it is important to think about stress and pausing. An alternative way of approaching this practice is to do the following exercise.

  1 Ask the students to change the past forms to present forms.

  2 Read out the passage so that students can check their answers.

  3 Let the students listen to the passage again, and this time mark strong stresses and where there is a pause.

  4 Check the answers with the whole class, then ask the students to practise retelling the story in pairs. This way, when they tell the stories, they are more likely to stress and pause correctly, and thus make the anecdote more natural and interesting.

  5 You may wish to record the anecdote onto a cassette before the lesson, and provide the answers below on a handout or OHT.

> It's 'Tuesday / and I'm driving to 'work / when my mobile 'phone rings. / The 'traffic's very busy / and by the time I pick up the 'phone to 'answer it, / it's stopped 'ringing. / It's my 'girlfriend's number, / so I 'call her back. / While I'm waiting for her to 'answer, / a po'lice car over'takes me / and 'flags me down. / I 'stop the car / and 'open my window. / The po'lice officer / points out that it's an of'fence to use a mobile 'phone while 'driving / and 'fines me 'forty pounds on the 'spot. / As soon as I get to 'work, / I ring my 'girlfriend to find out 'why she was 'calling. I ask her why she's 'phoned. / She says she's 'missing me / and wants to 'check I'm OK.

© Oxford University Press PHOTOCOPIABLE

2 Read the joke as a class, and make sure all the students have got it.

- Students often can't think of a joke. It is a good idea to ask round the class and find a few students who can think of a joke. Then divide the class into groups of three with at least one person with a joke in each group. Give the group a few minutes to prepare the joke to tell the rest of the class.

- If nobody can think of a joke, tell the joke below, (or one of your own), then write the prompts which follow on the board. Ask the students to retell the joke using the prompts.

  A man runs into a pub, and says to the barman, 'Quick, give me a beer before the trouble starts!' The barman pours a glass of beer and gives it to the man who drinks it quickly. 'Quick,' says the man, 'give me another one before the trouble starts!' The barman pours another, and gives it to the man, who drinks it quickly. The barman is starting to get worried now. 'What's happening?' he asks. 'What's the trouble?' 'I haven't got any money,' says the man.

  Man / pub / say / barman / beer / trouble / pour / drink / another / quickly / worried / happening / money

- Feedback any errors made with the Historic present.

Writing

Aim *To write an account of a first visit to a place.*

1 Read through the instructions with the students.

- Ask them to think of a place, then to write down ideas under the following headings: *Images and arrival; A description of the place; What I saw/did.*

- Ask them to write a paragraph, linking the ideas they have come up with, and using the Historic present. You could give them the opening line for each of the headings above:

  Before coming to _____ , I think of it as …

  I arrive, and it's …

  As I walk into the centre, I see …

- You could set this for homework. Refer them to the Writing guidelines on p.151.

2 Ask the students to exchange their paragraphs with a partner. Their partner should read the story, then think of questions to ask about the visit.

- You could also ask the students to suggest improvements and correct each other's work. They discuss the improvements with each other, then rewrite the paragraphs.

- If you set this for homework, you could put the corrected accounts on the wall, if this is OK with your students. The students have to walk round and read each person's piece of work, then find somebody who has written about a place they are interested in. Then they have to interview that person about the town.

Exploring words
p.78

Aim *To introduce and practise compound nouns, with particular emphasis on form and stress.*

This section could be worked through as a whole. It does, however, split easily into two shorter lessons. Exercises **1** and **2** could be done as an introduction to form and stress, with exercises **3** and **4** done a lesson or two later as an extension with the emphasis on fluency.

- As a lead-in to compound nouns, you may wish to do the following:

- First, elicit what a compound noun is. (It's a noun formed by putting two or more words together). Then divide the students into teams of three or four and ask them to write down the following categories: *Travel, Sport, Clothes, Work, School*. The teams must think of and write down one compound for each category. The first team to think of a compound noun for each category is the winner.

  Some suggested compounds:

  Travel: *flight attendant, air traffic, railway*

  Sport: *tennis court, football boots, windsurfing*

  Clothes: *raincoat, sweat shirt, swimsuit*

  Work: *job interview, lunch hour*

  School: *playground, exercise book, head teacher*

1 a–b Read through the rules with the students, then put them in pairs to match the rules with the examples, and think of other examples.

> **A** noun + noun: beach holiday; hotel room; town centre; car engine
> **B** noun + verb + -*er*: dishwasher; window cleaner; sheep farmer; cigarette lighter
> **C** noun + verb + -*ing*: bullfighting; housekeeping; windsurfing; town planning
> **D** adjective + noun: grandparents; greenhouse; highway; easy chair
> **E** verb + particle: break-in; checkout; take-away; passer-by
> **F** particle + verb: bypass; input; outbreak; uptake

c Do the first as an example, then put the students in pairs to match the verbs and nouns.

> 2 sports commentator
> 3 antique dealer
> 4 interior decorator
> 5 bus driver
> 6 fire fighter
> 7 clothes manufacturer
> 8 portrait painter
> 9 road sweeper
> 10 piano tuner

2 a–b Put the students in pairs to think about the stress, then play the recording for them to listen and check. (This is not included in the tapescript section of the Student's Book.)

10.3

1 I really like horse-riding – I can't stand bullfighting.
2 He's a window cleaner not a fire fighter.
3 Let's go on a beach holiday this year, not an adventure holiday.
4 This is a hotel room not a campsite.
5 Use the dishwasher, not the washing machine.
6 Can I work on the checkout instead of in the storeroom?

> The stress goes on the first word or part of most compound nouns.

3 Put the students in pairs to think about why the stress is on the second word.

> **1** In this group the first word specifies where something is.
> **2** In this group the first word specifies what something is made of.

4 Create a prediction task by asking students to look at the picture of the market. Ask them to tell you what sort of things they might find in such a place. Then ask them to read to see if they were right.

- Put the students in pairs to find and underline the compound nouns, and decide which type of compound noun each is. Note that most are noun / noun compounds, the most common type.

> | | |
> |---|---|
> | eye-opener B | drinking coconuts A |
> | lemon grass A | scorch marks A |
> | lime leaves A | coconut juice A |
> | weekend market A | street markets A |
> | rubbish bag A | flyscreens A |

5 a Put the students in pairs to write the paragraph. Ask them to decide what sort of place they are going to write about, then make sure they are clear that they have to use at least five compound nouns.

- Monitor and help with ideas and vocabulary.

  b–c When they are ready, ask one person in each pair to read out their paragraph. Ask the class to vote on which place sounds the most attractive when all the students have finished.

- If you have a large class, you may wish to put students into groups to read out their paragraphs, or you could put the paragraphs on the wall or circulate them so that the students can read them before voting.

11 Remember

Theme: memories, memory, and remembering to do things

11.1 Memories

Childhood memories

- **Reading:** gist
- **Listening:** specific information
- **Exploring natural speech:** reference words
- **Language focus:** *must, can, can't (+ have)*: certainty and deduction
- **Speaking:** memories
- **Writing:** an account of an early memory

11.2 Memory

Different types of memory

- **Vocabulary:** *remember, remind, recall*, etc.
- **Reading:** gist and matching paragraphs to descriptions
- **Language focus:** relative clauses
- **Speaking:** a memory test

11.3 Help!

What people remember and forget

- **Listening:** gist
- **Reading:** general information
- **Language focus:** articles
- **Speaking:** devising an online service

Exploring words

Loan words used in English

Workbook

- **Language focus:** modals *must, can, can't + have*; relative clauses; articles
- **Vocabulary focus:** memory and memories; words often confused
- **Vocabulary expansion:** *rise, raise, arise, arouse*; the prefix *re-*
- **Listening:** earliest memories

11.1 Memories p.80

In this stage a reading text introduces the topic and a listening contextualizes *must have* and *can have*.

Lead in

Aim *To prepare students for the theme of the unit by reading a highly descriptive account of an Irish writer's childhood memory. It is a full and rich description; you may want to explore it as a reading passage, not just as a lead-in.*

1 Ask students to look at the pictures and the title of the unit, and predict what it is about.

- Focus on questions **a** and **b**.

- Give the students quiet time to read the passage, or read it aloud to the class. (Pronunciation of Cnoc on Oir: /nɒkɒnˈuːr/)

- If they are just listening to you, teach some of the unknown vocabulary first.

2 Ask them to compare their answers in pairs. It isn't necessary to go into detailed explanations of vocabulary, but there may be some questions.

> **Possible answers**
> a It's his first memory of the country. It's very clear.
> b Sights – great detail: donkey and cart / fuchsia and bramble / empty milk churn / metal casing / pasture: snipe grass and dark loam of the bogs
> Sounds – tapping fingers / clicked tongue
> Smells – new-mown hay / ripening blackberries / sea salt

Note

fuchsia – flower, usually pink / purple / red, ballerina-like
brambles – thorny bushes, often in hedges
creamery – place which makes butter and cream, not very common today
milk churn – the large metal container in which milk used to be transported
reins – the guiding ropes from the horse / donkey for the rider to hold
pasture – field for animals to graze on
snipe grass – type of spiky grass
loam – rich, dark soil
bogs – marsh, wet ground

Listening

Aim *To listen for specific information in natural conversation.*

1 Outline the task and play the recording.

11.1

B Okay, so what are your earliest memories?

G Erm, well, I think probably one of my very earliest memories was when I was in Canada. Erm, I must have been about five or six years old at the time…

B Right okay…

G …and erm, basically, I was on a family holiday with my mum, my dad and my brother and we were staying with erm my uncle and his wife and they erm had some very strange rules of their house that you had to abide by if you stayed with them and I was quite sort of fussy as a kid. Anyway they had these rules and we had to stick to them, as we were staying there, and we sat down to dinner one one night and one of his rules was that you had to eat everything that was on your plate …

B No!

G Yeah, you had to completely finish your food.

B What if you didn't like it?

G Well, you weren't allowed to not like it, basically.

B OK …

G Erm, and anyway I was quite fussy and my mum had made sure that he did make something that I liked, so I had this hamburger. Anyway, I was talking to my uncle, telling some kind of story and basically I was putting ketchup on my hamburger and I was talking and I didn't basically realize how long I was talking for, and turned to look at my meal and there was ketchup everywhere all over my plate.

B Oh no!

G And, basically, I had to eat everything that was on my plate and my uncle, cruelly, actually made me sit there and finish it, and I was sick afterwards for about two days.

B Oh my.

G So, yes, that's mine …

B Well, let me see.

G … not a pleasant one.

B No, I don't think mine was good either, erm.

G Go on then.

B I can only have been about four, maybe slightly older.

G Yeah.

B And, er, I was in my mum and dad's house and I was messing about on the stairs and of course my mum was, like, you know 'Be careful, you'll fall down the stairs.' (Yeah) But I didn't really listen to her, and of course I did, fell down the stairs and tumbled all the way down the stairs and cracked my head open on the radiator at the bottom of the stairs.

G Oh dear.

B Yep. So of course I was crying and screaming …

G Did you go to hospital?

B Yeah, my head was bleeding and I had to go to hospital and have thirteen stitches.

G Err!

B 'Unlucky for some,' my mum said. So that's another bad memory as well.

G Yeah.

B Can you think of any …

G good ones?

B Erm, not …

G So we've both had really bad childhoods.

B I think I think you tend to remember the bad things, more than the good things.

G Yeah.

- Ask students to compare their answers.

> **1** five or six
> **2** In Canada, on a family holiday at an uncle's house
> **3** mother, father, brother, uncle, aunt

Exploring natural speech

Aim *To raise awareness of reference words in natural speech.*

1 Focus students on the task.

- Play the recording and ask students to follow this section in their books.

- Ask them to decide what the words in bold refer to. They could work individually or in pairs.

- Let them compare their answers in pairs.

> **1** *we* = my mum, my dad, my brother and I
> **2** *they* = my uncle and his wife
> **3** *them* = my uncle and his wife
> **4** *them* = the rules
> **5** *there* = in my uncle's house
> **6** *his* = my uncle's
> **7** *it* = the food

2 Deal with this question quickly as a whole class; elicit guesses, then provide the answers.

> *Unlucky for some* is a common expression used when talking about the number thirteen. Another example might be 'We had our meeting in room 13.' 'Unlucky for some'.

React and discuss

Aim *To give students a chance to talk about what they've been listening to.*

- Outline the task and ask students to discuss the questions in pairs or small groups. Set a short time limit.

Language focus: *must, can, can't (+ have)*: certainty and deduction   p.81

Aim *To extend students' recognition of advanced constructions with modal verbs.*

- Students will be familiar with the use of modal verbs to express certainty and deduction but they will probably have difficulty with the more unusual uses (*I must have been about six years old*) and with *can have* in the affirmative (*I can only have been about three years old*).

1 Ask the students for different ways of showing that we're certain or uncertain about something. They'll probably suggest things like *I'm sure … / I'm not quite sure*. Accept these answers and then ask them to look at the sentences. You may want to do the first one with them, and also refer them to the Language commentary on p.87.

- Now ask them to do the others in pairs or individually, then check the answers with the whole class.

> **a** *must have been* = almost certain
> **b** *probably* = almost certain
> **c** *I know* = certain
> **d** *no doubt* = certain
> **e** *I might have been* = uncertain

2 Focus students on the task. You may want to do this as a whole-class activity.

- Give students a few moments to read the sentences.

- Ask them why they think *can* has been used here, and why it is possible.

> *Can* to express deduction is only used in questions and, as practised here, in sentences with *never*, *hardly*, and *only* – all of which have a negative connotation.
> Using *can* gives greater emphasis, making the situations sound more surprising.

3 Outline the task and go through the example with the students.

- Ask them either to work in pairs, or to work individually and then to check their answers in pairs, then check the answers with the whole class.

> **3 Possible answers**
> **a** never liked using phones. / never phoned me before.
> **b** the only one who knows my phone number.
> **c** because there was water all over the roads.
> **d** There are empty bottles all over the place.

Note

Pronunciation: The students will need practice of the double contraction *can't 've*. / ˈkɑːntəv/ It is also a good idea to get students to practise saying the sentences aloud, with the right emphasis or stress, as this is a crucial part of the meaning.
Try a 'Mumble drill'.
Focus students on the problematic part of the phrase (*must 've* /mʌstəv/, *can't 've* / ˈkɑːntəv/, etc.) Provide / elicit a model for the phrase. Allow students to mumble – practise saying the phrase (*must 've been, must 've been*) quietly and repeatedly to themselves – before trying to say it out loud.

- Very often when teachers demonstrate sentences they change the way they say them without realizing. This is obviously confusing for students, so it's a good idea to decide first which word you are going to stress, in other words how you are going to say the sentence, and then stick to it.
Model these sentences for students to copy with the stress as shown in bold.

  a Someone phoned while I was out, but it **can't** 've been my brother.
  b It can **only** 've been my sister.
  c It must 've rained very **hard** there.
  d Somebody must 've been having a **party** here.

4 Outline the task then ask students to try and work out the differences in pairs.

- Check the answers with the whole class.

> **a 1** This whole episode is in the past.
>   **2** This is happening in present time. She's on her way but she hasn't arrived **yet**.
> **b 1** This is happening now.
>   **2** This refers to a past event – for which there is present evidence.

Exploitation

Aim *To give the students some relatively controlled speaking practice using the structures learned.*

- Ask students to look at the pictures.

- Choose one, and elicit comments about it, steering students towards using the structures learned and away from easier structures, e.g. *maybe, it could be that, I think*. Then recap yourself, using the structures and vocabulary you are expecting from them, e.g. *The woman jumping might have won the Lottery / passed an exam / had good news.*

- Now ask the students to work in pairs or small groups and do the same. Monitor and help as necessary, encouraging them to extend their language and use a wider range of structures and language than they might otherwise be tempted to.

- Round up by asking different pairs or groups to talk about the different pictures.

Speaking

Aim *To give the students some guided speaking practice to prepare them for the writing task that follows.*

- Outline the task. You might like to try the following technique, called Guided Visualization, to encourage students to immerse themselves in the subject they are going to speak and write about. It can be very useful in allowing students to remember or imagine something in greater descriptive or emotional depth.

- Ask the students to close their eyes. If they haven't done this before in class, they may feel self-conscious about doing it. Reassure them, but don't make a big issue of it.

- Now ask them to think back to an early childhood memory. Ask them to try and remember how old they were, where they were. Ask other questions for them to think about but not answer out loud: Was there anyone else around? Who? Can they remember any smells? Sounds? How did they feel?

- As you ask these questions, allow plenty of quiet time for students to do what you are asking them to do, i.e. cast their minds back to another time and place.

- When you feel you have asked enough questions and given them enough time, tell them to really focus on that time and feeling in their mind's eye.

- Then ask them to open their eyes slowly and come back to the present time.

- When they are ready, ask them to work in pairs or small groups and tell each other about their memory, in as much detail as possible. Remind them to use modal forms from the *Language focus* and expressions from the box.

- Monitor and join in, if appropriate, taking notes of mistakes made if you like, but don't correct now. Allow enough time here; remember that this is not only speaking practice but preparation for writing.

- Conduct a correction session if necessary, writing up the mistakes made and asking students to correct them.

Writing

Aim *To give students practice in writing a descriptive paragraph.*

1–2 Following on from the speaking activity, ask students to make a few notes about the memory they described (or a different one), using the aspects listed.

- Ask them to list a few phrases or particular words they might use. Remind them of the richness of description used in the *Lead in* text and refer them to the Writing guidelines on p.151. Set a time limit for note-making.

- Monitor and help during note-making.

3 Ask the students to write their paragraph. You could do this in class or set it as a homework activity.

4 Ask students to exchange paragraphs and read about each other's memories. As well as asking more questions, they could also be asked to comment on words or phrases they particularly liked in the description.

Note

It is useful for students to realize the importance of an 'audience' in writing activities; too often they view writing as an exercise to satisfy the teacher. Asking other people to read their work and respond to it, rather than merely correct it, can be a useful way of helping students realize that writing is written to be read!
Tell them before they actually start writing that someone in the class as well as you will be reading and commenting on their work.

11.2 Memory   p.82

The reading text on memory in this stage contextualizes relative clauses.

Lead in

Aim *To get the students thinking about memory by doing a memory game. This also serves as preparation for the reading text that follows.*

1 Ask students to do the task on their own, then to check quickly with a partner to make sure there are no problems with vocabulary.

> **From left to right:**
> p82: zip, ticket, pipe, screw, lipstick, duck, rose
> p83: sunglasses, pill, mousetrap, biscuit, shoe, match, boy, rhino

2–3 Make sure students close their books. Explain that they can use their own language, if they like, to write down all the objects they remember.

- Students then compare their lists with each other before checking with the book.

- Students may want to talk about what they remembered / forgot, what was difficult, and why, so hold a brief feedback session.

4 This question checks the distinction between an important vocabulary set. Set up the task quickly, perhaps doing the first sentence with the students as an example.

- Ask them to work through the others on their own or in pairs, then check the answers with the whole class.

> **a** remember / recall   **d** memorize
> **b** reminds   **e** Remind
> **c** remember / recall   **f** recognize

Reading

Aim *To develop students' ability to read for general information (gist) and also to read intensively.*

- This text is quite a detailed factual account of what we mean by memory. Although it is quite long and fairly dense, the language used is relatively straightforward, with few new words that are not explained in the text itself.

1 Explain to the students that they are going to read a text about memory. Tell them that they will be reading it in detail later, but for the moment you want them to focus on questions **a** and **b**. Ask them to keep questions about vocabulary until later.

- Give them a strict time limit and ask them to find the answers to the two questions as quickly as they can.

- When most of them have finished reading, ask them to compare their answers in pairs, then check the answers with the whole class.

> **a** There are 7 types of memory mentioned:
> short-term / long-term / working / procedural / declarative / eidetic or photographic. A distinction is also made in the article between recognition and recall (though these are not necessarily different types of memory.)
> **b** how all the different brain processes combine to produce coherent conscious experience

Close up

- Ask students to do these individually and then to compare answers in pairs, before checking with the whole class.

- At this stage the students may well want to know other items of vocabulary. Deal with these as you see fit, trying to balance the students' wish to understand every single word, with your need to focus on comprehension of a text, a great deal of which is possible *without* knowing every word.

1.2–1.3   There are 10 centuries in a millennium.
          10 years is a *decade*.
1.3   hardly / scarcely
1.44   photo'graphic / pho'tographer / 'photograph

Note

Here are two tips on how to deal with being pestered for vocabulary:
Tell students you will only explain a limited number of words (say 3), and they can decide which ones.
Tell students to try to find the meaning of new vocabulary at home. Reassure them that you will help with anything they couldn't find at the beginning of the next lesson.

Glossary

saddles – place where you sit on a bicycle or a horse
handlebars – things you hold on to on a bicycle
Alzheimer's disease – illness affecting the brain which causes people to lose memory
myriad – any immense number (quantity)

2 Ask students to do this individually or in pairs, then check the answers with the whole class.

> **a** C **b** D **c** F **d** A **e** G **f** B **g** E

Language focus: relative clauses   p.83

Aim *To practise use of relative clauses.*

- Students will have studied relative clauses before. It is an area of grammar which they do not generally find particularly difficult when analysing. However, even advanced students are often quite poor at actually using relative clauses, whether in speaking or in writing. It is important therefore, to keep reminding students about this feature of language, highlighting it in texts that they read and showing them how their own writing, and speaking, could be made more sophisticated by the use of relative clauses. Some students may be concerned about the difference between *which* and *that*. They can mostly be used interchangably (see the Language commentary on p.87) as subject or object of relative clauses when referring to things. However, to summarize the Language commentary:

    1) *which* is used (not *that*) when referring to an idea expressed by a clause: *There was absolutely no-one there,* **which** *was terrifying.*

    2) *which* is used (not *that*) as the subject of a non-defining relative clause: *Pelota,* **which** *is a Spanish ball game, is quite popular in Japan.*

    3) *that* can refer to a person as well as a thing, whereas *which* can only refer to a thing: *He's the man* **that** *I was telling you about.*

1 a Before you begin the exercise, you may want to brainstorm with the students the various relative pronouns: *who, which, whom, whose, that, when, where, what, why*.

- Now ask them to do task **1a** on their own or in pairs, then check their answers with the article.

> **1** who **2** which **3** what **4** by which **5** with which

1 b Ask them to identify the relative pronouns that haven't been used.

> whom; whose; that; when; where; why

2–3 Students can probably work these out together, in pairs. If, however, you feel they need greater teacher control, you could lead the tasks yourself, eliciting answers from the whole class and dealing with any queries or problems as they arise.

- Students sometimes find it difficult to see the difference between defining and non-defining relative clauses (task 2) and feel that it isn't really important anyway. The sentences in 2b show how there can be a real difference in meaning between the two. You may want to explain that in speech we tend to use pauses to show the difference, as well as to use a more roundabout way of expressing the same idea: *My daughter, you know, the one who works as a teacher, well she has a photographic memory.* Students can also find it quite difficult to identify a relative clause, especially when there is no relative pronoun (task **3a**).

> **2**
> **a** The relative clauses in the first two sentences of 1a are non-defining clauses. The others are all defining. (Non-defining clauses can be taken away without changing the sense of the main clause. They are separated by commas.)
> **b 1** I have more than one daughter. The one with the photographic memory is the one who works as a teacher. (defining relative clause)
> **2** I have only one daughter and she works as a teacher. (non-defining relative clause)

> **3**
> **1** photos *that* / *which* they have seen before and new ones
> **2 a** person *that* / *whom* you met yesterday
> **b** A relative pronoun which is the object of a defining relative clause can be left out.
> Relative pronouns can never be left out of non-defining relative clauses.

4 Ask students to do this in pairs or individually, then check the answers with the whole class.

> **a** *which* refers to the house.
> **b** *which* refers to the act of remembering going past the white house.
> Note the use of the comma in **b**.

Exploitation

1 It's a good idea do the first sentence with the class as an example, then ask the students to do the rest in pairs or individually.

- Check the answers with the whole class.

> **a** the apartment **that** / **which** we're in now
> **b** the person to **whom** this parcel
> **c** the one **that** / **who** has just come
> **d** people **whose** opinions I despise
> **e** her job **which** surprised me
> **f** by **which** time people had already left

2 Ask the students to do this on their own, then check answers quickly together.

> The relative pronouns could be left out in **a** and **b**.
> **b** ... the person this parcel is addressed to ...

3 Outline the task, then write the following example definitions on the board.

  a An adult is a person over the age of 18.
  b An adult is someone who is mentally and emotionally mature.
  c An adult is someone who has stopped getting taller and started getting fatter.

- Ask students to work in small groups to write their own definitions. Monitor and help as necessary. Since this is a very focused activity, it would be appropriate to correct too, in order to ensure that students really understand the structures.

- Students may want to read out some of their sentences to the whole class. You could ask for comments on the clearest, most amusing, etc.

Speaking

Aim *To round up this section of the unit in a light-hearted way by referring back to the beginning of the unit and checking their own memories again.*

1 Ask students to close their books.

- Now ask them to try and remember the pictures and objects they tried to remember in *Lead in*. Give them a short time to write down as many as they can remember, using their own language if they want to.

2 Put them in pairs to compare their lists. How many did they remember? How similar are they? What did they both remember? Why?

3 Now ask them to open their books and look at the pictures on pp.82–3. Still in their pairs, ask them to talk about why they think they didn't remember certain objects.

- You will probably want to conduct a brief class feedback simply to round up the activity and this stage of the lesson.

The light-hearted reading text in this stage contextualizes the use of articles.

Lead in

Aim *To introduce the topic.*

1–2 These tasks can either be done as a whole-class activity with books closed, with you asking the questions and eliciting answers, or as a discussion in pairs or small groups.

- You might want to ask the class briefly if there is anything they always remember or never remember.

- There is no need for group feedback.

3 Ask students to read questions **a** and **b**.

- Play the recording and ask students to compare their answers.

11.3

Speaker 1 I think I'm at the age when I'm starting to for... realize that I'm forgetting more things than I used to. Erm, I cert..., I've always found it very difficult to remember directions how to get to places. Erm, but I've now, I've had to start to use a diary which is an admission I think that I'm forgetting more than, than I used to or maybe I'm just doing more things, erm, so using a diary really is how I try to remember things as much as possible – maybe repeating things to myself that are very important just so I realize how important they are.

Speaker 2 I'm very good actually. I don't forget many things – I'm one of these people that's quite good at remembering birthdays, anniversaries, friends and family. I tend to remember most things and I remember because I am a compulsive list-writer, which is very tragic in my life ...

Speaker 3 I'm quite proud of never forgetting anything – erm I have a system erm which revolves around post-it notes erm which, depending on what I have to remember, I'll write it down on a post-it note and stick it to the inside of my front door, erm so I never forget anything – amazing.

Speaker 4 I always forget when I have to pay my bills, and I always forget to water the plants. With bills I have to leave them sitting in front of me so that I actually remember to pay them, but most other things, birthdays, names, phone numbers, useful things I can remember, but just not the bills, the serious stuff.

Speaker 5 My memory's getting worse and worse and worse and it's very difficult to say what kind of things I forget because I forget everything, erm I used to have an extremely good memory for numbers and faces and dates and people and general information and now that's just got worse and worse and because it is something that I didn't use to have problems with, I actually find it quite difficult to find a good way to remember things. I, I write lists and keep books and leave myself notes, but none of those works as well as actually having a memory that works and unfortunately mine doesn't do it so well any more.

- If necessary, play the recording again before checking the answers with the whole class.

Speaker 1	a	directions to places	b	keeps diary
Speaker 2	a	nothing	b	writes lists
Speaker 3	a	nothing	b	post-it notes
Speaker 4	a	pay bills, water plants	b	leaves things visible
Speaker 5	a	everything	b	lists, books, notes

Reading

Aim *To extend students' abilities to extract essential information from a piece of writing.*

This is an article about an Internet service which enables people to remember important personal events. It is quite chatty and colloquial and contains a lot of information in relatively few words.

1 Outline the task and ask students to look at the text together.

• Check the answers with the whole class.

> It is a sample e-mail reminder sent by RememberIt.com.

2 Ask students to read the article quickly in order to answer the questions. Set a time limit.

• Ask them to compare their answers in pairs, then check with the whole class.

> **a** birthdays; anniversaries; special occasions; appointments; goals (ambitions)
> **b** gift shop; wish list; personal calendars; New Year's resolutions; losing weight; saving for an important purchase

React and discuss

1–3 Ask students to discuss the questions in small groups. Monitor but don't interrupt, except to join in if appropriate.

• You could extend this topic by asking students to brainstorm the kind of reminders people might need in relation to these categories:
Auto, Entertainment, Health and Beauty, Family and Friends, Finance, Holidays, Home, Pet Care, School, Travel and Vacation, Work.

Close up

• Ask students to do the tasks in pairs. Give them time to work out their answers before checking with the whole class.

> **1.1** /fæm fæˈtæl/ Woman who is attractive in a mysterious way, leading men into danger and causing their destruction. Example: Marilyn Monroe
> **1.9** forty-six point seven / twenty-seven point five
> **Note:** You may want to do a quick check here of pronunciation of other numbers, dates, times, e.g. 3,672, 1989 (the year), 12/05/01 (both the American way – month, day, year; and the British way – day, month, year); 10:25 (both analogue and digital ways, i.e. ten twenty five and twenty-five past (British) / after (American) ten
> **1.11** *birthday* is the day on which you were born; *anniversary* is the day each year when something (but not a birth) happened, for example *wedding anniversary*.
> **1.20** *the site which was easy to use.* (note no hyphens)

Language focus: articles   p.85

Aim *To review the use of articles.*

This section reviews the use of articles and gives students the opportunity to prepare a summary of use.

1 Ask students to do the tasks in pairs, then check their answers by referring back to the article on p.84.

• Refer students to the Language commentary on p.87 which can be used to check their answers to 1 and 2, and also to check the *Exploitation* exercise which follows.

> **a** 1 the   2 the   3 a   4 a   5 the
> **b** 6 a   7 an
> **c** 8 the   9 the
> **d** 10 ^   11 ^   12 a   13 ^

2 Ask students to do this task in pairs, using the extracts in 1 to help them. Then check answers with the whole class.

> **Examples, from extracts where used**
> **a** a(n): *a loved one's birthday* (3); *a quick e-mail* (4); *A new survey* (6)
> **b** the: *the solution to your dilemma* (5)
> **c** ^ (no examples)
> **d** the: *the most unforgettable public events* (9)
> **e** a (no examples)
> **f** the: *the White House* (2)
> **g** the: *the survey polled* (8)
> **h** a: *a loved one's birthday* (3); *a quick e-mail reminder* (4)
> **i** a(n): *an information management and online reminder service* (7)
> **j** ^: offers, online tools (10); help, users (11); such as, birthdays (13)

Exploitation

Aim *To practise and test what students have learned from the previous activity.*

• Ask students to do this individually, then compare answers in pairs.

• Monitor and encourage, referring them to the appropriate section in the Language commentary on p.87, but avoid giving them the answers.

• Finally check answers with the whole class. Make sure everyone is clear about why the answers are correct.

> 1 the   2 the   3 a   4 the   5 ^   6 a   7 A
> 8 the   9 a   10 the   11 ^   12 ^   13 the
> 14 ^   15 a   16 ^   17 a   18 a   19 ^
> 20 ^   21 the   22 the

Speaking

Aim *To give the students some free speaking and writing practice.*

1 Put students into small groups to discuss the question and make a list. If your students have not used Internet services, omit this question.

2 Ask groups to discuss what the sites might do; you could have a quick feedback session to compare ideas.

3 Make sure groups first decide what their service is to be, then choose a catchy name for it, then write a two-line description for it. Monitor and make suggestions as necessary.

• When they are ready, put them in larger groups, or a whole class, and let them try to 'sell' their service to the others.

Exploring words   p.86

Aim *To extend students' knowledge of commonly-used loan words.*

Most languages borrow words from other languages, but English is unusual in the huge quantity of words it has borrowed. Students generally find it useful and interesting to look at these words and this section extends their knowledge of commonly-used 'foreign' words.

1 Read the introduction with the class. The process has been going on for many years! *bungalow* comes from Hindustani, *village* and *femme fatale* from French.

• Ask students to work in pairs to complete the tasks.

• Check the answers with the whole class.

• If relevant, you could ask if there are any words from their own language that are used in English.

> *junta*: government formed by group of military officers following a coup d'état – Spain
> *ballet*: form of classical dance – France
> *paparazzi*: photographers who specialize in spying on famous people in order to get photos of them in unguarded moments – Italy
> *Czar*: ruler, usually used negatively today, a despot – Russia
> *robot*: automaton – Czech
> *pizza*: bread-like food with topping – Italy
> *trekker*: person who walks on a long, hard journey – Holland
> *café*: place where you can eat or drink – France
> *menu*: list of food available – France
> *tandoori*: style of cooking, in a clay pot – India
> *sauna*: steam room – Finland

2 Outline the task and ask the students to complete it in pairs.

• Ask them to try and guess the pronunciation. Don't let them spend too long on this.

• Listen to the recording, check pronunciation and practise saying the words. (This is not included in the tapescript section of the Student's Book.)

11.4

a After the performance the star was presented with an enormous bouquet of roses. **bouquet**

b Many of the friends I was at university with now live very bourgeois lives. **bourgeois**

c It took undercover police officers three months to find the terrorists' cache of weapons. **cache**

d The televised debate between the two presidential candidates was full of political clichés. **cliché**

e It's very convenient – they're going to start a new crèche at the place where I work. **crèche**

f People like living in cul-de-sacs because they're usually quiet and traffic-free. **cul-de-sac**

g We have two duvets – a light one for the summer and a heavier one for the winter. **duvet**

h Paul Getty was one of the twentieth century's most successful entrepreneurs. **entrepreneur**

i I'd love a slice of that chocolate gateau. **gateau**

j Novels and poems belong to different literary genres. **genre**

a	bouquet	collection of flowers /bʊˈkeɪ/
b	bourgeois	belonging to or typical of the middle class /ˈbɔːʒwɑː/
c	cache	secret hiding place /kæʃ/
d	cliché	an expression or idea which is overused /ˈkliːʃeɪ/
e	crèche	place for pre-school children /kreʃ/
f	cul-de-sac	a road which is blocked off /ˈkʌl də sæk/
g	duvet	bedding /ˈduːveɪ/
h	entrepreneur	someone who starts and runs a business /ɒntrəprəˈnɜː/
i	gateau	large rich cake /ˈgætəʊ/
j	genre	particular type /ˈʒɑːnrə/

c Ask students to try this in pairs or small groups if you feel they know enough French words. Otherwise go through some with the whole class.

> **Possible answers:**
> ending in -*é(e)*   café; papier mâché; résumé; fiancé(e)
> ending in -*et*   ballet; beret
> ending in -*eau*   bureau; plateau
> ending in -*eur*   de rigueur; raconteur; bon viveur
> Others: cuisine; contretemps; rapport; carte blanche; fait accompli; faux pas; savoir faire

3 Ask students to complete the task on their own before comparing answers with a partner. There is no need to monitor.

• Check the answers with the whole class.

> *hoi-polloi* /hɔɪpəˈlɔɪ/ – poor, common people
> *siesta* /sɪˈestə/ – short sleep
> *sauna* /ˈsɔːnə/ – hot steam bath
> *patio* /ˈpætɪəʊ/ – paved area
> *blitz* /blɪts/ – violent attack
> *crescendo* /krɪˈʃendəʊ/ – peak in volume
> *macho* /ˈmætʃəʊ, ˈmækəʊ/ – aggressively masculine
> *spiel* /ʃpiːl/ – persuasive speech

4 Focus students on the questions and make sure they understand them.

• Give them a few minutes to discuss the questions in small groups or pairs.

• Conduct a feedback session to round off the activity.

12 All the rage

Theme: crazes, fashions, and favourite films

12.1 Crazes

Past and current crazes

- **Listening:** gist and interpretation
- **Exploring natural speech:** repetition and the use of *whatsoever*
- **Language focus:** *used to* and *would*
- **Speaking:** talking about childhood interests

12.2 Fast food fashions

The rise of the hamburger

- **Reading:** prediction and interpretation
- **Language focus:** ellipsis

12.3 Films

What makes a successful film

- **Listening:** gist and specific information
- **Exploring natural speech:** contrasting natural speech with a formal talk
- **Vocabulary:** phrasal verbs with *off*
- **Speaking:** describing a scene in a film

Exploring words

Fashion

Workbook

- **Language focus:** *used to* and *would*; omitting words
- **Vocabulary focus:** phrasal verbs with *off*
- **Vocabulary expansion:** verbs like *throw*; idioms with *back*
- **Listening:** childhood pursuits

12.1 Crazes   p.88

Stage 1 consists of a listening text about past crazes which contextualizes uses of *used to* and *would*.

Lead in

Aim *To define* craze, *and get the students talking about the theme of the lesson.*

1 Read the definition of *craze* with the students, and ask them to look at the pictures. Put them in pairs to guess what they are.

> **From left to right:** Lego®, hand-held computer games, diabolo, skateboarding, pogo sticks, in-line skating, soft toy collecting
>
> **What they have in common is that they are all crazes, past and present.**

- You could personalize the discussion by asking the students which crazes they are / were into. Or talk about current crazes sweeping the country you are in.

Listening

Aim *To listen for gist and interpretation.*

1 Read through the questions as a class, and check the words *taste*, (personal preference) and *obsession* (in this case, a sport or hobby that you can't stop doing – for example, spending ten hours a day on computer games).

Glossary
_____

Lego® – system of building bricks for children, with which they can make intricate constructions.

- Play the recording.

12.1

Speaker 1   When I was a girl I suppose I was completely ballet-mad – erm I used to go to ballet classes two or three times a week, erm used to get books about ballet from the library, used to read novels about ballet and always wanted to be a ballerina and of course never managed to do that – but I was absolutely obsessed with ballet and all my friends were as well.

Speaker 2   Actually one time, I had a birthday party and I invited about twenty kids and I told them all what I wanted was a stuffed animal and every single one of them got me a stuffed animal and my mother was so mad and it was like 'What are you doing?'

Speaker 3   Slightly embarrassing childhood, not exactly an obsession, but I used to be a great fan of heavy metal music erm which now seems incredibly embarrassing – I was about 14 years old and wore blue jeans and a sort of blue anorak with a grey rabbit fur hood and went around listening to what now seems to be the most awful music in the world …

Speaker 4   When I was really young I was really keen on playing with Lego® and I had to have every set and I really wanted to go to Legoland in Denmark, but never made it and then I was too old and when it came over here and there was one in Windsor, but erm I was a member of the Lego® club and I had lots of sets and I used to play for hours and hours with it making different buildings and houses and cars …

Speaker 5   I think probably from about the age of 7 or 8 until 11 or 12, I was completely obsessed with football – erm all my spare time was spent playing football with friends. Every break time every lunchtime at school we would play football in the playground. Erm it had a disastrous effect on my shoes – my mother was having to buy me shoes, I remember, every, every three or four months or so cos I wore them out so quickly erm I used to buy regularly a football magazine which I would read avidly every Saturday morning – I knew the names of all the teams in the football league, I knew their grounds, I knew their colours, I knew the names of most of the players in all the teams – it was a complete obsession and the odd thing is that now I have absolutely no interest in football whatsoever …

- Let the students check in pairs before going through the answers with the whole class.

> **a**   3 the music he listened to and the clothes he wore
> **b**   4 Lego® club
> **c**   1 ballet-mad girl
> **d**   5 football-crazy boy
> **e**   2 girl with the stuffed toys

2   Focus the students on the question, then play the recording again. Let them check in pairs before going through the answers with the whole class.

> **Possible answers**
> Speaker 1 – sounds a little *sentimental*
> Speaker 2 – sounds *amused*, perhaps *nostalgic*
> Speaker 3 – sounds *amused* and *embarrassed*
> Speaker 4 – sounds *nostalgic*
> Speaker 5 – sounds *factual*, *unemotional*

▶   A natural follow-up here is to focus on some of the language involved with talking about crazes. You may wish to do the Extra activity on p.142 at this point.

Exploring natural speech

This activity looks at two features of natural speech: firstly, the way that the rhetorical repetition of a phrase can add emphasis to what you're saying. Secondly, the use of *whatsoever* at the end of a sentence for emphasis.

1–2   Put the students in pairs to discuss the questions.

- You may wish to read through the extract as the students listen and read, or re-play the last extract from the recording. Not only will this help the students to work out how the two features in question work, it will also show how the words are strongly stressed to show emphasis.

> Every break time every lunchtime at school we would play football in the playground. Erm (It) had a disastrous effect on my shoes – my mother was having to buy me shoes, I remember, every three or four months or so cos I wore them out so quickly erm I used to buy regularly a football magazine which I would read avidly every Saturday morning – I knew the names of all the teams in the football league, I knew their

grounds, I knew their colours, I knew the names of most of the players in all the teams – it was a complete obsession and the odd thing is that now I have absolutely no interest in football whatsoever …

> **1**   The effect of the repetition of the phrase *I knew* is to emphasize how obsessed he was with football.
> **2**   Like *at all*, *whatsoever* follows *no* + noun, *none*, and *nothing* to emphasize what is being said. It is a little stronger than *at all*.

React and discuss

Encourage a whole-class discussion, or let the students discuss the questions in small groups, then present their ideas to the class.

Language focus: *used to* and *would*
p.89

Aim   *To revise and practise* used to *and* would *to talk about past states and past habits.*

The assumption here is that students have come across *used to* and *would* before. Consequently, the form and use are initially checked in a quiz, which encourages the students to discuss their understanding of the structures.

At this level, students may still have problems remembering the complex form of *used to*, making mistakes like **I didn't used to live in London*, or **I was used to live in Paris*. In the latter case, they may still be getting confused with the similar-looking structure *to be used to + -ing*. These are all checked in the quiz.

The students may also have problems with pronunciation, and it is worth including some repetition work to practise the correct production of /juːstə/.

The major problems, however, are with use. Students tend to avoid them, but it is important to encourage them to start using them when talking about memories, or being nostalgic, as it sounds unusual and dull not to in English. Although the basic rules are straightforward, and students usually grasp the idea that *used to* is for habits and states that are no longer true, but you cannot use *would* for states, watch out for errors of the following types:

> **When I used to be twenty, I used to live in a bedsit.*

(The second part of the sentence, *used to live*, is fine, as it is a past state that is no longer true. In the first part *used to be twenty* may look like a past state that is no longer true, but the word *when* suggests that the speaker sees it as one event in time. Consequently, it should be *When I was twenty*.)

> **I used to live in Bristol for seven years.*
> (You can't use *used to* to say how long.)

> **I use to play tennis all the time.*
> (You can't apply the form to present habits.)

> **I would live in London when I was younger.*
> (You can't use *would* for states, and here *live* is seen as a state.)

It is also worth noting that we tend to focus on *used to*, but that *would* is a very frequent form which learners often avoid.

- Put the students in pairs to do the quiz. If there is a lot of debate, let them double check their ideas with another pair before feedback. You may wish to refer the students to the Language commentary on p.95 to check their answers.

Quiz answers
1 True
2 False – we use the Past simple.
3 False
4 a – implies that this habit has been stopped.
5 False (*would* can't be used to refer to a habitual past state.)
6 a is correct. b is an example of the rule in 5 above.
7 b
8 If a time or length of time is specified *used to* cannot be used.
9 a could mean *I went once* or *I went more than once* – no indication is given.
  b means *I went more than once.*
10 a = *I am accustomed to*
  b = *I did this several times in the past, and don't any more.*

Exploitation

1 Ask students to work individually to complete the extract, then check their answers in pairs.

Note: Usually, but not always, there is a choice of forms. The important thing to impress upon students is that they should vary the forms they use so that the text as a whole does not sound repetitive.
1 was
2 used to collect / collected
3 were [**Note:** *used to be* would imply that they are no longer free – which is not true; so although grammatically possible, could only be used if you now have to pay for cheese labels and stones.]
4 was
5 moved
6 went
7 used to go / would go / went
8 would take / used to take / took
9 became
10 used to insist / would insist / insisted
11 went
12 I'd remove / used to remove
13 had

2 Read through the example with the students, then ask them to write sentences. Monitor and help. Make sure they are varying the use of *used to* and *would*.

- Ask some students to read out some of their sentences for the class. Alternatively, put the students in small groups to use the sentences as a basis for discussion, or do a mingle activity if space in the classroom allows. Ask the students to walk round and try to find people in the class they have something in common with. You could also set this task for homework.

Speaking

Aim *To get the students talking about crazes and using* used to *and* would, *and 'enthusiasm' expressions.*

1–2 Set the scene by eliciting a few things that the students were interested in as children. Then ask them to work individually and write a list, then use the list to say how interested they were in each activity.

3 Put the students in small groups to discuss their lists and find out whether anyone shared their interests.

- If you didn't do a mingle activity in the *Exploitation*, you could ask students to walk round and find people who shared their interests.

12.2 Fast food fashions   p.90

Stage 2 consists of a reading text about the rise of the burger. It looks at ellipsis, i.e. omitting words unnecessary to meaning in English.

Lead in

Aim *To get the students talking about the theme of the lesson, fast food, in a personalized discussion.*

1–3 Put the students in small groups to discuss the questions.

Reading

Aim *To develop prediction and interpretation skills.*

1 Put the students in pairs or threes to do questions **a–d**. Don't give the answers at this stage. The aim here is to get the students interested in the topic, and to create a prediction task for the first reading.

2 Ask the students to read the article and check their predictions.

a B (1904)	b B	c C	d C (7%)

Close up

- Put the students in pairs to do the exercise. Encourage them to make guesses from context rather than rely on their dictionaries.

1.2	person – hero / heroine
	quality – heroism
1.1–1.8	galloped – *to gallop* describes how horses run fast
	saddle – the thing a horse rider sits on
1.26	*Hamburgers* are people from the German city of Hamburg.
	hamburgers are the flattened circles of minced beef you eat in McDonald's.
1.48	*one* can refer to people in general or the speaker / writer in particular. The writer of this article uses the phrase to show that he has no evidence for the 'information' he is giving us.
1.50	potato
1.65	quickly
	to scoff also means *to mock / speak with contempt.*
	Stop scoffing. You're always scoffing at me.

- This reading text has a lot of difficult vocabulary. If you think your students are having difficulty, the following exercise extends the *Close up* and will help the students to understand the text. Since there are so many words, you may wish to deal just with the ones you think your students will have most problems with.

Write these words and phrases on the board and ask the students to work in pairs to find words in the passage with a similar meaning:

1 flat, grassy plains
2 attacking and robbing
3 tried for the first time
4 places in a market or fair with special permission to sell a product
5 new idea or invention
6 pressed into shape with your fingers
7 a tightly-packed ball
8 very hot cooking surface
9 an American coin worth five cents
10 really enjoy
11 buying and selling
12 unskilled worker
13 salesman
14 sell
15 a company with permission to sell a product
16 not considered properly
17 likely to

1	steppes	**10**	relish
2	pillage	**11**	merchandising
3	pioneered	**12**	menial
4	concessionaire stalls	**13**	vendor
5	innovation	**14**	peddle
6	kneaded	**15**	franchise
7	pellet	**16**	glossed over
8	hotplate	**17**	prone to
9	nickel		

3 Ask students to look back at the text and answer the questions in pairs. Expect some discussion in the feedback as the task necessitates interpreting the writer's words, so the students may have more than one possible answer.

Suggested answers

a It's easy and quick to make and cook / It was brilliantly marketed / Because no one got a trademark on the word, anyone could make it so there were many people selling it / Children particularly like food of this kind.

b They're cheap, quick, and you can buy one at all hours of the day.

c These foods seem to have no connection with meat. They certainly don't look like meat.

d He is saying that when we call them *cheap hamburgers* what we really mean is *poor quality hamburgers*. The word *anonymously* means that they have no brand name.

e Because of various diseases connected with meat, specifically new variant CJD – the human form of *mad cow disease*.

Glossary

CJD – Creutzfeld-Jakob's disease

mad cow disease – bovine spongiform encephalopathy (BSE)

Note

Creutzfeld-Jakob's disease (CJD) affects the brain of sufferers, causing damage to all functions, and eventually death. The development of BSE, which affected cattle, and its link to new variant CJD, began to be explored in 1990, with the first cases of nv CJD being found in 1994. These cases in humans were linked to the consumption of beef from infected cattle – hence the danger of eating meat from a source you don't know.

React and discuss

Encourage a whole-class discussion.

Language focus: omitting words   p.91

Aim *To introduce and practise the use of ellipsis – leaving out words and phrases which are unnecessary to the meaning – in spoken and written English.*

This section looks at the way subject pronouns, auxiliary verbs, articles, and others, are left out in order to avoid giving or repeating information that is already clear from the context. Conceptually, this is quite a straightforward idea. However, some students at this level often avoid ellipsis when they're speaking in favour of being 'grammatically correct'. It is difficult to 'feel' when and which words to leave out. The emphasis here is on recognition rather than practice – getting students to think about which words to leave out and why.

1 Put the students in pairs to look at the sentences and answer the questions. Refer them to the Language commentary on p.95.

a		**b**
1	*It's / They're*	Subject pronoun and verb
2	Q *Have you*	Subject pronoun and auxiliary verb in question
	A *No, I'm*	Reply to question; subject pronoun and verb
	I haven't.	Short answer
3	*The*	article
	I've	Subject pronoun and auxiliary verb
4	*I*	Subject pronoun
	Are you	Subject pronoun and auxiliary verb in question

2 Read through the examples as a class.

Exploitation

1 Do the first as an example, then ask the students to work in pairs to cross out the unnecessary words.

- After checking the answers, you could get the students to practise the conversations with their partners.

> **a** Q ~~Is there~~ any chance of ~~you giving me~~ a lift?
>   A Sure ~~I can give you a lift~~. Get in.
> **b** Q ~~Have you~~ seen my dad recently?
>   A Yes, ~~I have seen your dad recently~~. I saw him this morning.

- To give the students more fluency practice in this area, you could do the following extra activity.

  1   Put the students in pairs. Write a list of questions on the board. You could use the list below, or make up your own to reflect your students' interests. Student A must ask Student B the questions, using ellipsis, and Student B must give short answers, also using ellipsis.

  2   Get the students started by eliciting suggested short answers then modelling the activity.

  Example:
  Done your homework?
  Not yet. No. You? Too busy. Haven't had time. Sort of. Couldn't be bothered.

  Suggested questions:
  Have you done your homework?
  Are you tired?
  Do you fancy a coffee?
  Have you got a pen?
  Are you coming to the party on Friday?

2 Do the first sentence as a class, then ask students to work individually to do the first exercise.

- Ask the students to compare their versions in pairs, and do exercise **c**.

> **Possible answers**
> Since last Friday been from Perth to Adelaide then to Mount Gambier, a remote farming town. Climbed a volcano, saw koalas and kangaroos in the wild. Tuesday hired a car and Tina and I drove along Ocean Road past rocks in the picture. Views really breath-taking. Never seen anything like it. Planning to visit rainforest tomorrow. (57 words)

- As a follow-up or homework activity, ask students to write their own postcard about an adventurous holiday they have been on.

- Alternatively, give students in pairs a postcard with an interesting picture of a well-known place on the front, and ask them to write about the place using ellipsis. Or you could ask each pair to write the text in whole sentences, then give their text to another pair who have to cross out unnecessary words.

Stage 3 consists of two listening texts: one in which a speaker describes successful films, and another in which people describe a frightening scene in a film.

Lead in

Aim *To get students to describe their favourite film in a personalized speaking activity.*

1–2 Elicit as many different types of film as you can from the students. Then put the students in pairs to tell their partner which is their favourite type of film and why.

> **Suggested answers**
> thrillers; horror films; romantic films; sci-fi; animated; comedy; action; classic; westerns; gangster

3 Check that students understand the language in the box, then give them a few minutes to prepare how to describe their favourite film. *Dubbed* means translated into another language and recorded over the original soundtrack.

Listening

Aim *To listen for gist and specific information.*

Note

Crouching Tiger, Hidden Dragon (2000) – film directed by Ang Lee, starring Chow Yun-Fat and Michelle Yeoh. A beautiful blend of martial arts and romance which won four Oscars and was nominated for six more.
Julia Roberts – American actress who won an Oscar for her role in *Erin Brockovich* (2000), and received nominations for *Steel Magnolias* (1989) and *Pretty Woman* (1990).
Michael Douglas – actor and producer. Son of actor Kirk Douglas and one of only two people ever to have won Oscars both for best picture (*One Flew Over The Cuckoo's Nest*, 1975) and best actor (*Wall Street*, 1987).
Braveheart (1995) – film directed by and starring Mel Gibson, about 13th century Scot William Wallace who united the Scots in a battle to overthrow English rule. It won five Oscars, including Best Film and Best Director, and was nominated for five more.

1 Outline the task, then play the recording.

12.2

I think in the past obviously classic films, things like *Casablanca*, things that have endured over the years, but I think also films in the past that were popular were very strict to their genre, things like Westerns, which had a very strict set of rules that were always followed. They were based around the same thing – that actually have a fairly universal appeal. I think a Western is actually an example of a sort of myth, a legend, almost like a fairy tale – the good guy and the good guy always wins, and the bad guy. But the good guy never quite integrates into society – the good guy always goes off riding into the sunset and these rules are very very strict, but I think that that's part of the appeal, but that that genre really, I think, has had its day, erm I think it's being eclipsed by other things and I think an example of that is *Crouching Tiger, Hidden Dragon*, which is a similar sort of thing actually, in some ways.

Looking at things in the cinema at present and I think there's the two main types of film erm there's blockbusters, box-office smash films, romantic comedy, there's, you know, things, I don't know, any Julia

Roberts film, anything, you know, some of the Michael Douglas films, whatever, erm and then there's the big action films, things like *Braveheart*.

  a classic; Western; romantic comedy; action
  b Julia Roberts; Michael Douglas

2 Play the recording again and ask students to complete the sentences.

  a classic film
  b a myth, legend, or fairy tale
  c the good guy; the bad guy
  d the good guy riding into the sunset

3 Play the second part of the recording.

12.3

As for where films are going, I think the idea that the genre is no longer applied as strictly as it was once that erm genre is something which is increasingly you know that and a good example of that is *Crouching Tiger, Hidden Dragon*, that what kind of movie is it? Well it's a feminist, art house, martial arts movie – very very difficult to pigeonhole. It comes across much more like something like a computer game than a film in some ways, the fighting scenes and the flying scenes and the treetops and the canopy of the forest, you know it's an incredible mixture of of different influences and yet it's got this nineteenth-century China, star-crossed lovers erm, and the honour code and you know this this amazing story behind it that it's a really interesting film and I think what's interesting about it is that it doesn't fit into the rules of any one genre.

I think that actually is the key to what makes a good film is if it really carries you into that film and involves you in it and has you somewhere else for two hours and I think that's what film does probably better than any other art form. A book does but you're still having to read it and yeah I love books, don't get me wrong erm, but I I feel that a film really can do that – it transports you it's the, the whole atmosphere, the music and that especially when you see it at the cinema and you have to go and make an effort to go see it, erm and you sit there in the dark and this massive movie is is playing – and you know there's the music and the effects and the sound and the pictures and it's just the whole experience.

I really think that's the essence of a good movie is a movie that carries you away that takes you from your normal life for a couple of hours – it's an escapist thing.

A good film is one which involves and absorbs the audience. It provides an escape from real life.

Exploring natural speech   p.93

Aim *To contrast natural speech with the language used in a formal talk.*

1 Read through the introduction as a class, then put students in pairs to turn the passage into a formal talk.

Possible answer
A film transports you. It's the whole atmosphere and the music. That's especially true when you see a film at the cinema; probably because you have to make an effort to go see it. You sit there in the dark with this massive movie playing. There's the music, the effects, the sound and the pictures. It's the whole experience which makes a film successful or not.

React and discuss

Do this as a class discussion or in small groups.

Vocabulary: phrasal verbs with *off*

Aim *To introduce and practise phrasal verbs with* off.

This section introduces a number of phrasal verbs by looking at the different meanings of *off* when used as a particle.

1 Discuss the sentences as a class.

  a *goes riding* – this describes a simple activity
  b *goes off riding* – this means he is leaving on horseback, and probably not coming back.

2 **a–b** Ask students to work in pairs to match the phrasal verbs with the meaning groups, and say which single verb could be used as an alternative.

a		b	
1	call off	B	cancel / postpone
2	spark off	C	start / begin / cause
3	divide off	D	separate
4	set off	A	begin / start
5	kick off	C	start / begin (The football match starts with a *kick off*.)
6	break off	B	end
7	block off	D	close
8	blast off	A	leave

c Students remain in pairs to categorize the phrasal verbs and illustrate the meanings. Monitor and help, and get some students to read out their best sentences in the feedback.

close off **D**	ring off **B**
drive off **A**	seal off **D**
lead off **C**	take off **C**
put off **B**	wave off **A**

Some possible sentences
The police closed off the area after the accident.
He drove off at top speed.
The captain led the players off the pitch to collect the trophy after their victory.
They decided to put off the race meeting because of the bad weather. / Don't put me off when I'm trying to concentrate.
She was so angry that she rang off without answering his question.
Because of the gas leak, we will have to seal off the factory so that no-one can enter.
The plane took off. (beginning a journey) The craze for micro scooters took off very quickly.
Their families waved them off as they left for Australia.

Listening and speaking

Aim *To listen for gist, and to practise describing a scene in a film using the Historic present.*

1 Set the scene by asking the students what was the most frightening film they have ever seen, and why it was so frightening.

Note

Psycho (1960) – classic thriller directed by Alfred Hitchcock and starring Anthony Perkins as the deranged Norman Bates who famously stabs a young woman in her motel room shower. Nominated for four Oscars.
Misery (1990) – film directed by Rob Reiner, starring Kathy Bates (who won an Oscar for Best Actress) and James Caan. A famous novelist is first rescued from a car crash and then held prisoner by an obsessed fan.

- Outline the task and play the recording.

12.4

T There's that bit in *Psycho* when I think there's a girl hiding under the staircase, isn't there, and whoever it is, is coming in, he runs up the stairs and you're you're not quite sure if he's noticed her or not and he's sort of looking around the house and you know that he's about to come down and find her and then obviously the shower scene.

R Hitchcock is always good for suspense really.

K Definitely.

R I love the bit in I think it's *Misery*, is it called *Misery*? with Kathy Bates (Yes) where where she's she's gone out for a drive and he's in the house and he has to try and get out of the room which she's locked him in and, you know, he gets all the way …

K (Does it) with hairpins or something? He finds …

R Yeah, he has to unlock all sorts of doors and of course he's wheelchair-bound as well and then she … you see the car coming back and the camera keeps cutting to the car coming back and he's got to get back into the position that she expects to find him in.

J And obviously, he just makes it.

R Just in the nick of time.

J In an amazingly short period of time. Apart from the fact that when she comes back in, one of her china erm ornaments is the wrong way round.

R That's right, she notices something's just slightly been moved.

J Total psychopath because she's noticed that.

R Picks up the sledge hammer and breaks his legs.

J That is an absolutely horrible scene.

> a Personal answers
> b Suspense: characters and audience not quite sure what's going to happen next.

2 Put the students in pairs to read the extracts and discuss the questions.

> **Extract A**
> - *bit* = part of the film / scene
> - The speaker is trying to get the agreement of the people with him. He is assuming they have seen the film and will support his opinions.
> - Present tenses are used to make the action come alive. (Compare with the text, *Welcome to the Pole!* in Unit 10.)
> - *you* = the cinema-goer, the person watching the action, everyone
>
> **Extract B**
> - *where* refers to *the bit in Misery. When* could be used instead.
> - The Present perfect is used in combination with Present tenses. If the main narrative had been in the Past simple and Past continuous, this verb would be in the Past perfect.

3 Elicit from the class what makes film scenes frightening. Some suggestions include: dramatic music, sound effects, lighting, rapid editing, unusual camera shots.

- Ask the students to think of a frightening scene, and take five or six minutes planning how to describe it. Ask them questions **a** and **b**, and use some of the language in exercise 2, particularly the Historic present. Refer them to the Language commentary on p.79.

- If your students find it difficult to be creative, they could do this in pairs, and think how to describe a frightening scene they have both seen.

- When they are ready, put the students in groups of four or five to describe their scenes. Monitor for errors.

- A natural follow-up for homework is to ask the students to write a film review. Refer them to the Writing guidelines on p.156.

Exploring words   p.94

Aim *To introduce and practise phrases based around the key word* fashion, *and adjectives used to describe clothes.*

1 Ask students to work alone or in pairs to complete the gaps.

> a fashion-conscious
> b the latest fashion
> c come (back) into fashion
> d fashion victims
> e went out of fashion
> f unfashionable

2 a Ask students to divide the adjectives into three lists.

> **Positive:**
> *cool; elegant; flattering; posh; smart; snazzy*; special; stylish; tasteful; trendy*
> **Negative:**
> *conservative; dressy*; dull; flashy; naff*; ordinary; shocking; unflattering*
> **Neutral:**
> *bright; casual; classic; formal; neat; neutral; presentable; sensible; sporty; traditional*
> * snazzy = very fashionable
> * dressy = too smart or elegant for a particular occasion
> * naff = bad taste / unfashionable

b–c Students work in pairs or small groups to look at the pictures, describe them, and discuss the questions in **c**. Monitor and help.

d Outline the task and play the recording.

12.5

1

M1 This looks kind of office wear.

W1 Quite conservative, isn't it?

W2 Yeah. It's a bit sensible.

M1 I like her red dress though.

W2 Really?

W1 Yeah, but you wouldn't actually wear it. I wouldn't.

W2 Remind me not to go shopping with you.

M1 No I wouldn't wear it either, actually, funnily enough.

M2 I prefer the one in the middle – she looks kind of …

W2 Yeah, she's a bit more snazzy.

M2 Yeah, definitely.

W1 Yeah, OK.

M2 Whereas the one on the right – not very flattering.

W2 No.

M1 Well, she's chosen pale colours, hasn't she, …

2

W2 Right what about him? Now that's very office.

M2 Very office.

M1 But it's kind of casual office.

W1 It works.

W2 It's kind of special, but in a stylish way.

W1 I think he looks neat.

M1 Nice tie.

M2 Presentable.

W2 Definitely – if you're going for an interview, you know – it's fine.

W1 You could take him home to your mum …

3

W1 Ooh look at her!

M1 Now that's saucy secretary, isn't it?

W2 That's kind of air hostess actually, isn't it?

W1 It's quite scaring.

M2 She looks quite powerful – you know bit of a power suit there, powerful suit …

W2 It is powerful definitely – yep, she knows where she's going – she knows what she's doing …

4

W2 So, what about this guy?

W1 Hello.

W2 No, he does look pretty fit, do you know what I mean?

W1 Yeah, but what about the clothes?

W2 OK, let's look at the clothes.

M2 That's classic.

M1 Chinos, black T-shirt.

M2 Yeah.

W2 Casual again.

W1 Quite neutral.

W2 Yes.

M2 Uncomplicated.

W2 Definitely.

M1 Smart.

W2 Classic.

W1 Yeah.

M1 That's it, really, isn't it?

W2 Yeah.

M1 And I think everyone likes it.

W2 You could wear that anywhere, really, couldn't you?

5

W2 OK, let's move on to her.

W1 Ooh.

M2 Right. Action.

W1 I like the colour.

M2 It's bright.

W1 I know.

M1 It's sporty-ish.

M2 Yeah. That's what I'm thi … I'm thinking outdoor wear.

All Yeah / Definitely.

M1 Could be good snowboarding …

W2 All weather, all weather.

M2 Yeah it's kind of got that snowboard look, hasn't it, it's sort of …

W1 Yeah – it's still trendy, it's cool.

M2 Yeah.

W2 Like the boots.

M2 Yeah good boots.

W1 Hiking.

M1 Sturdy boots. She's got sunglasses on her head, as well.

W2 Has she?

M1 Yeah. I think she's thinking she's …

W1 She's quite trendy.

M2 She could be going sailing. …

Adjectives in **bold** are not from the list in 2a.
***office**(wear); conservative; sensible; snazzy; (not) flattering; casual; special; stylish; neat; presentable; ***saucy secretary; *air hostess; scaring; powerful**; classic; neutral; **uncomplicated**; smart; bright; sporty(-ish); trendy; cool
*These are nouns used as adjectives, i.e. clothes such as might be worn in an office (dull, boring), or by a 'saucy' secretary (too sexy, maybe a bit cheap) or an air hostess (smart suit, formal elegance).

3 Put the students in small groups to look at the questions in the two lists, and decide which ones they are going to discuss.

· Monitor the discussions.

· When they have talked about four questions, ask the students to stand up, if possible, walk round the class, and find and sit down with other students who have discussed the same questions. They can then compare answers.

13 Conflict

Theme: how people deal with different kinds of conflict

13.1 Personal and professional

People talk about how they deal with conflict in their personal and professional lives

- **Listening:** matching and specific information
- **Exploring natural speech:** 'echoing' for emphasis
- **Listening and speaking:** role play – a conflict situation

13.2 Only a game

An article about conflict in the playground

- **Reading:** gist and specific information
- **Language focus:** -ing forms
- **Writing:** a story

13.3 Families at war

Relationships and conflict within families

- **Listening:** causes of argument within families
- **Reading:** gist, analysis, interpretation
- **Language focus:** singular or plural?
- **Speaking:** formal discussion

Exploring words

Conflict

Workbook

- **Language focus:** -ing forms; adjective + preposition + -ing form; verb + (object +) preposition + -ing form; singular or plural?
- **Vocabulary focus:** conflict – collocations and idioms
- **Vocabulary expansion:** idioms with *big*; idioms with *word / words*
- **Listening:** trouble at work

13.1 Personal and professional
p.96

This stage includes two listenings which look at the topic of conflict in different ways.

Lead in

Aim *To get students thinking and talking about conflict in people's lives.*

Note
Throughout this unit, and particularly in the speaking and discussion-based activities, it is important to remember that different cultures define and resolve conflict in very different ways.

1 You could elicit ideas from the whole class before asking students to discuss the question in pairs or groups.

2 Check vocabulary, then ask students to do the task. Do not get feedback at this point as this can be done after *Listening* 1.

Listening

Aim *To practise extracting the main idea of what is being said (the gist) from different speakers talking quite informally.*

1 Outline the task and play the recording.

13.1

Speaker 1 Well it's very different in personal and professional, but erm I think I probably find it easier to deal in a professional context because you have some sort of structure that you can you have recourse to, but in personal life I find it very stressful.

Speaker 2 Conflict – I'm getting better at it – much better than I used to be, but it's not enjoyable, it's never enjoyable having to deal with conflict, erm but I can stay much calmer now than I used to be in those kinds of situations, which always helps, because then you can step back from it and decide what's really happening without getting upset or excited or angry or any of those things.

Speaker 3 Absolutely impossible I would always avoid conflict whenever I possibly could, which I think is always, if if you want to avoid conflict badly enough you can avoid it Which is cowardly I know, and I see it as a a failing I think, because I think some people can make something constructive out of conflict but I can't. I don't like it at all.

Speaker 4 In my personal life I find it erm probably a bit easier than in my professional life. I would say that, erm I like to deal with it absolutely immediately and er can't rest until it is dealt with whereas professionally although I would like to do that it's not quite as easy to do that.

Speaker 5 I find it very difficult, but you need to be able to deal with conflict in order to to progress.
So how do you approach it – what do you do about it?
You've got to be sure of your facts before you start, and I think you've also got to be aware of some position of compromise.

Speaker 6 … I feel professionally I deal with it pretty well, but personally that's a whole nother ball-game for me – I really have a problem with it personally – when someone yells at me, even if it's totally unjust, rather than argue back or yell back, I cry which isn't very helpful in resolving the conflict, but I just, I get so upset I …

Speaker 7 Well conflict – I'd rather not talk about it, that's basically how I deal with conflict. I'm I'm very uncomfortable with conflict quite honestly and – personally and professionally – and I'll do just about anything to avoid it. I like to be an easy-going laid-back kind of person and it really takes a lot for me to confront someone on something even if they've treated me badly – it's actually an area that I'd like to get better at, but erm I have a boyfriend who is, loves conflict so we actually make a great pair because …

- Ask students to compare their answers. Play the recording again, if necessary.

- Check answers with the whole class. you may want to hold a brief feedback on their own answers at this point.

| a 3 / 7 | b 1 / 6 | c 5 | d 2 | e 6 | f 4 |

2 Ask students to read the statements a–g.

- Go through any difficult vocabulary with them, for example:

step back = to try to become more objective about a situation, by 'stepping back'

failing = a weakness, a character fault

laid-back = having a relaxed attitude

- Check students understand the task.

- Play recording **13.1** again. It is probably a good idea to pause after each speaker to give students time to write their answers.

- After the whole recording, ask students to compare their answers before checking with the whole class.

Possible answers
a There is a *structure* for dealing with conflict at work. / There is a *structure* to fall back on.
b She stays calmer if she is able to *step back* from the situation. / She tries to *step back* from the situation and see what's actually happening.
c He thinks it's a *failing*. / He see it as a *failing*.
d He can't *rest* (relax) until he has dealt with the situation.
e You have to be prepared to *compromise*. / You have to try to think of a *compromise* position.
f It doesn't help him to *resolve* the conflict. / Crying and being upset makes it more difficult to *resolve* the conflict.
g She is more *laid-back* than her boyfriend.

React and discuss   p.97

Aim *To give students a chance to talk about themselves and how they have dealt with conflict.*

Be prepared by having a conflict situation of your own that you are willing to talk about. Tell the students your story in as natural a way as possible.

Exploring natural speech

Aim *To draw students' attention to* fronting, *the way in which natural, spoken English often has a different word order from the one the students are taught.*

In natural speech the subject of the discussion, and of the sentences, can be brought to the front of the sentence (see Unit 15 Language commentary on p.116) in order to add emphasis and / or to give the speaker time to think about what they want to say (*Conflict … I'm getting better at it*).

Although students are given the chance to practise some fronting themselves, the main aim here is to increase awareness of it so that they are then better able to follow natural speech. Students will have more opportunity for practice in Unit 15.

1 Either play excerpts **a** and **b** from recording **13.1** or read the sentences yourself, in as natural a way as possible. Then ask students to think about the question.

There are two possible explanations:
They are deliberately 'fronting' the key idea to give it emphasis.
They are giving themselves time to think of what they want to say.
In either case, starting with the word *conflict* focuses the listener's attention.

2 You could go through these with the whole class first, eliciting possible answers so that students are sure of the word order, then ask them to practise in pairs or small groups.

Possible answers
a Family rows, can't say they worry me too much.
b Well, war, now that's a big question.
c Disappointments, well I guess you've just got to put up with them, haven't you?
d My neighbours, now there's something I could talk about all night!

Listening and speaking

Aim *To identify and practise language used to calm people down.*

1 Outline the task briefly.

- Play the recording. Give the students a few minutes to complete any notes they might be making.

13.2

M1 What do you think you're doing?

M2 I was following you. I wasn't that, I wasn't that far behind – you stalled …

M1 You, yeah, you wait till I move off, right? The lights turned green. You are behind me and you wait till I've moved off.

M2 Yeah, all right, all right.

M1 Look at this.

M2 I know, well look at my headlight mate.

M1 Well look at my rear lig… They're not even working.

M2 All right. We're not going to get anywhere by shouting, are we? (I've got to go) We're not going to get anywhere by shouting.

M1 I've got to go and pick my kids up and it's getting dark.

M2 All right. You gonna get, all right look I've got a mobile phone if you wanna use it. It's fine, you can call, you can tell em you're gonna be late.

M1 I don't believe this.

M2 Look there's no point getting upset. Look – you've lost a bit out the back. I've lost me headlight. It's fine. It's not serious. It's absolutely not serious. If you've got your insurance …

M1 It's your fault mate.

M2 I don't …

W Excuse me.

M2 I don't think it's right to start blaming people.

M1 It is.

M2 I mean this is, this is it's easily remediable.

W Look, excuse me, but you're really causing quite a tailback, back here.

M1 What's it got to do with you?

- Ask them to compare their answers in pairs, then play the recording again so that they can check and add to their notes.

> **a** A minor road accident. One car has driven into the back of the car in front. There is damage to the headlights of one car and the rear lights of the other.
>
> **b** The driver in front is very aggressive, rude, and angry. The other is polite, conciliatory, and ready to compromise.
>
> **c** all right, all right
> We're not getting anywhere by shouting, are we?
> there's no point in getting upset
> It's not serious
> I don't think it's right to start blaming people
> It's easily remediable.

---

2 Before starting the role play, spend some time practising the pronunciation of the expressions in the box.

- It is usually a good idea to spend some time setting up a role play; if students are really involved and feel they can imagine the situation and their role quite well, they generally have more to say.

- Taking Situation 1 as an example, ask the students to look at the picture and describe the scene to you, then try to get them to fill in some details. What day is it? When is it? (When is rush hour?) How do they think the people are feeling? The cyclist? The pedestrian? The other pedestrians? Check some vocabulary with them: *Walkman; mobile phone; knock someone over / down; hit / hurt; in a rush; dashing across a road.*

- When you feel that the situation has been well described from a variety of angles ask students to divide up their roles: cyclists, pedestrians, and probably two different other pedestrians.

- If any groups decide to practise the other situation, ask them to follow the same procedure: think about the situation and fill in details before assigning roles.

- Group the students so that they are sitting with other people of the same role (all the cyclists together, the pedestrians together, etc.).

- Now ask them to think about what happened from their perspective. Ask them to consider how they feel now. Get them to decide which language from the box and expressions they noted from **1** they might want to use. Set a time limit for this (probably a few minutes only).

- Regroup the students so that each role is represented in each group. Tell them they have a few minutes to practise their

role play. This is a rehearsal. As they rehearse, go around and monitor, noting any problems of language and especially intonation.

- Stop the rehearsal. Give them a few general tips as a whole group based on your observations and then get them to do the role play again, this time as well as they possibly can. Monitor and take notes.

- If appropriate, ask one of the better groups to demonstrate their role play to the whole class.

- Ask the listeners / observers to comment on the kind of language used, the effectiveness of the participants, what worked / didn't work, and how well the situation was resolved.

13.2 Only a game   p.98

This stage includes a reading which contextualizes *-ing* forms.

Lead in

Aim *To start the students thinking about childhood conflict and to prepare for the reading text that follows.*

1–3 Read through the questions quickly with the students, dealing with any problems that arise.

- Ask them to work in pairs or small groups to discuss the questions.

- You might like to share the answers to **1** to help lead in to the reading.

Reading

Aim *To develop the students' ability to read a semi-formal text, extracting the most important points and arguments from fairly dense writing.*

1 Briefly outline the task and check the vocabulary with the whole class.

> **a** *bully* = to frighten or hurt a weaker person. *Bullying* can be mental as well as physical.
> *fight* = to struggle against physically
> *Bullying* may include *fighting*, but *fighting* isn't necessarily *bullying*.
>
> **b** *hit* = to strike
> *hurt* = to damage, possibly as a result of *hitting*. You can *hurt* someone psychologically as well as physically.
>
> **c** *uncoordinated* = not good at controlling your movements, clumsy
> *unfit* = unhealthy or not fit due to lack of exercise

---

2 Outline the task and give students quiet time to read the text.

- When most of the class has finished, ask them to compare their answers in pairs, then check with the whole class. Avoid dealing with other comprehension or vocabulary questions here – they may come up in the *Close up* section or in question 3.

- Children's identities are formed through competition and conflict.
- Fighting is a form of role play. It allows children to see the effects of their actions.
- Fighting helps children to become aware of the need for rules and compromise.

Close up

- Put the students in pairs to do the exercise. Encourage them to make guesses from context rather than rely on their dictionaries.

1.6 climb
1.6 hang (*dangle* = to hang loosely)
1.17 water

3 Ask students to answer these questions in pairs or small groups, referring to the text as necessary.

- When you have checked the answers, you can ask the students if there are any other words they want to know. Even if it is not necessary for general understanding of the text, some students, especially at advanced level, like to feel they understand every word of a reading text. Be careful to avoid word-for-word translation though, as this is generally unhelpful for both comprehension and vocabulary development.

a Children are bored, unfit, uncoordinated, and depressed.
b They make their own rules (in order to *make the outcome more unpredictable*).
c He thinks children should not be left alone (unsupervised). If they are not supervised, he says, there will be bullying.
d The experiment supports Flemmen's ideas.

Glossary

tyres – the rubber outside of wheels
presided – ruled, governed
intervene – physically interrupt
thrilling – exciting

React and discuss

- Ask students to share their own ideas and discuss in small groups whether they agree with Asbjorn Flemmen's views.
- You may find that the whole class want to talk about the article. Give them time to do so, as the kind of speaking that will happen here is different from that practised earlier.

Language focus: *-ing* forms   p.99

Students will have come across the *-ing* forms before (and they may have learnt the terms gerund or participle). However, even at advanced level, students often make mistakes with the *-ing* forms, tending to use the infinitive instead (**He's a man who thinks to fight is good for children.*) or using a whole phrase (*After the boy fell off his bike, he had to go to hospital.*). In this section the various uses of the *-ing* form are reviewed and students then practise using some of the more difficult ones. You may wish to refer them to the Language commentary on p.103.

1 Give students time to do the task on their own to begin with; long enough to read the task properly and to try to separate the different types.

- After about five minutes, let them compare their answers in pairs before checking with the whole class.

Use	Extract
a	5 (*were fighting*)
b	3 (*boring*)
c	2
d	1 (*saying* after *listen*); 3 (*sitting* after *keep*); 5 (*hitting* after *started*)
e	4 (*interacting* after *while*)
f	1 (*Listen to the designer **who is** saying* …); 6 (*adults **who were** supervising*)

2 Go through the example sentence with the whole class. You may also want to do the next sentence with the class to demonstrate.

- Ask the students to complete the task in pairs, then check answers with the whole class.

a He ran out of the playground, *slamming* the gate behind him.
b Parents don't let their children play in the street, *thinking* they may get into trouble.
c She sent a text message, *not realizing* the teacher was watching her.
d The woman was interviewed several times before *being* arrested.

Note

-ing forms are often used after conjunctions in participle clauses (use e in 1). They tell us when actions took place in relation to each other.
Examples
Children should be careful *when crossing the road*.
While travelling in Scotland, I met someone I used to play with as a child.
Since studying abroad, he's been much better at looking after himself.
The subject of the verb in these participle clauses is the subject of the main clause: *when (they are) crossing; while (I was) travelling*.

Exploitation

- Outline the task briefly.
- Start the first passage off with the whole class, going through the first one or two with all the students until they are sure of what they have to do. You may decide to do the whole of the first text together. Some of the sentence linking may be quite difficult to begin with but the students should soon get better at manipulating language in this way.
- Ask the students to do the second text on their own or in pairs, and to check their answers together.

1 Passengers travelling (**1**) on a flight from Miami to Puerto Rico were amazed when a deranged passenger walked to the back of the plane and then started to run up the aisle, slapping (**2**) passengers' heads along the way. He then kicked a pregnant flight attendant and bit a young boy on the arm. Cabin crew restrained the man by jumping (**3**) on him and holding (**4**) him down. He was arrested when the plane landed.

2 On another flight, for some unknown reason, a passenger who had been drinking (**1**) started throwing peanuts at a well-built man sitting (**2**) with his wife minding (**3**) his own business. When the first peanut hit him in the face, he ignored it. After being struck (**4**) by a second peanut, he looked up to see who had thrown it. He gave the man a dirty look, expecting (**5**) him to stop immediately. When a third peanut hit him in the eye, he'd had enough. 'Do that again' he said, 'and I'll punch your lights out.' But the peanut-thrower couldn't resist throwing (**6**) one last peanut. Getting out of his seat, the victim (**7**) punched the man so hard that witnesses heard his jaw break.

Writing

Aim *To give students practice at writing short texts for a fairly informal context.*

1 Draw students' attention to the Writing guidelines on p.151.

• Put the students in small groups and ask them to tell a conflict story of their own, or to talk about a story with one of the suggested endings in **b**.

• Monitor and join in if appropriate, but don't correct.

2 Now ask the students to plan their stories. Give them a few minutes to note down the key points and to ask you for any vocabulary or phrases they might need.

• Give them time to write their stories in class or set for homework.

The 60 seconds game

If your students are confident speakers, you could do this extra speaking activity where students have to speak for 60 seconds about something without repetition, hesitation, or deviation from the subject. (You will need to demonstrate it yourself first.) These are the rules:

1 Students work in groups and take turns to start talking about one of these subjects:
   • Smoking in public places
   • Sending and receiving e-mails
   • Buying birthday presents
   • Learning to drive
   • Getting married
   • Leaving school

2 One member of the group should keep time.

3 The student talking must try to speak fluently without:
   • repeating a word or phrase
   • hesitating
   • changing the subject

4 The other students in the group should listen and interrupt the speaker if they break any of these rules.

The student who notices the mistake continues with the same topic for the remainder of the 60 seconds.

5 The student speaking at the end of 60 seconds wins the round.

Demonstrate the game yourself first.
Act as the speaker, (making sure you don't speak too fluently!) and ask the students to interrupt you if you repeat, hesitate, or change the subject.
Now continue the activity with the whole class. When they have got the idea, they could do it in groups.
Once the rules are clear, and if they enjoy it, this can be a good warm-up or filler activity for subsequent lessons. Make sure you have some topics handy.

13.3 Families at war   p.100

This stage includes two reading texts, which provide an initial context for the *Language focus*, singular or plural.

Lead in

1 Set up the task with the whole class then ask the students to discuss the questions in pairs or small groups.

2 Tell students that they will now hear five people discussing the same subjects. The students need to make notes of their answers. (They may find it useful to draw up a chart or grid to make notes – see Answers below.)

• Play the recording.

13.3

Speaker 1   Mess, I think is the biggest cause of arguments in our house, erm, who made it, whose turn is it to clear it up, who makes more mess, who clears up more mess, erm, can't think we argue about anything else really, just general tidiness, organization and mess.

Speaker 2   Me and my family have argued about very few things really. Erm, I mean, I suppose the only things I can remember would be playing Scrabble and arguing over whether a word was actually a word, but that's always sorted out by getting the dictionary, and occasionally what to watch on TV, but that's pretty much it really.

Speaker 3   Erm – my family and I have argued a lot about food, erm. My mother likes meat and my sister's a vegetarian so often we have to cook more than one meal – causes a lot of problems.

Speaker 4   We tend to argue about really silly things, I think. It's very often something and nothing and the argument is is basically simply because somebody feels in a bad mood and just needs to have the release of possibly picking a fight of some kind, so erm we can argue about anything and everything. It really is impossible to say whether there is anything specific that we we argue about.

Speaker 5   My family always argue about holidays. My mum always wants to go abroad, but my dad doesn't like to fly, so he always wants to stay in the country. My brother and sister like a seaside-type holiday, but my mum likes to do sightseeing and I always argue, because I never get an opinion.

• Ask students to compare their answers in pairs. Play the recording again if necessary.

• Check answers with the whole class.

	a	b
S1	mess; tidiness; organization	not mentioned
S2	wordgames; TV	family
S3	food	mother; sister
S4	bad moods; anything and everything	not mentioned
S5	holidays	mother; father; sister; brother

Reading

Aim *To provide students with texts they can compare and contrast in terms of style and attitude, and to give them further intensive reading practice.*

1 Go through the task with the whole class. Make sure they realize they have to read both texts. Tell them not to worry about unknown vocabulary at this stage but to focus on the questions.

• Give students time to read the texts quietly.

• Ask them to compare their answers in pairs, then check with the whole class.

> **a A** father
> **B** mother
> **b A** had three sons / school teacher / very old-fashioned / he used to shout at his children
> **B** black hair / small ears / looks after son

2 Go through the task with the students, making sure that they are clear about what they have to do. (Again, unknown vocabulary is not important yet).

• Ask students to complete the task in pairs, then check answers with the whole class.

> **Possible answers**
> **Focus**
> Text **A** focuses on single event. Son makes a remark to father who demands apology. Son refuses and walks out.
> Text **B** Here the focus is on the developing relationship between the son and his mother.
> **Attitude**
> **A** The son feels sorry / pity for his father. He has just refused to continue being subservient to him, so he also feels proud to have asserted his independence.
> **B** Mother amuses son / he's fascinated by her / feels protected by her / feels he knows her better as time goes by.
> **Style**
> **A** is more conversational, i.e. *I suppose, I'd say, blew his top, slunk out*
> **B** is more formal, literary, especially because it includes a poem.

3 Ask students to answer the questions on their own, then check their answers in pairs.

• Briefly check answers with the whole class.

> **Key points from text**
> **a 1** (He blew his top)
> **b 3** (I'd cracked it. He's never behaved like that to me again.)
> **c 2** (Our eyes are locked together)

Glossary

about to – very useful, very common phrase meaning 'on the point of doing'
blew his top – got very angry
in the wrong – wrong
slunk out (to slink out) – left quietly, in a cowardly way
I'd cracked it – I'd solved the problem. Colloquial

Language focus: singular or plural? p.101

Aim *To focus on nouns which can be considered as either singular or plural.*

Students will, of course, be very familiar with singular and plural verb forms and they may have little difficulty in using them appropriately. However, they may be unsure of which form is correct after certain nouns (*family, the government*, etc.). This section aims to point out any distinctions that exist and provide practice in using the forms correctly. It also shows the flexibility in English where it is acceptable, with certain nouns, to use a plural verb with a singular subject. You may wish to refer students to the Language commentary on p.103.

1 Go through the three sentences with the whole class. Encourage discussion. The point here is that these nouns can be used with either a singular or a plural verb.

> **a** is / are **b** has / have **c** has / have

2 Again, this is probably best done as a whole class. Try to get the students to work out that these are all collective nouns. They are singular in form but refer to a group made up of a number of individuals, so can be thought of as either singular or plural.

> **Possible answers:**
> audience; class; club; committee; company; congregation (in church); council; crowd; gang; group; jury (in court); staff; team; union

3 Ask students to look at this in pairs, then check with the whole class.

> A singular verb tends to be used if the group word is thought of as a single, unified entity. If we think of the group as a collection of individuals, then a plural verb is more likely to be used.

4 Again, ask students to do this quickly in pairs, then conduct a quick feedback.

> **Possible answers**
> **Organizations:** NATO; The EC; The BBC; The World Bank;
> **Companies:** Sony; Benetton; Shell; BMW; Coca-Cola

Exploitation

Aim *To give students the chance to practise using singular and plural verb forms in a less controlled context.*

1 Outline the task briefly. You may want to do the first sentence together to show students what to do. Note that both singular and plural verbs are possible; it depends on whether you are thinking about the subject as a singular entity (the whole of the older generation) or the mass of individuals (all the various old people).

- Ask students to complete the task in pairs.
- Conduct feedback and check answers.

> **Possible answers**
> a In my experience, the older generation *is* / *are* more conservative than the younger generation.
> b The local council *is* / *are* working hard to repair the damage caused by the latest floods.
> c My favourite football team *is* / *are* going to win the cup.
> d The government in my country *has* / *have* just cut taxes by 5%.

2 Ask students to work in pairs. Encourage them to be adventurous with language and to speak at length about each subject, whether or not they agree with what they are saying.

- Monitor and make notes of mistakes made with singular and plural verbs.
- Write the mistakes up on the board, and ask students whether the correct verb was used / whether you could use singular or plural.

Speaking

Aim *To develop the students' semi-formal oral English in the context of a debate.*

1 Outline the task, checking that students understand the language and what they have to do.

- Put them in small groups to gather their thoughts about the issues and prepare for the discussion. Set a time limit.

2 Re-organize the groups so that they are now sitting with new people.

- Outline the task, making sure everyone knows the procedure and that this is a fairly formal discussion. You may need to go through the characteristics of a formal discussion, i.e. the importance of turn-taking and suitable language. (**Not** 'Rubbish!', 'No way!', 'Yeah!', etc.)
- Conduct the discussion. Monitor but don't interrupt. You can make notes for some error correction later.
- At the end of the activity (stop it just before you think they will run out of steam) ask the class to vote on the statement.
- Do some error correction from the board, using examples of mistakes heard in the discussion.
- If you have time, you could get students to discuss the following statements:
  - Extended families have less conflict than nuclear families.
  - The generation gap has a serious effect on family relationships.

Aim *To become familiar with the adjective–noun and verb–noun collocations that are typical in the vocabulary of conflict.*

1 Briefly check the meaning of the verbs with the whole class.

- Ask students to work individually and then compare answers with a partner, or if you feel they will not be able to work out collocations, it would be better to do this as a whole-class exercise.

> a reach   b quell   c spark off   d settling / resolving
> e avoid / create   f avoid

2 a Ask students to work in pairs to find the words and phrases in the headlines, then check answers with the whole class.

> fury   fight   rioting   challenge   row /raʊ/
> wins battle   attacks rival   expels   clash

b Ask students to work in groups. Check that they understand the task.

- Check answers as a class.

> **Possible answers**
> Passengers (probably) with those who have increased the rail fares (government or rail companies)
> The government and those who impose / use child labour
> Soldiers with civilians
> An ex-spy and those who have introduced laws about secrecy (presumably the government)
> Presumably the government which owns the plane that was spying and the country in which / over which it was spying
> A supermarket and the government (who allow cheap imports)
> The leader of a political party and his / her rival
> The USA and the ten diplomats
> The managers of various top European football clubs

c Show the students what they have to do by going through the first example with the whole class. The language of newspapers and newspaper headlines is quite difficult, so be prepared to offer assistance. Monitor and help.

- You could set this task for homework, after you have done one or two with the whole class.

> **Possible answers**
> There was fury among passengers on the south-east network at the proposed 23% fare increase.
> Governments of all the EU member countries said that they are fighting to end child labour in their countries.
> A former UK spy is to challenge the secrecy laws of the country after being arrested at his home in South London.
> British and American leaders argued fiercely that the plane shot down over British waters last night had no right to be there.
> The ASDA supermarket chain has won a historic battle to have the right to refuse to stock cheap European imports.
> Michael Portillo launched a bitter attack on his rival Kenneth Clarke at the Conservative Party Conference yesterday.
> The US government has expelled 10 Chinese diplomats accused of spying in Washington.
> The UEFA cup will be decided when AC Milan and Benfica play next Saturday.

Theme: the world of work

14.1 Time management

Improving time management

- **Reading:** interpretation and summarizing
- **Language focus:** ability or possibility
- **Speaking:** planning a work schedule

14.2 The big wide world

Young people talk about getting a job

- **Listening:** gist and specific information
- **Exploring natural speech:** the use of colloquial adjectives
- **Vocabulary:** phrasal verbs with *out*
- **Language focus:** *someone, everybody, anything*
- **Speaking / writing:** a job description of the ideal job

Exploring words

Euphemisms

Workbook

- **Language focus:** ability and possibility; indefinite pronouns
- **Vocabulary focus:** the prefix *co-*; phrasal verbs with *out*
- **Vocabulary expansion:** expressions with *time*; expressions with *come*
- **Listening:** career choices

14.1 Time management   p.104

Stage 1 consists of a reading text about time management which contextualizes the language of ability and possibility.

Lead in

Aim *To get students talking about the theme of the lesson, time management, by means of a personalized quiz and a short listening exercise.*

1 Start by asking the students whether they think they are good or bad at managing their time. Ask questions like:

Can you do two things at once?
Do you put off until tomorrow what you can do today?
Do you make lists, and tick things off when you do them?
Do you often leave tasks unfinished?

- If you have a class that are used to this subject – business people perhaps – ask them to share experiences of occasions when poor time management has resulted in funny or disastrous situations.

- Let the students do the quiz, then check answers with a partner.

- Talk through the quiz as a class, encouraging discussion.

2 a Ask the students to listen to Lorna, the management trainer, and answer question **2a**.

14.1

I think one of the most common problems people have is that they simply just try to do too much. They have too many tasks on the go at once. Rather than concentrate on one task at a time. So at the start of the day they might have several things on their 'to do' list but they'll try and do a bit of everything all in one go. So they'll try and be writing a report and answering the phone and talking to people at the same time. Secondly I think we tend to take on too much in the first place because we are not very good at saying no to other people. Particularly it is hard to say no if it's our boss or other managers asking us to do a task and that doesn't help because we're too quick to give their task priority over our own. Thirdly I think interruptions are a big time management problem for people. There's two types of interruptions, firstly, interruptions caused by other people either dropping in for a chat or dropping in to get some information, or ringing you up to see if you've got their e-mail. And the second type of interruption is the interruptions that we cause ourself, so procrastination, which is the art of putting off till tomorrow the things that we should be doing today. And we are our own worst enemy because we tend to put off particularly large or difficult tasks and instead we do easy short tasks to avoid doing the long ones.

She mentions 1, 2, 4, 7.

b Ask the students to listen to the second part of the recording and answer question **2b**.

- If your class are used to this subject, you could ask them to predict what advice for improving time management Lorna might give.

14.2

What would be your top tips for improving time management?

Lorna   Well I think leading on from what I was just saying about using your time well, is is first of all to be really clear about what it is you want to achieve. Not only at work but in your home life as well. And then focus your time and effort on those things. The principle being that if you don't know what you want to achieve, it's very much, it's much more easy to get side-tracked. Secondly I think, be realistic about how long things really take. When we are planning tasks I think we assume that they'll only take an hour or two hours, when in reality, once you have been interrupted several times they might actually take three or four hours. And then, once you have decided how long tasks really will take, put them in your diary. I think people could use their diaries more effectively to make appointments with their tasks not just appointments with other people. And my last tip I think, is to break down big tasks into manageable chunks. It makes it much more easy to get started if you if you break it down into short steps and then start with an easy one to get the ball rolling.

> **Suggestions:**
> 1 Be clear about what you want to achieve. Focus your time and effort on those things.
> 2 Be realistic about how long things are going to take.
> 3 Write down what you are going to do in a diary.
> 4 Break down big tasks into manageable chunks.

c Put the students in pairs to discuss, then feedback as a class.

- With younger, pre-work students, elicit and list some areas of their lives where they could apply time management suggestions. For example, doing their homework, doing a school project, revising for their exams, writing compositions.

Reading

Aim *To read for interpretation and summarizing.*

1 Check that the students understand the words in italics, then put them in pairs to discuss the questions.

- The aim of this activity is to pre-teach some of the key phrases from the text. You may wish to get the students to use their dictionaries to check unknown words, or explain them yourself.

Glossary

collect your thoughts – take a few minutes to regain control of yourself and what you think – after a shock, perhaps
onerous – very hard
impending – approaching, coming up soon

2 Ask the students to read the text and answer the gist question.

> humorous

Close up

- Put the students in pairs to do the exercise. Encourage them to make guesses from the context, rather than rely on dictionaries.

> 1.8   whoever; whenever; wherever
> 1.12 personal answer
> 1.16 colleague
> 1.22 coffee break / tea break / drinks break

3 Ask the students to read the passage again and match a summary to each paragraph. Let them check in pairs before feedback.

> **a** 3   **b** 5   **c** 1   **d** 4   **e** 2

Language focus: ability and possibility
p.105

Aim *To revise and practise the language of ability and possibility.*

Can, can't, and *could* are not as easy to use as they may appear. In many languages, different words and phrases are used to express the notions of ability and possibility. Consequently, although familiar with *can, can't,* and *could,* many students at this level avoid using them, instead using convoluted structures such as 'it is possible to', and overusing 'maybe' and 'perhaps'.

Other confusions include the fact that *could* refers to a past ability, but refers to present or future when talking about possibility. *Could* is also used to talk about a general past ability, for example, *I could swim when I was five,* but is not used when referring to a specific past ability in the affirmative, in which case *manage to* or *be able to* are used, for example, *I managed to open the door.* However, it is possible to use *couldn't* to talk about a specific past ability in the negative, for example, *I couldn't get in last night.*

Note that *can* and *could* are modal verbs, and have other uses than those dealt with here. See the Language commentary on p.109 for examples.

1–2 Put the students in pairs to discuss which extracts refer to ability and which refer to possibility. Do the first as an example. Tell the students to check by trying to rephrase each sentence with 'is / are possible to' or 'is / are able to'.

> **1**
> Ability   b
> Possibility   a, c, d
> **2**
> Ability   a, b, d
> Possibility   c

3 Students discuss the questions in their pairs. You may wish to refer them to the Language commentary on p.109 at this stage.

3

Sentences **b** and **c** can be rephrased:
b *I had so many interruptions* **I couldn't reply** *to your e-mail.*
c *If left with many hours on your hands* **you could compose** *an uplifting …*
Sentence **a** cannot be rephrased because *can / could,* etc. cannot be used to refer to ability in the future.
Sentence **d** cannot be rephrased because *could* cannot be used to refer to specific abilities in the past.

Exploitation

1 Check the students understand *pump, puncture,* and *touch (his) toes.* Use mime (blowing up a tyre and touching your toes – if you can!) to get across the meaning of these words.

- Do the first as an example, then ask the students to work individually to complete the rest of the text. Put them in pairs to check their answers before doing a whole class feedback.

> **1** haven't been able to get / can't get / haven't managed to get / haven't succeeded in getting
> **2** can still ride / is still able to ride
> **3** I'll be able to cycle / can cycle
> **4** couldn't ride / wasn't able to
> **5** managed to stop / succeeded in stopping / was able to stop
> **6** could / was able to (general not specific ability)
> **7** couldn't do it / can't do it / wouldn't be able to do it
> **8** can still touch / is still able to touch
> **9** haven't been able to touch / haven't managed to touch

Speaking

A group discussion in which the students plan a weekly schedule. It rounds off the theme of time management.

You may wish to do this short discussion activity, either as a lead-in to the *Speaking,* to get the students thinking about how little time office workers take off, or as an alternative short group discussion. Write the survey findings on the board.

1 Read these findings from a survey of 2,000 British people.

- *Less than one in five British people take an hour off for lunch.*
- *Most people take only 20 minutes for lunch and many just grab a bite to eat while sitting at their desks. 14% of workers skip lunch altogether.*
- *Britain's sandwich market, worth 3.2 billion pounds a year, has become the largest in Europe.*

2 How do you react to these facts? How does this compare with the situation in your country?

1 Divide the students into groups of three or four.

- Give one student in each group an A4 sheet divided into five boxes headed Monday, Tuesday, Wednesday, Thursday, Friday. Or get them to copy the headings from the board. This helps the students do the activity because they have a framework to fill in with their ideas. Ask one student to play the role of 'secretary', taking responsibility for noting down the other students' ideas.

- Read through the factors with the students and elicit a few ideas to get them started. For example, flexi-time so that they can drop off or pick up their children from school.

- Ask the students discuss the factors and complete the schedule. Monitor and help.

- When the students have finished, exchange the schedules among the groups, or ask the 'secretaries' to present the ideas to the rest of the class.

14.2 The big wide world p.106

Stage 2 consists of a listening text in which young people discuss their future plans. It revises indefinite pronouns.

Lead in

Aim *To get the students talking about different types of jobs in preparation for the listening text.*

- As an example, elicit from the class the plus and minus points of being an office worker. Some suggestions include:
Plus points a clean, warm working environment, regular hours, not dangerous.
Minus points a lack of fresh air, a lack of exercise, having to wear a suit, office-related illnesses like stress, headaches.

- Put the students in pairs or threes to discuss the other jobs. Monitor and help with vocabulary, then elicit some of the best ideas to put on the board.

- Alternatively, choose one of the jobs – teacher, perhaps – and divide the class into two halves. Half the class, in pairs, have to think of as many reasons as they can why teaching is a great job. The other half have to think why it is a terrible job. Redivide the students into new pairs with opposing views, and ask the students to persuade their partner why teaching is a great / terrible job. This creates an opinion gap, and mixes the students.

Listening

Aim *To listen for gist and specific information.*

1 Put the students in pairs to discuss the meaning of the phrases. Ask them to guess from the context before checking in a dictionary. The aim here is to pre-teach vocabulary, and introduce the subject of the listening passage, before playing the recording.

> **a** *get stuck* = become unable to move or leave
> **b** *get kicked out* = be forced to leave
> **c** *get sucked into* = attracted to (almost against your will)
> **d** *get head-hunted* = be offered a job with a high salary without having applied for it. Often used to refer to the habit of attracting senior, key, or bright people already in work to change jobs.
> **e** *fund yourself* = pay for yourself / pay your own fees and living expenses
> The use of the verb *get* in sentences **a–d** shows that the speakers do not feel in control of their situation. These things will happen to them, whether they like it or not.

2 Focus the students on the questions, then play the recording.

14.3

T I'm just worried that I'll get stuck in some sort of boring job or that I won't get a job and I won't have enough money and that I'll have to pay off my student debts and it will be impossible and stuff like that. Hopefully something more exciting will happen.

K Meaning what?

T I'll get a great job, I don't know, maybe, I don't know something in theatre or TV, or something fun but everyone wants to do that.

R Everyone's dream.

T Totally.

K It's everyone's real hope, isn't it? To be able to be paid for something that they really enjoy doing.

R Yeah.

T A hobby.

K Yeah.

J I can't work in an office. I mean at the moment my major hopes and fears are that I won't get kicked out of university but beyond that, I could not work in an office. (Yeah)

K You might have to.

J I have to do something where I stand up.

K Where you stand up?

J Or move around at least.

T You are allowed to move around in an office, you can go to the photocopier, get some tea.

K Yeah, (Four walls) it is those first sort of couple of years of making tea, isn't it that just seem a bit …

R It's just immediately what you are going to do once you leave university really, what really scares me – the big wide world.

K I work in a café – I make coffee all the time.

J You make coffee all the time?

T We keep on getting leaflets at college or posters and things saying wouldn't you just love a job in the city? – which is not what you want at all.

K Well, (It's a lot of money) everyone I know who's started working in the city within a year they absolutely hate it.

J But it's the kind of thing that you don't need to really love, I mean it would be amazing to do it for a year. It, it's hard work but it's an awful lot of money.

T But once you start having that sort of lifestyle, like a really nice flat and a mobile phone and everything then you want to keep it.

R And you probably get sucked into it, don't you?

T Yeah, you stay there for two or three years.

J Everybody says that and maybe it's just very naïve of me not to believe it but why can't you just save?

K Because you are so miserable, your work makes you so miserable that you you are desperate to go out.

J Because it's the perfect way, yeah but you can go out I mean it's not as if anyone's saying that you can't spend any money. You've got double the amount of money that you'd have in any other job.

T I think that if you tell yourself that it's just going to be for a year or two and that you've got better things you want to do.

K Yeah.

J Everybody says that, though, don't they?

T It's dangerous.

J And then stays there.

R And then you get head-hunted. (Yeah)

J Yeah, and that's probably very flattering but it's the perfect way to make a lot of money and then go and be an actor. Do you know what I mean? Because, you know … (You make it sound so …)

K Yeah, and then I'm going to go and be an actor.

J No, but you, but you've sorted out enough money to …

R Fund yourself.

J Yeah, to be able to maybe go to drama school or to not have to worry about things.

K Yeah. Someone said to me a couple of months ago, 'Oh isn't it so scary you know going out and going into your first real grown-up job in a couple of months' – and I was … 'Well it's actually more scary that I'm not going into my first adult grown-up job in two months because I don't have a job at all.'

J What are you gonna do?

R What are you doing at the moment?

K Well, I am working at the moment but I'm saving up to go away over the summer. (On holiday) Yeah. Six weeks in China.

All Wow!

K That's what I am hoping to do.

> **a** They worry about jobs being *boring*. / They don't want *office jobs*. / They worry about *money*. / They think once they have a well-paid job they may not be able to give it up because they have come to depend on the money. / They worry about not being able to get a job at all.
> **b** A creative job – 'something in theatre or TV'.

3 Allow the students time to read through the questions, then play the recording again.

> **a** Having to sit down all the time.
> **b** They would hate it, but would find it difficult to give up the high salary.
> **c** They think you might get trapped by the lifestyle associated with jobs of this kind.
> **d** Your job makes you so bored you just want to go out. *Go out* here means going to clubs, pubs, shopping, etc. and inevitably spending money.
> **e** Making a lot of money quickly would allow them to do what they really want to do – become actors.

Exploring natural speech

Aim *To explore the use of colloquial adjectives in natural speech.*

Do the first as an example, then put the students in pairs to complete the exercise.

> **a** rewarding (both the salary and the job satisfaction)
> **b** comfortable / pleasant / attractive
> **c** more challenging / more satisfying
> **d** serious
> **e** frightening / worrying / alarming

React and discuss

1 Discuss as a class.

2 Allow the students time to think about the sort of job they would like, then put them in small groups to discuss.

Vocabulary: phrasal verbs with *out* p.107

Aim *To introduce and practise phrasal verbs with* out.

This section introduces a number of phrasal verbs by looking at the different meanings of *out* when used as a particle.

1 Read through the introduction as a class, then put the students in pairs to match the verbs with the meanings. Do the first as an example.

1	cut out **C**	6	locked out **C**
2	deal out **A**	7	run out **B**
3	died out **B**	8	shared out **A**
4	stamp out **B**	9	voted out **C**
5	handing out **A**		

• In the feedback, you could check understanding by asking students to try to think of single-word verbs that could be used instead of these phrasal verbs.

Suggestions:	
cut out	exclude
deal out	distribute
die out	disappear
stamp out	eradicate / eliminate
hand out	distribute
lock out	exclude / bar / ban
run out	expire
share out	distribute / divide
vote out	reject

Language focus: *someone, everybody, anything*

Aim *To revise and practise indefinite pronouns.*

Students at this level are probably clear about the basic uses of *some* and *any*. Problems that arise are confusions about whether indefinite pronouns are used with singular or plural verbs, or used in positive negative statements. Common errors, for example, are:

*Everybody like chocolate.

*No one can't come to the party.

*I haven't done nothing today.

Other problems include the often subtle difference between *any* and *every*, and some of the more complex constructions involving indefinite pronouns. See the Language commentary on p.109 for details of these.

• Read through the extract as a class, then put the students in pairs to answer the questions.

a	1 T
	2 T
	3 F
	4 T – Note that some grammars may say that they should have singular pronouns, but now it is acceptable to use 'they' rather than 'he' or 'she'.
	5 F
	6 T
b	Sentence 4 is incorrect. *Nothing* cannot be used with a negative verb.
c	any job – one but it doesn't matter which one
	every job – all the jobs

Exploitation

1 Do one or two examples to get the students started, then give them a few minutes to prepare sentences about their family and friends. Monitor and correct errors.

• Put the students in small groups to discuss their answers, or, if you have a small class, ask the students to walk round and find other people with similar answers.

2 If your students are of the same nationality, put them in pairs to prepare generalizations. Monitor and correct, then ask pairs to tell the class some of their sentences.

• If your students are from different countries, let them make their own sentences, then share ideas with other students in small groups.

• Alternatively, ask students to use the phrases to make controversial generalizations, for example: *Hardly anyone nowadays votes in elections, so we should abolish them.*

• Put the students in small groups to read out and discuss their controversial statements.

Speaking and writing

Aim *To describe an ideal job, and write a job description.*

Note that a job description is a formal, official document which defines the limit and responsibilities of a post. This will affect the style.

1 Check that the students understand the vocabulary in the headings, and elicit one or two suggestions from the class to get them started. Alternatively, you could describe *your* perfect job as a model of the sort of thing you want them to say.

• Give the students a few minutes to prepare what they are going to say.

2 Put the students in pairs to describe their ideal jobs to each other. Tell them to remember as much as they can, or to write notes.

3 Read through the headings for the job description with the students, and elicit the sort of information required under each heading. Point out the structures used in a job description. You may wish to make a list on the board, and elicit other phrases the students might use. For example:

You will spend …

You will be expected to …

You will have to …

The ideal candidate should be / have / be able to …

• Ask the students to work individually to write brief job descriptions for their partner.

• Monitor and help as necessary.

4 When the students have finished, ask them to exchange job descriptions with their partner and ask them if they would like to apply for the job.

• You could extend this activity into a role play by telling the students that they are going to do a job interview based on one of the job descriptions. Ask each pair to choose one. The person who wrote the job description has to think of five or six questions to find out whether their partner is suitable for the job. The partner has to think of five or six questions about the job to check that it is the job they really want.

- When they are ready, ask the students to roleplay the interview. Monitor and listen for errors.

Exploring words p.108

This section looks at euphemisms. It divides into two sets of vocabulary. Exercises 1 and 2 look at euphemistic expressions. Exercise 3 looks at using negative words to create a euphemism. Consequently, you could do all four exercises in one lesson, or split it into two shorter lessons comprising exercises 1 and 2, and then exercises 3 and 4.

1 a Read through the introduction and the categories as a class. Ask the students if they can think of any euphemisms that could be put in any of the categories mentioned.

- Put the students in pairs to match the euphemisms with the subjects.

A **Wealth and poverty**	
comfortably off	rich
from a deprived background	poor
hard-up	poor
B **Death, illness, etc.**	
to pass away	to die
to slip away	to die
C **Dishonesty**	
disinformation	rumours and lies to confuse and mislead
(to be) economical with the truth	to be a liar
imaginative journalism	lies published in a newspaper
D **Ability**	
hard of hearing	deaf or almost deaf
less able	unintelligent / academically slow
visually handicapped	blind or almost blind
E **Age**	
in your golden years	old
mature	old
F **Alcohol**	
to enjoy a drink	to be a frequent, probably heavy drinker
to have a drink problem	to be an alcoholic
G **Employment**	
between jobs	unemployed
economically inactive	unemployed
unwaged	unemployed

b Put the students in pairs to match the euphemisms with the contexts.

1 He / she is economical with the truth.
2 They're a less able class.
3 He / she is between jobs / economically inactive.
4 She enjoys a drink. / He has a drink problem.
5 He / she is comfortably off.
6 He's mature. / He's in his golden years.

2 a Focus the students on the question and play the recording.

`14.4`

1
A If anything happens to me, I'd like you to take over the business.
B I'm sure everything will be OK – it's only a minor operation.

2
A The papers accuse you of being tired and emotional after the party, Minister. Is that true?
B No, certainly not.

3
A The figures clearly show that the economy is doing very well. Incomes are up and inflation is down.
B Yes, but everyone knows that figures can prove anything. Our party thinks the government has been involved in creative accounting here.

4
A I was sorry to hear about your grandmother. Had she been ill long?
B No, only a couple of weeks – she's always been very healthy.

5
A You wanted to see me, Mr Birch.
B Yes, John. I'm afraid your work has not been satisfactory recently. We're going to have to let you go at the end of the month.

1	death
2	alcohol
3	dishonesty
4	death
5	employment

b–c Ask the students in pairs to make a note of the euphemisms the speakers use, then discuss what they think each one might mean. Do the first as an example.

1 *If anything happens to me* = If I die
2 *tired and emotional* = drunk
3 *creative accounting* = false accounting / fraud
4 *I was sorry to hear about your grandmother* = I'm sorry your grandmother has died.
5 *to let you go* = to sack you / to fire you

3 a Read the introduction as a class, then students in their pairs discuss the meaning of the negative expressions.

1 *no scholar* = dull / unintelligent / non-academic
2 *non-industrialized* = poor / underdeveloped
3 *not all there* = of low intelligence / old, with failing mental abilities
4 *not as young as you were* = quite old / middle-aged
5 *no longer with us* = dead
6 *not the most sociable of people* = unsociable / unfriendly

b Students in their pairs think of some negative euphemisms of their own.

Possible answers
1 not particularly bright / not the most intelligent person
2 not the clearest of thinkers
3 not unaccustomed to alcohol / no stranger to the bottle
4 not in work
5 not easy to make friends with / not easy to get to know
6 not very well / not in the best of health

4 Put the students in small groups to discuss the questions.

Theme: unusual behaviour – strange competitions, attitudes to cheating, avoiding work

15.1 Why do they do it?

Competitiveness and strange competitions

- **Listening:** gist
- **Reading:** jigsaw – retelling
- **Language focus:** alternatives to relative clauses ('reduced relative clauses')
- **Speaking:** designing a strange competition

15.2 Honesty?

People talk about whether they have ever cheated

- **Listening:** matching and specific information
- **Exploring natural speech:** auxiliaries to add emphasis
- **Language focus:** fronting

15.3 How to skive

A light-hearted article about avoiding work

- **Reading:** gist, matching, and specific information
- **Language focus:** -ing forms and infinitives
- **Speaking and writing:** 'How to …'; presenting ideas and writing an article

Exploring words

Competitions

Workbook

- **Language focus:** alternatives to relative clauses; fronting; -ing forms and infinitives
- **Vocabulary focus:** the prefix out-
- **Vocabulary expansion:** dishonesty – words and expressions; ways of laughing
- **Listening:** stories of dishonesty

15.1 Why do they do it?   p.110

This stage includes a reading text – a newspaper article which contextualizes alternatives to relative clauses.

Lead in

Aim *To start students talking about competitiveness in general as an introduction to the listening and reading which follow.*

1 Focus students on the task, and put them in pairs to discuss and compare ideas. Set a time limit.

2 **a** Let the students stay in pairs. Make sure they understand the listening task.

- Play the recording.

15.1

Speaker 1 I don't think I'm a particularly competitive person. I suppose like most people I don't like it if I feel something good or worthwhile that I've done hasn't been recognized, but I'm not actually competitive, I'm not particularly bothered about being the best or being number one or getting to the top, being the star and being the boss and all those sorts of things …

Speaker 2 I don't think I'm very competitive, although I find lately that in some ways I am, but I never did any sports I never got into the habit of beating other people or being defeated. I always just try to achieve things or be good at what I do on my own and not compete with others.

Speaker 3 I'm very, very, very competitive – having an older brother definitely is why, erm. We had a pool table – it was my brother's and he could always beat me – he's three years older. I thought 'Right! I'm going to beat him,' and I used to practise on the pool table, for like, three hours a day and I beat him finally – it was brilliant and now I'm quite good at pool actually.

Speaker 4 I wouldn't say I'm particularly competitive – only at things like games and quizzes where I do like to win, but that's just showing off …

- Ask students to compare their answers. Play the recording again if necessary.

> **Suggested answers**
> From most competitive to least competitive: 3, 4, 2, 1

b Ask the students to discuss the question.

Reading

Aim *To give students practice at extracting sufficient information from a short newspaper article to be able to tell a partner about it.*

1 Ask students to look at the pictures and to guess or predict what they will be reading about (strange competitions).

- Split the class into two; half the class are As, the other half Bs. Tell them they are going to read different stories but their task is the same.

- Ask them to read through the task and questions **a** and **b**, making sure they have understood.

- Now ask the As to turn to p.159, read the news story there and make notes of the key facts.

- Ask the Bs to read the story on this page and make notes.

- Watch the class carefully to gauge when most students have finished, then ask them to pair up with someone who has read the same passage, and to compare answers.

- At this stage you may need to monitor, trying to get round the pairs quickly to make sure they have all understood.

> **Student A**
> a Geoff Smith had himself buried alive for 5 months (147 days) in a wooden box.
> b He wanted to get into the Guinness Book of Records. Wanted to make himself and his family world famous. (His mother had held the world record for human endurance until 1968 and then lost it.)
> Ironically while he was under ground the Guinness Book of Records removed the human endurance category for safety reasons.
>
> **Student B**
> a A Polish woman became world screaming champion with a scream of 126 decibels.
> b World fame. / Attention-seeking.

Close up

- Ask students to work through their *Close up* questions with a partner who read the same text. (Student A's questions are with the text on p.159). You will need to check their *Close up* answers at this point, either orally with each group, or you could produce a handout of the answers and give them to each pair for final checking. Encourage them to make guesses from context rather than rely on their dictionaries.

> **Student A**
> 1.2   a coffin
> 1.13   supporting
> 1.14   lunacy
> **Student B**
> 1.11   *outrun* = to run faster than; *outlive* = to live longer than; *outnumber* = be more in number than; *outplay* = play better than
> 1.6   *25-year-old Dagmara Stanek / Dagmara Stanek, who is 25 years old, …*
> 1.12   *35-year-old Pawel Dabrowski / Pawel Dabrowski, who is 35 years old, …*
> 1.28   *Each of the winners took home a colour television set. The winners took home a colour television set each.*

2 Ask the students to close their books now and pick up their notes. Regroup them so that they are in AB pairs.

- Tell them they are going to tell each other their stories. The person listening has to make sure they understand it, so can ask questions for clarification.

- The students can then spend a few minutes discussing the strange behaviour they have read about.

- If you have time and feel it would be useful, you could then ask the students to read the text they haven't read yet.

React and discuss

Aim *To give students a chance to discuss what they've read and to round up this stage of the lesson.*

Discuss these questions briefly as a whole class.

Language focus: alternatives to relative clauses   p.111

Aim *To show students how to make their writing more concise or clearer by using alternatives to relative clauses.*

1 You will probably want to do this with the whole class so that you can talk them through alternatives to relative clauses. Give them time to read the introduction and the examples, then elicit and discuss possible answers.

> Relative clauses can sound clumsy and sometimes confusing if several are used in the same sentence (as in sentence **b**). Leaving them out (as in sentence **a**) means that more information can be conveyed in relatively few words. In newspapers space and immediacy are important factors.

2–3 You might want to start the students off by doing the first one with the whole class, and then ask them to work on their own or in pairs. Refer them to the Language commentary on p.116.

- If students are having difficulty, you could provide the relative clauses (or the relative pronouns) on the board and ask them to work out where they go. Alternatively you could tell the students how many relative clauses there are in each sentence if you think they just need a little help.

- Give them time to compare their answers, if they have worked on their own, then check answers with the whole class.

> a Dagmara Stanek, **who is 25**, **and who comes** from the Baltic resort of Sopot, emitted a scream of just over 126 decibels, **which is** equivalent to the noise of a racing car **which is** travelling at top speed.
> b Europe's only vocal noise competition, **which is** modelled on an annual screaming festival in Japan, took place in the town of Goldap …
> c The judges measured the highest scream level of each contestant with equipment **which is** normally used to check noisy workplaces and neighbours.
> d Mr Sokolowski is also behind Poland's first kissing championship, **which is** to be held in October.
> All these added relative clauses are **non-defining**.

Exploitation

To extend the practice that students have had and get them to work on alternatives to relative clauses at text rather than sentence level.

In doing exercise 1 they are also practising the skills of summarizing and writing, which they will need for the following writing task.

1 a Give students a few minutes to read the story, then outline the task.

- You could start the students off by doing the first line or sentence with them, then ask them to work in pairs. Monitor and help as necessary.

b–c When they have finished, outline this next task.

- Set a time limit for this and encourage them to enjoy the activity – it's quite fun slashing a text down! Monitor and help, as before. If pairs are having trouble, draw their attention to the phrases which can be reduced, e.g. *addiction to gambling.*

- When most pairs have finished, ask them to exchange their final text with another pair.

> **a** John Philips, ~~who is~~ 37, ~~years old and comes~~ from the North West, said his wife ~~who is called~~ Edwina had left him because of his 10-year addiction to gambling. Philips, ~~who works as~~ a senior accountant with a company ~~which is~~ based in the centre of Manchester, appeared in court, ~~where he was~~ accused of dangerous driving. Colleagues and others ~~who are~~ close to Mr Philips say he is heart-broken. Tim Roberts, ~~who has been~~ a friend of Philips since the two were at school together said he can't stop thinking about his wife. 'John's doing everything he can to win Edwina back.'
> **[104 words originally / 82 words with cuts]**
>
> **b** John Philips, 37, from the North West, said his wife Edwina had left him because of his 10-year **gambling addiction**. Philips, a senior accountant with a **central Manchester-based company**, appeared in court accused of dangerous driving. Colleagues and close friends say he is heart-broken. **Old schoolfriend** Tim Roberts said he can't stop thinking about his wife. 'John's doing everything **possible** to win Edwina back.'
> **[64 words]**

2 This is a short writing activity so you can do it in class with students working together in pairs, which they usually find more enjoyable. Alternatively, if you are short of time, you could set it as a homework task. Either way, try to get students to choose quickly which story they are going to write.

- Circulate the stories and ask students to decide which is the clearest, funniest, most interesting. Strong classes could be asked to write in *exactly* 80 words.

Speaking

Aim *To round off this stage of the unit and give students some free, light-hearted oral practice.*

1–2 Outline the task. Make sure that the students understand that they are to think of crazy, lunatic ideas for a record-breaking competition.

- Ask them to work in small groups and set a time limit for getting ideas. Monitor and encourage.

- Now ask the groups to present their ideas, either to the whole class or to other groups.

15.2 Honesty?   p.112

This stage includes a listening text which provides an initial context for *fronting*.

Lead in

Aim *To start students thinking about cheating and what kinds of actions they consider right or wrong.*

1 Ask students to look at the photographs and think what the connection is.

> The three pictures are all connected with cheating. The student is cheating, possibly in an exam; the painting shows someone cheating at cards; the photograph of the race shows Ben Johnson, who was stripped of his Olympic medal in 1988 for having taken anabolic steroids.

2 Outline the task, focusing on the questions.

- Give students a few minutes to read, then ask them to compare their answers in pairs or small groups.

- Conduct a class feedback so that the focus is back on the whole group.

> **Possible questions**
> Would you lie, cheat, or sleep with your boss if it helped you to get on?
> How would you define success?
> Would you sleep with your boss if it advanced your prospects?
> Would you be willing to do something ethically or morally wrong if it advanced your prospects?
> Would you be willing to be dishonest if it advanced your prospects?

3 Go through the task with the whole class.

- Ask them to work in small groups. Monitor, but don't interrupt.

Listening

Aim *To develop students' ability to match information and to listen for detail.*

1 Outline the task. Draw students' attention to the fact that there are five speakers and six statements, i.e. one statement doesn't match any of the speakers.

• Play the recording.

15.2

Speaker 1 Yeah, I did cheat once – it wasn't an exam exactly – it was a course I was doing – a sort of training course where in preparation for the exam we had to do a timed essay – like a like a little mock exam and we had one hour to do this timed essay and I wasn't very well prepared for it and I decided that I would get more out of it if, instead of writing an essay that was complete rubbish – because I hadn't particularly studied the topic we were writing about – if I took a little crib sheet in with me and wrote a very good essay – and so that's what I did – I mean it was one of these subjects where there are basically ten major points, so rather than desperately try to remember them in the two minutes before the exam, I just wrote them down on a little piece of paper about the size of cigarette packet and took it in – it wasn't it wasn't sort of (a) sneaky childhood thing – I was probably in my mid-twenties and and cheated in a very sort of mature kind of a way and wrote quite a good essay – not surprisingly …

Speaker 2 Cheating, erm, have I ever cheated in anything? I think as a very young child I found it very hard to lose at Monopoly and I did cheat once and my family has never forgotten erm – they mistakenly put me in the bank and I must have been about seven and I thought the bank was there to give me money and erm I took it. I think apart from that I'm too cowardly to cheat. In an exam I was given a very stern warning at age seven that my exam would go in the bin if I smiled or talked to the person next to me and since then I, I haven't risked it. Sports I don't want to win that badly and competitions I'm probably not competitive enough.

Speaker 3 I haven't actually cheated in anything that I can remember – the only very very small thing I did was in the first year there used to be about four of us who sat round a table and we had a science test – and (we'd) all sort of copy each other, sort of – that's the only sort of thing I can remember but erm, no I've never tripped anybody up in a sports event or anything – would have liked to, would have broken my ankle or something.

Speaker 4 I haven't ever cheated in an exam or any other kind of competition and I think the main reason for that is that I haven't really had an opportunity to do that but I probably wouldn't if it came to the crunch.

Speaker 5 I've never cheated in an examination and never would erm but that I think is to do with the fear of being found out as much as anything else. I occasionally slightly cheat at sport, I think, and in fact I don't know anybody who doesn't, so when you're playing a game where it's a very close decision where something is 'in' or 'out' – depending on how I'm feeling and whether we're winning or losing – I might say something was 'in' when it was 'out' or vice versa, but not very often – maybe once in every five or six games and it doesn't worry me at all – I think it's part of the game.

• Ask students to compare their answers, then check with the whole class.

> a Speaker 2
> b Speaker 4
> c Speaker 5
> d Speaker 1
> e Not mentioned by any of the speakers
> f Speaker 3

2 **a–b** Go through the questions.

• Play the recording again.

• Ask students to compare and check their answers in pairs.

> Four of the speakers admit having cheated:
> Speaker 1 took notes into an exam. (These notes are sometimes called a *crib-sheet*.)
> Speaker 2 cheated at a game (the board game Monopoly).
> Speaker 3 cheated in a school test – she and her friends copied from each other.
> Speaker 5 cheats slightly at sport.

c Ask students to do this in their pairs. Set a time limit.

Exploring natural speech   p.113

Aim *To raise awareness of the correct use of extra auxiliaries for emphasis and to give students controlled practice in using them.*

The use of auxiliaries for emphasis was introduced in Unit 2 – you may wish to refer students to the Language commentary on p.19.

1 Focus on the extracts from the recording.

• Ask students to answer the questions quickly in pairs, then check with the whole class.

> They use the auxiliary for emphasis.

2 Now ask students to do the same themselves. You could do the first one with them if you feel they need another example, then ask them to do the others individually or in pairs.

• Let them compare answers briefly.

> a I have to confess, I **did take** a crib sheet into the exam with me.
> b I'm ashamed to say, I **did copy** from my friend in a science test.
> c I must admit, I **did write** a very good essay.
> d It's hard to believe, but she **does** occasionally **cheat** at sport.

3 Play the recording. (This is not included in the tapescript section of the Student's Book.)

15.3

> a I have to confess, I did take a crib sheet into the exam with me.
> b I'm ashamed to say, I did copy from my friend in a science test.
> c I must admit, I did write a very good essay.
> d It's hard to believe, but she does occasionally cheat at sport.

• Ask them to check their answers with the recording. Students can use the recording to improve their own pronunciation by imitating the emphasis put on the auxiliary verb. By getting students to emphasize, even over-emphasize, the auxiliary verb you can often get them to smooth out the rest of the sentence, so that it sounds natural. Some students will tend to emphasize or stress every other word, which can sound very jumpy, while others may use too little stress or emphasis.

• Now play the recording section by section, drawing students' attention to the way the speakers said the sentences.

- Ask them to repeat the sentences aloud after each section, paying particular attention to the emphasized auxiliary.
- When they have practised all four sentences together ask them to work in pairs and to practise reading the sentences to each other.
- You can call on individual students to say their sentences, emphatically, to the whole class.

4 Focus on the first part of the sentences in **a–d**:

I have to confess …
I'm ashamed to say …
I must admit …
It's hard to believe …

- Ask students what they have in common.

> These phrases prepare the reader for some important or surprising information. What follows includes the use of the auxiliary verb *did* for emphasis.

- If you have time, ask students to practise saying them. Demonstrate yourself first, then ask them to practise altogether, before getting them to work in pairs to practise with each other.
- You could extend the activity slightly by asking the students in their pairs to think of other ways of continuing the first parts of the sentences in **a–d**.

Language focus: fronting

Aim *To draw students' attention to the common practice in spoken English of starting a sentence with a key word – the object or the complement – instead of the subject.*

1 Go through the task with the students. You might want to read sentences **a–d** aloud as these are examples of spoken, not written, English.

- Ask students to rewrite the sentences, using more normal word order, individually or in pairs. Refer them to the Language commentary on p.116.
- Check answers together.

> a I don't want to win sports that badly, I'm probably not competitive enough for competitions.
> b I absolutely hate doing washing up and ironing when I'm tired.
> c That was a brilliant film!
> d I don't mind eating in pubs, but I can't stand fast food restaurants.

Note

You may want to point out that when we front a sentence with a singular countable noun + adjective we often leave out the indefinite article necessary in a sentence with more 'normal 'word order. This is another way of bringing the important idea to the very beginning of the sentence:

Great guy, your father! (Your father is **a** great guy.)
Terrible song, that is! (That is **a** terrible song.)

2 Outline the task briefly and ask students to do this in pairs. Point out that these phrases are possible in written English as well as spoken English and that inversion (*Not once did I cheat at anything*) is actually more common in the written form. You may wish to refer them to the Language commentary on p.43, which covers inversion.

- Check together.

> a We visit friends or relatives **nearly every weekend**.
> b There's a bus stop **at the end of the road**.

3 You can discuss this question together as a whole class.

> The effect is to emphasize particular information in the sentence, information that would not be highlighted if the normal word order was retained.

Exploitation

Aim *To give students the chance to practise fronting.*

This is not necessarily difficult for the students but it may well feel slightly strange and uncomfortable for them. Don't worry at this stage; what is more important is that by practising saying sentences like this, they actually learn to hear them when they are used by others.

1 Briefly run through the phrases in the word list and explain the task quickly.

- Ask the students to do the task individually or in pairs, then to check their answers with each other.
- Check answers with the whole class.
- Once they have all got correct sentences, ask them to practise saying them to each other.

> **Possible answers**
> a *Opposite the library* there are tennis courts.
> b *Most of the time* she sits staring into space.
> c *(An) awful accident* I saw on the way to work.
> d *My next-door neighbour* I've only spoken to two three times in the last ten years.
> e *(The) best meal I've had for ages,* that was.
> f *Dates, times, and phone numbers* I just can't remember.

2 Ask students to work on their own sentences in pairs.

- As before, give them the chance to practise saying them once they have the ideas and language in place.

3 Go through the task with the students and make sure they understand the questions.

- Now put them in pairs or small groups and ask them to do the task, continuing or extending the conversations in any way they see fit. Encourage them to speak freely and confidently, not worrying too much about the exact sense of what they might be saying!
- If you want to, ask some of the more confident students to demonstrate their conversations to the whole class.

15.3 How to skive   p.114

In this stage the reading text about skiving (getting out of or avoiding doing something) contextualizes -ing forms and infinitives.

Lead in

Aim *To get students thinking and talking about excuses.*

1 Go through the task with the students. You could do this with books closed.

• Give the students a few minutes to talk to a partner about the excuses they made.

2 Outline the task briefly and ask the students to compare their excuses in groups.

• Ask each group to choose their 'best excuse' to present to the whole class.

• Conduct a whole-class feedback session to discuss answers together.

Reading

Aim *To extend students' reading skills by asking them to read a fairly long article written in a particular tongue-in-cheek style. In other words, it appears to be serious but is in fact light-hearted and is making fun of the whole subject.*

1 Set the task; make sure the students understand they are only going to read the first paragraph.

• Ask them to compare their answers in pairs, then check with the whole class.

> *skive* = to avoid work

Glossary

skive – a very colloquial term to describe getting out of work or school: *He **skived** (off) the last days of term*, or generally avoiding work: *She manages to **skive** out of the things she doesn't want to do.* It is very informal; students need to be made aware of this.

2 Ask students to read the rest of the article quickly. They are only going to answer the two questions. Set a short time limit. You don't want them to get too involved in the text yet.

3 Give students time to read through the paragraph summaries. Ask them to do the task individually and check in pairs.

> **Key phrases**
> a Paragraph 2 *has a long history / Trojan wars / 1960s and 70s*
> b Paragraph 4 *A more creative approach was called for*
> c Paragraph 5 *The day of return*
> d Paragraph 3 *An employee could be absent for up to 8 weeks*
> e Paragraph 6 *ensure a tool of your trade ... walk briskly ... leave a jacket*
> f Paragraph 1 *Skiving is a skill. The good skiver... attracts no attention*, etc.

4 Give students time to read through the questions, then ask them to complete the task on their own or in pairs.

• Ask them to check their answers with each other, then check with the whole class.

> a At school and at work.
> b It sounds serious and is impossible to prove or disprove.
> c Employees did not need to get a doctor's note until they had been off work for eight weeks (so-called *self-certification*).
> d To give the impression that the illness is serious. To intimidate employers and discourage them from questioning the illness.
> e The scarf is a sign that the skiver has not fully recovered. The paper bag would contain medicines still being taken.
> f These are signs that the skiver is actually busy.

Glossary

flourish – to do well / succeed, thrive
fit the bill – to suit the circumstance well
flagged up – signalled for attention
tucked – put neatly, folded
slung – thrown casually

Note

Paragraph 2
• National service (military service) lasted in Britain from 1945 to 1961.
• The 'spectacular results in the 1960s and 1970s' refers to a period when militant trade unions frequently called their workers out on strike.

Paragraphs 3/4
• Until the 1970s, you could only be off work for two days (later extended to three) before having to get a certificate from your doctor, confirming to your employer that you were unfit for work. It was sometimes possible, by claiming to have a 'bad back' or another ailment equally difficult to diagnose, to obtain a doctor's certificate under false pretences, and so avoid returning to work.

Close up

- Put the students in pairs to do the exercise. Encourage them to make guesses from context rather than rely on their dictionaries.
- Check answers with the whole class.

1.4	*personal* = adjective: to do with an individual person /'pɜːsənəl/
1.54	*personnel* = noun: people employed by an organization /pɜːsə'nel/
1.30	*is refined*
1.83	the main basis: bread and butter stands for basic foods, staple diet

Language focus: *-ing* forms and infinitives p.115

Aim *To give the students further exposure to and practice of these forms.*

Students will have been introduced to *-ing* and infinitive forms before, but it is an area that they continue to find difficult. One of the problems is that they simply have to learn which verbs take which verb form. Another is that some verbs can be used with either form with a difference in meaning (*remember to do / remember doing*).

1–2 Set up the tasks quickly and ask students to complete them in pairs.

- Ask them to check their answers with the article.

> **1**
> **a** forgetting to tidy
> **b** managed to bunk off
> **c** need to produce
> **d** start questioning
> **2**
> In extract **d** the *-ing* form or the infinitive would be equally correct: *start questioning* or *start to question*.

3 Go through the task with the whole class to make sure they understand what to do. You may want to do the first example with them.

- Ask students to complete the task in pairs. Monitor and help as necessary.

> **a** the infinitive without *to*. Examples: *must / should / might / can / could / would*, etc.
> **b** the *-ing* form. Examples: *loathe / enjoy / hate / can't stand / dislike*
> **c** the *-ing* form. Examples: *give up / end up / take up / look forward to / put off*
> **d** the infinitive with *to*. Examples: *teach someone / tell / ask / order / persuade*

▶ There is an extra exercise on p.142 which gives some useful practice on the different meanings some verbs have, depending on whether they are followed by the *-ing* form or the infinitive. If you have not taught this before, make sure you are very well prepared! Check the Language commentary on p.117 and make sure you are confident about the differences between each of the two sentences in this task. Drawing a time line on the board when you come to check the answers can be helpful.

Exploitation

Aim *To give free practice of using* -ing *or infinitive forms.*

1 Give students time to complete the sentences on their own, then put them in pairs and ask them to tell each other their sentences.

- If the students know each other quite well, you could ask them to guess how their partners would complete the sentences.

> **Possible answers**
> **a** I wish I could afford **to take a trip to the moon**.
> **b** There's no way anyone will ever persuade me **to do a parachute jump**.
> **c** I'd really like to give up **smoking**.
> **d** I'll always be grateful that my parents taught me **to cook**.
> **e** I'm not looking forward to **taking my final exams**.

2 Go through the task quickly with the students and check that they know the meanings of the key phrases:

put off = postpone
give up = stop doing something

- Give them some quiet thinking time to prepare for the task.
- Now ask the students to stand up and move around the class, trying to find people who have some of the same responses.

Speaking and writing

Aim *To give an opportunity to develop an article in a similar 'tongue-in-cheek' style.*

1 Put the students into small groups.

- Give them time to prepare their ideas. Monitor and help the groups as necessary.

2 Go through the phrases in the language box.

- Give the groups a few minutes to finalize their presentations, then ask them to make their presentations either to the whole class or to other groups.
- Monitor and make notes of mistakes made.
- Go through some of the mistakes with the whole class, choosing to focus on language they might want to use for the writing activity.

3 Set up the writing activity. Check that students realize that it is important to try and use the same 'tongue-in-cheek' style, i.e. using quite formal, instructional language about a trivial subject.

- Ask the students to write the article in 150–170 words as a homework activity. Refer them to the Writing guidelines on p.154.

Exploring words   p.116

Aim *To look at the language of sport and competition and extend students' vocabulary through word families.*

1 Briefly set up the task, making sure the students read the questions before you play the recording. It may be helpful to tell them that there are eight speakers, and eight different competitions.

• Play the recording. (This is not included in the tapescript section of the Student's Book.)

15.4

1 This year's top prize, a cheque for £5,000, has gone to a first-time novelist.

2 For the third year running, David Jones has taken the title of champion jockey with 25 wins in 30 rides.

3 The race was abandoned after three cars skidded off the track and burst into flames.

4 This year's competition was held in Paris. In addition to the first prize of £20,000, Miss Europe was awarded a modelling contract with a top agency.

5 All you have to do is complete this sentence in no more than ten words: *'Hi there' is my favourite magazine because* … . Got any ideas?

6 If you're ambitious and you've got talent, just complete the form and send it with a video of one of your performances. Fifty lucky contestants will compete in a series of 10 weekly programmes and the final winner will be awarded a recording contract.

7 Brazil is through to the final after beating Norway 5–4 on penalties. The match went into extra time and ended in a penalty shoot-out.

8 The winning yacht, captained by Richard Merryweather, came in nearly two days ahead of its nearest rival.

• Ask students to compare answers in pairs, then check with the whole class.

Speakers	Types of competition
1	literary / writing / book
2	horse-racing
3	motor-racing
4	beauty contest
5	magazine competition
6	TV talent contest
7	football competition, e.g. The World Cup
8	yacht race / sailing
Least dependent on skill or ability is the beauty contest.	

2 Ask the students to read sentences **a–h**. Give them a few minutes to try and remember or guess the missing words in pairs.

• Play the recording again and ask students to check their answers in pairs.

a prize; gone to
b taken; title
c race; abandoned
d held; awarded
e complete
f winners; compete; final; awarded
g beating
h winning; rival

3 a Complete the first line with the whole class as an example.

• Students complete the rest of the chart in pairs. Monitor and help as necessary.

b Ask students to check how they think the words are pronounced. They should mark the stress on each word.

Person	Other noun	Verb	Adjective
1 com'petitor	compe'tition	com'pete	com'petitive
2 'champion	'championship	X	X
3 'rival	'rivalry	'rival	X
4 de'fendant	de'fence	de'fend	de'fensive
5 con'testant	'contest	con'test	X
6 'winner	win	win	X

c Play the recording for students to check and practise the correct pronunciation.

15.5

1 Twenty competitors went in for the race.
2 The competition was won by the youngest athlete.
3 All athletes should compete hard.
4 The winner was by far the most competitive of the lot.
5 The contestants were all under 30.
6 The contest was held in London.
7 The winner will be too old to contest the race next year.

1	competitor	/kəm'petɪtə/
2	competition	/kɒmpə'tɪʃn/
3	compete	/kəm'piːt/
4	competitive	/kəm'petətɪv/
5	contestant	/kən'testənt/
6	contest	/'kɒntest/
7	contest	/kən'test/

4 This exercise checks a number of common collocations. Ask students to do this individually or in pairs, then check answers with the whole class.

1 set	2 beat	3 broke	4 holds	5 wins

5 Divide the class into pairs or small groups.

• Go through the task and set a time limit.

• Monitor and help, but don't interfere or interrupt too much.

• Ask students to present their competition ideas to the rest of the class, who could then vote on the most original / the funniest / the most practical.

16 Processes

Theme: how people do things / how things are done

16.1 Getting to sleep

Talking about sleeping habits

- **Listening:** matching and specific information
- **Exploring natural speech:** *thing* and *stuff*
- **Language focus:** habits and predictable behaviour
- **Speaking:** designing a survey

16.2 Animation

The process of animation

- **Reading:** checking predictions
- **Listening:** specific information
- **Language focus:** the passive
- **Writing:** a report
- **Speaking:** discussion

16.3 Interviews

Dos and don'ts for interviewees

- **Reading:** general information and matching
- **Vocabulary:** applying for a job
- **Language focus:** verb + object + *to* + infinitive
- **Role play:** interview
- **Writing:** a personal profile or a letter of application

Exploring words

British and American English

Workbook

- **Language focus:** habits and predictable behaviour; the passive; verb + object + infinitive; verbs with other patterns
- **Vocabulary focus:** applying for a job
- **Vocabulary expansion:** *-ing* adjectives; *dream* and *sleep* – words and expressions
- **Listening:** dreams

16.1 Getting to sleep   p.118

The listening text contextualizes the range of structures used to describe habits and predictable behaviour.

Lead in

Aim *To introduce the topic of sleep, and prepare for the listening tasks which follow.*

- Ask students to complete the survey on their own first, then put them in pairs to compare and discuss answers.
- Round off the activity by asking the students to report back to the class any unusual behaviour or situations they have discussed.

Listening

Aim *To listen for detail and match information.*

1 Focus students' attention on the task. Make sure they know that some speakers mention more than one thing.

- Give them time to read through the list.
- Play the recording.

16.1

Speaker 1   If I don't go bed when I'm completely and utterly exhausted like when your head is about to, you know, just drop off regardless of where you are – **if I don't go to bed at that time, then I will actually stay awake for an awful lot longer when I actually do go to bed. I have to make sure that I'm completely relaxed, and completely unwound before I actually go to bed, otherwise then, you know I'll just be lying awake for ages. Erm my mind starts to wander** and I start thinking about all the things that I haven't done or that I've got to do, so I have to sit in front of the television for an hour or something or two hours and er just make sure that I'm completely exhausted and completely tired and my eyes are closing before going to bed, otherwise I just stay awake for hours. In terms of position, well, I mean, if I'm that tired I, I just go to bed in any position and I'll probably sleep anywhere when I get to that stage – on a bus on a train you, you name it erm and if I can't get to sleep, well, I dunno I try all sorts of things of, try to think of erm, relaxing thoughts of you know waterfalls and fields …

Speaker 2   I don't have a fixed routine of going to bed – I panic if I'm going to get less than about eight hours – I always have done and always will. I sleep always on my left side – **I start off always on my left side er but that can switch. And what keeps me awake is usually either hunger or anxiety, so if I can't sleep I'll either eat something or I'll usually e-mail now actually** which'll, which is very bad because then I definitely get at least an hour less sleep than I should have, but I'm addicted to it, or I'll read a novel or listen to Radio 4 and yes I can sleep absolutely anywhere, if I'm knackered enough, but er also feel terribly, terribly vulnerable doing that and get off at wrong stops and drool and stuff so try not to but er if I can't sleep I can panic because I do have a thing about getting enough hours – and it'll affect me the whole next day – so it's a psychological thing probably more than a physical.

Speaker 3 To be honest, being an English student sleep isn't really much of a problem for me – I spend a lot of time sleeping. Erm I often lie in till about 2 o'clock in the afternoon when I'm supposed to be writing an essay or making notes or something and then just end up working really late – so get into sort of bad patterns anyway. If ever I can't sleep – which as I say isn't really often the case, I often listen to music to try to get to sleep or I'll just sit up and read a book if, basically if I can't sleep, then I don't try.

Speaker 4 I tend to drink quite a lot of coffee, so sleeping is often quite difficult, and it drives me mad. If I can't sleep I tend to get up and read or watch TV. Some nights I just don't go to sleep at all, which is very bizarre and then just continue the next day as if I have been to sleep, cos once it gets light I then can't get back to sleep – like I went to a ball the other day and we didn't go to sleep all night and then by nine o'clock the next morning as far as I was concerned it was the next day so I just carried on which is quite bizarre.

Note
Radio 4 is a BBC radio channel which is devoted mainly to news, current affairs, and other fairly serious documentary programmes.

- Ask students to compare answers in pairs, then check with the whole class.

> a Speaker 3
> b Speaker 2
> c Speakers 2 / 3 / 4
> d Speaker 2
> e Speaker 1
> f Speaker 4 (Speaker 1 also watches TV to make himself tired enough to go to bed.)

2 Give students a couple of minutes in pairs to see if they can remember any of the answers, but tell them that you will play the recording again so they can check their answers.

- Play recording **16.1**.

- Ask students to check their answers together, then check with the whole class.

> a He lies awake for a long time. His mind starts to wander and he thinks of things that he hasn't done or that he has to do in the future.
> He has to make himself completely exhausted, by watching TV, etc.
> b Hunger or anxiety may keep her awake. She eats something, sends e-mails, reads a novel, listens to the radio.
> c Because he often stays in bed until late (2 p.m.) and then has to finish his work.
> d On nights when she doesn't sleep, she just continues on into the next day.

▶ If you feel your students would benefit from some additional sleep vocabulary work, there is an extra exercise on p.143.

Exploring natural speech

Aim *The vague words* thing *and* stuff *are extremely common in spoken English (they came across sort of in Stage 2 of Unit 4). This section aims to familiarize students with these words and give them some practice in using them.*

1 It's probably a good idea to go through this with the students. Make sure they understand the key words:

knackered = extremely tired – a very colloquial word
vulnerable = able to be harmed, exposed
drool = to water at the mouth, salivate

> *stuff* = other embarrassing things like these (getting off at the wrong stops / drooling)
> *thing* = obsession / fixation
> *thing* = issue / matter / problem

2 Ask students to answer the questions in pairs, then check with the whole class.

> **Possible answers**
> a *things* possessions / belongings
> b *thing* problem / dilemma / difficulty / point
> c *Things* activities / business / matters
> d *stuff* material / substance
> e *stuff* belongings / possessions (the same here as *things*)

- The following activity provides speaking practise of the words *thing* and *stuff*. It is probably a good idea for you to demonstrate it first.

1 Put students in groups.

2 Each student thinks of an object or a substance and then describes it to the rest of the group using only the words *thing* and *stuff*. They must not use the name of the object or substance. The other members of the group have to work out what is being described.

Language focus: habits and predictable behaviour p.119

Aim *To focus attention on the frequency with which* will *is used in preference to the Present simple in informal speech to refer to typical or predictable behaviour.*

The language here is not difficult in itself, but the students may simply find it strange that *will* can be used in this way when they will have previously learnt to use the Present simple.

1 Ask students to read through extract **a** and to try to remember, or guess, what the verb forms were.

- Check with the whole class, highlighting the fact that *will* is sometimes used, not the Present simple. (But give the answers yourself, without letting the students refer to the tapescript themselves yet).

> a ... If I don't go to bed at that time, then I **will actually stay** awake for an awful lot longer when I actually do go to bed. I **have to** make sure that I'm completely relaxed, and completely unwound erm before I actually go to bed, otherwise then, you know I'**ll just be lying** awake for ages. Erm my mind **starts** to wander.

- Now ask students to try **b** and **c** in pairs.

- When they have finished, refer them to the tapescript on p.148 to check their answers.

b I **start off** always on my left side er but that can switch. And what **keeps** me awake is usually either hunger or anxiety, so if I can't sleep **I'll either eat** something or **I'll usually e-mail** now actually …
c If ever I can't sleep – which as I say isn't really often the case, **I often listen** to music to try to get to sleep or **I'll just sit up** and read a book.

- At this point it might be useful to do some extra practice of the contracted *will*. Advanced students usually have no problem with *I'll, he'll, she'll, we'll*, but still find it difficult to say *you'll, we'll, they'll*, and usually find contractions like *it'll, what'll* and *who'll* very bizarre and unreasonable! They need to be able to recognize these contractions, and if they are able to use them themselves, their speech will sound more fluent and natural.

3 You could do this task with the whole class, or ask students to do it in pairs.
- Check answers with the whole class.

a future	**b** predictable	**c** predictable	**d** predictable
e predictable	**f** predictable		

4 This is probably best done with the whole class.

> typical behaviour
> recent / temporary habit

- Refer students to the Language commentary on p.125 for more information on habits and predictable behaviour.

Exploitation

Aim *To give students the opportunity for some freer speaking practice using* will *to describe habitual or predictable behaviour.*

1 Focus students on the photos and outline the task, emphasizing that they will need to use their imagination.
- Put the students into groups to talk about the pictures. Monitor and correct as necessary. Interruption and correction is appropriate here because the students are being asked to practise a particular language structure.

2 Outline the task and look at the example together, mentioning the addition of *possibly* or *probably*.
- Ask students to work in pairs. Again, monitor and correct as necessary, helping particularly with pronunciation.

Speaking

Aim *To give the students free speaking practice with a task outcome.*

1 Ask students to work in small groups of three or four.
- Tell them they are going to design a survey. Make sure that they all write down the questions. Encourage them to follow the pattern of the Sleep Survey on p.118.
- Set a time limit. Monitor and encourage as necessary.

2 Regroup the students so that they work in pairs, with someone they were not working with before.

- Ask one person in the pair to try out their survey on their partner(s). Set a time limit.
- Now ask them to change over. They can try out their survey on as many other students in the class as time permits.
- At the end of the activity, ask the students to go back to their original groups to report back to each other on what they found out from their survey.
- Conduct a general class feedback on the students' findings.

16.2 Animation   p.120

The reading and listening texts in this stage contextualize the use of the passive.

Reading

Aim *To develop students' ability to read a fairly detailed text in order to extract information.*

1 Start with books closed.
- Before the class find out the names of some animated films your students will know or have heard of. Write the titles on the board or tell the class the titles, and ask them to tell you what they have in common. Once they have some concrete films in mind they will find the brainstorming easier.
- You can either ask students to brainstorm what they know about animated films in groups, or you can do it with the whole class. Either way, make sure that they write down anything and everything they come up with, whether or not they can agree it's true.
- Set a time limit.

2 Now tell them they are going to to read an article about making animated films.
- Ask them to read and find out whether the ideas they brainstormed are correct or not. The article may not answer or deal with all the points they raised – this is not important.
- When the students have finished reading, ask them to work in pairs to check their ideas, or those of the group.
- Conduct a feedback if this is appropriate.

Close up

- Put students in pairs to do the exercise. Encourage them to make guesses from context rather than rely on their dictionaries.
- Check answers with the whole class.

Listening

Aim *To practise listening for very specific information.*

- Outline the task and play the recording.

16.2

So, once rough sketches of the character have been made and it's been decided how the character will move, the modelling process begins.

First of all a detailed drawing is made showing the model's armature or skeleton.

Then the armature is made using twisted wire or ball and socket joints.

This enables a basic clay model to be created and this in turn becomes the finished character.

Next the storyboard is filmed and the voices are added, allowing the director to check that the scenes, and the movie as a whole, work. This stage is followed by a very simple animation known as a 'blocking rehearsal' where the director checks characters' movements and how they look on set.

Once the voices of the characters have been recorded the animators are able to match the shape of the mouth to the dialogue. The mouth forms different shapes depending on what sound is coming from the character. This process is called lipsynch.

Then finally there's the actual filming of the movie. This is a painstaking process. The final action may be fast and furious but Chicken Run took four years to make. Every aspect of the character has to be carefully adjusted for each frame, 1,400 times to produce one minute of film time. This means that actions like the blinking of an eye can take hours to film.

- Ask students to check their answers in pairs, then check with the whole class.

The correct order of illustrations: B / C / A / E / D / F

▶ There is an extra vocabulary exercise on p.143 which could be done as homework with students using their own dictionaries.

Language focus: the passive p.121

Aim *To review the form and use of the passive.*

1 Ask the students to do the task in pairs, then check with the whole class.

para 2	has to be changed; needs to be repeated
para 4	will be used
para 5	have been made; has been decided

2 You could complete this task together as a whole class in order to check that everyone is as familiar as they need to be with the form of the passive. You may wish to refer them to the Language commentary on p.125.

a Present simple   b Past simple   c Present continuous

3–4 Ask the students to answer these questions in pairs.

- Monitor and help as necessary.
- Check with the whole class.

3
a Reasons: A / E
b Reasons: B / C / D / E
c Reasons: C / D / E
4
a News report: radio, TV, or newspaper
b An encyclopaedia
c Public notice – in a shop
d Academic textbook

Exploitation

Aim *To raise awareness of the use of the passive form in formal or official contexts.*

1 Outline the task briefly.

- Ask students to write the sentences together, in pairs.
- Check with the whole class.

a Smart formal clothes must / have to / should / be worn for meetings.
b The party leader was blamed for the election defeat.
c The new town hall was opened on 15 September 2001.
d The boy was sentenced to six months in prison for 'borrowing' his father's car.
   Note: the judge does not need to be mentioned: it is only judges who sentence people.
e The government cannot be blamed for the recent increase in the price of petrol.

2 Set up the task carefully. It is important that students choose a process they have some knowledge of, although they should also be encouraged to use their imagination to fill in any gaps in their knowledge. The important point is that they are able to describe a sequence of actions involved in the process they choose.

- Ask students to work in pairs. They are speaking, not writing at this point.
- Monitor and help with vocabulary as necessary.

Writing

Aim *To use the ideas they have just been talking about to write a report about a process, using the passive voice.*

This is a second opportunity for students to write a report (the first was in Unit 7).

1–3 Refer students to the description of the task and make sure they know exactly what is required.

- Refer students to the Writing guidelines on p.155.

- You could ask the students to do the preparation work in class and then to write the report at home. If they have prepared the writing together, they might then like to read each other's final written versions.

Speaking

Aim *To give the students the opportunity for some free speaking. It also serves as a final round up for the unit.*

- If you have a fairly confident, communicative class, you could discuss these questions with the whole class, with you leading and directing the conversation to make sure that the points are discussed as fully as possible.

- If not, it is probably better to put the students into small groups. You could ask different groups to discuss different points, give them a time limit, and then ask them to switch over.

- As usual in this sort of activity, monitor and join in, if appropriate, but don't interrupt or correct.

16.3 Interviews   p.122

A light-hearted text about interviews contextualizes verb + object + infinitive.

Lead in

Aim *To prepare the students for the article they are going to read.*

1 Outline the task and give students a time limit to compile their lists.

- Conduct a brief class feedback.

2 Ask students to do this in pairs. When they have decided on a 'worst thing', the pairs could then team up to make fours, and compare their 'worst things'.

- Ask them to decide, in their fours, on one 'worst thing', then join the fours together so that you have groups of eight and again ask them to compare their ideas and then to decide on one 'worst thing'. (This way of building up groups for discussions is sometimes called a 'pyramid discussion'.)

- Eventually the whole class decides on a worst interview mistake.

Reading

Aim *To give students practice at reading and responding personally to a text before analysing it, and then to help them develop their detailed reading skills through a matching task.*

1 Outline the tasks briefly. You may want to point out that the text is in American English from a US newspaper.

2 When most of the students have finished, ask them to compare their answers in pairs. This becomes a discussion point, as there are no right or wrong answers to **a** or **b**, but in discussing their opinions it is likely that the students will actually improve their comprehension.

- You could conduct a brief whole class feedback if needed.

3 Now focus students on the questions **a–h**. Give them time to re-read the text and answer the questions individually.

- Ask them to compare their answers in pairs, then check the answers with the whole class.

> **a** F – he didn't know what the company did
> **b** G – doesn't like working with people
> **c** H – couldn't answer questions
> **d** B – 'not a nickel less'
> **e** C – thought references were people (confusion with 'referee')
> **f** A – 'I asked him not to eat it until later'
> **g** E – wearing a bathing suit
> **h** D – The only evidence of 'organizational skills' was being able to pack a suitcase.

Vocabulary: applying for a job   p.123

The students will probably know several of the vocabulary items here, so this section serves as a review and a reminder of some vocabulary associated with interviews.

- Ask students to do the task in pairs, then check answers with the whole class, paying attention to pronunciation and word stress.

> **1** applicants /ˈæplɪkənts/
> **2** personnel /pɜːsəˈnel/
> **3** C.V. /siːˈviː/
> **4** referees /refəˈriːz/
> **5** shortlisted /ˈʃɔːtlɪstɪd/
> **6** interview
> **7** candidate

Language focus: verb + object + *to* + infinitive

Aim *To review and categorize verbs which use this structure and which do not.*

Students will have come across many of the verbs that use this pattern but are unlikely to be aware that they tend to fall into certain categories (*influencing, causing, wanting*). They may also overuse the structure so that they apply it to verbs that use a different structure, saying things like *She insisted me to do it*.

1 Give students a few minutes to do this task quickly.

- Check answers – there is more than one possibility.

> **Possible answers**
> **a** asked / told
> **b** asked / told
> **c** get / persuade / convince
> **d** remind

2 a Set up the task. Go through the verbs in the list quickly, checking meaning and pronunciation as necessary.

- Give one or two examples of the **Influencing** category, to show students what is wanted. Then ask them to do the rest together in pairs.

- Check answers with the whole class.

> **A Influencing: ordering / requesting**
> advise; ask; beg; encourage; forbid; invite; order; persuade; tell
> **B Causing / helping**
> allow; enable; get; help; permit; teach
> **C Wanting / liking**
> want; wish; would like

b Ask students to work in pairs to do this task, then check answers with the whole class. You may wish to refer them to the Language commentary on p.125.

> *discourage* someone **from doing** something
> *insist* **on** someone **doing** something / **that** someone **does** something
> *let* someone **do** something
> *make* someone **do** something
> *prevent* someone **from doing** something
> *prohibit* someone **from doing** something
> *suggest* **that** someone **does** something

Exploitation

> Aim *To give the students some free speaking practice using the verb + object + to + infinitive structure.*

- Give students a few minutes to prepare their sentences. (They don't need to write them down, but they will need time to think.)

- Now ask them to team up with one or two others and to compare their answers.

- Monitor, but don't interrupt. Make notes of mistakes for a later correction task.

- After the speaking activity, conduct a correction task in which the students correct the mistakes you noted.

Role play

> Aim *To develop the students' oral English skills with a fairly formal role play.*

- Tell the students they are going to prepare for a role play.

- Divide the class into two halves, As and Bs. Ask the As to read the notes on p.158 and the Bs to read the notes on p.159.

- Give the As some time to prepare their roles together, and the Bs the same. Encourage the groups to be adventurous rather than safe with the language.

- Now regroup the students into AB pairs.

- Elicit / clarify the kind of language and behaviour expected at a job interview. You are trying to appear professional, organized, mature, responsible, etc.

- Ask them to conduct the role play. Encourage them to say as much as they can, to experiment with the language by practising words / phrases / structures they may not be entirely comfortable with yet. If appropriate, give them two stages; a rehearsal, where they can experiment, ask for help, etc., and a 'real' run-through.

- Monitor, but don't interrupt. Make notes. This time you could focus on words / phrases / expressions you hear that are good.

- At the end of the role plays you could ask one or two pairs to demonstrate to the whole class.

- Finish with a feedback session where you tell them or write up the good things you noted, explaining why they were good.

Writing

> Aim *To provide writing practice based on the theme of interviews.*

Students are given a choice here of writing an informal personal profile or a more formal application letter.

- Ask the students to decide on their type of writing (unless you are making the choice for them).

- You could group them so that those working on the profile sit together, and those doing the formal letter are together.

- Refer them to the appropriate Writing guidelines on p.152.

- Give the groups some time to decide on the key ideas, words, and phrases they want to use.

- Set the task for homework.

Exploring words

p.124

Students are often very interested in the differences between British and American English and enjoy finding out about them. It is also useful for students at an advanced level to be able to recognize some of the more common differences so that they are able to function in either language setting.

1 Briefly introduce the topic of this section and ask students to do the quiz on their own.

- Ask them to compare their answers with a partner.

- Now play the recording which will confirm the answers.

16.3

OK, here are the answers to the quiz. Give yourself a point for each correct answer.

A. How many more speakers of American English than British English are there? The answer is C – there are actually four times as many speakers of American English.

B. The most noticeable difference between British and American English is in fact B – pronunciation. There are relatively few differences in spelling and vocabulary.

C. The statement 'Where words are spelt differently in British and American English, the American spelling is usually shorter', is true.

D. The statement 'There are no differences in grammar between British and American English', is false. But there are only a few, for example in American English it is possible to use the time adverbs *already* and *yet* with the Simple past.

E. This statement is false. Pairs of words with different spellings in British and American English are usually pronounced in the same way.

And finally F. It is true that most British people understand American English without any problem. This is probably because British people are used to seeing lots of American films and TV programmes.

> **A** c
> **B** b
> **C** TRUE (Examples: color (colour) / traveled (travelled)
> **D** FALSE (Example: American English uses Past simple with *already / yet*)
> **E** FALSE
> **F** TRUE – this is partly because British people are constantly exposed to American films and TV programmes.

2 Ask students to try this in pairs. Between them, they will probably be able to work out most of these.

- Check answers with the whole class.

> **a** 5 **b** 9 **c** 10 **d** 8 **e** 2 **f** 7 **g** 4 **h** 1
> **i** 6 **j** 3

3 You could begin by asking students if they know of any differences in spelling between British and American English.

- Then ask them to complete the table in pairs and note any other examples.

- Go through it with the whole class.

British	American	Other examples – British English words
1 centre	center	theatre; fibre; sombre; litre
2 **rumour**	rumor	favour; flavour; humour; labour
3 offence	**offense**	defence; licence; pretence
4 **dialogue**	dialog	catalogue; monologue
5 travelled	**traveled**	jewellery

Speaking

Aim *To round up the unit with a free-speaking activity which gives students a chance to talk about the different forms of English that exist.*

- You could conduct the discussion in pairs, small groups, or as a whole class. Encourage students to discuss the questions in as much depth as possible.

17 Creativity

17.1 Mr Gormley's Angel p.125

Stage 1 consists of a listening text in which a sculptor describes his work. It contextualizes uses of dependent prepositions.

Lead in

Aim *To get the students talking about the theme of the lesson, and to introduce key vocabulary used to describe the sculpture,* The Angel of the North.

1 Ask the students to look at the sculptures (*The Angel of the North*, *Another Place*, and *The Iron Man*) in the photos, and discuss the questions as a class.

- Ask whether there are any large, famous 'motorway' sculptures near the students' home towns. If so, ask the students to describe them, and say how they feel about them.

- Alternatively you could get the students to work in pairs to describe and discuss the sculpture *The Angel of the North* in detail. This should preview some of the language used in later activities. Write these questions on the board:

    How would you describe The Angel of the North *to someone who hasn't seen it?*
    How do you think it was made?
    Why do you think it was placed near a motorway?

2 Focus the students on the questions, then ask them to read the factual information.

- Put the students in pairs to discuss their answers before feedback.

- Encourage the students to make guesses at these questions, but don't tell them whether their ideas are right or not. They will get more information about the sculpture when they listen to the sculptor talking.

    a *The Angel of the North* is located very close to a major road and so can be seen by thousands of passing motorists every day.
    b It is made of steel which will corrode after 100 years of exposure to the weather.

- Check that the students understand the more difficult vocabulary in the text. *Mound, wingspan,* and *steel* can be checked by referring to the picture on p.126.
    Plaster is the material used to immobilize broken bones while they heal.

Listening p.127

Aim *To listen for gist and for specific words, and practise summarizing.*

1 Read through the questions with the students, and point out that each of the four short extracts they are going to listen to is a response to one of the four questions **a–d**. Play the recording. (This recording was made in Antony Gormley's studio, and so the sound quality is less good – there is a slight 'echo' effect.)

17.1

Extract 1 Well it's a long process, but I think it starts always **with** the place, the location. The actual piece came about from a conversation that I had **with** councillor Pat Murphy who had been a miner himself – he was Irish – and er he said 'What we need Mr Gormley is is one of your angels,' and I said 'Well if you're serious **about** this, Pat, it's going to have to be 65 foot tall,' and that was the beginning of the whole thing.

Extract 2 I had told the people that I wasn't interested in making motorway art erm rather snobbishly – but, as it turned, out this relationship **between** this mound and the road got me very intrigued. There is always cars on it and we know that 90,000 motorists pass that point a day.

Extract 3 You would expect a work of that scale to perhaps express some heroic ideal or anyway monumental certainty and it doesn't, – I think it expresses as much anxiety as it does succour.

Extract 4 Not at all. Couldn't matter less. I mean I think these are the, these are the thoughts and feelings that I had in the process of making it, having made it er looking at it as a work amongst my other works erm, but for the average person I wouldn't even imagine they would begin to think in these terms, so that you know an ex-ship builder or an ex-miner or a housewife or the train driver or the schoolboy that passes every day – each of them will have their own particular relationship **with** this with this work.

a 4	**b** 1	**c** 3	**d** 2

2 **a** Put the students in pairs and play the recording so that they can complete the extract. You may need to play and pause while they write down the words.

17.2

What I'm more interested in is tripping people up you know on their way to the supermarket because I think that part of the problem with our culture at the moment is that we deal in a culture of you know snacking basically, er of highly-articulated highly-hyped, almost predigested experience. I hope the Angel makes you aware of the time of the day, of the shape of the landscape, your speed, erm, also, even though people wouldn't recognize that perhaps as part of their response to a work. The only value of art, I think, is as a instrument of reflexivity to make us feel more alive – there's no intrinsic value to art.

Note: The words omitted from the extract are important to the understanding of Gormley's ideas.

1 *tripping* – Gormley means that he wants people to be taken by surprise when, by chance, they come across his sculptures. This is quite different from taking the decision to go to an art gallery to look at art.

2 *culture*

3 *snacking* – Gormley seems to disapprove of the modern approach to art where the public is told what to expect from and what to think about art. (*Snacking* usually means eating small things like crisps, biscuits, and chocolate bars between meals.)

4 *experience*

5 *aware*

6 *landscape*

7 *value*

8 *alive* – Gormley sees art not as a commodity with a cash value, but as a means of making people aware of the natural world and their place in it.

b Discuss the questions as a class.

3 is the best summary.

• There are vocabulary exercises on the use of metaphor in the *Exploring words* section on p.132, which you could introduce at this stage if you wish.

React and discuss

• Put the students in small groups to discuss the questions.

Language focus: dependent prepositions

Aim *To revise and practise dependent prepositions.*

This stage looks at various forms:

Verb + preposition + noun: *to believe in …*
Verb + object + preposition + noun: *to arrest (someone) for …*
Noun + preposition: *a contrast between …*
Adjective + preposition: *I'm afraid of …*

In particular, it explores different possible combinations of adjectives with prepositions, *good for* and *good at*, for example, and examines the change of meaning.

It is a difficult area for students, because unless the dependent preposition happens to be the same as that in their own language it is very difficult to remember what it is. In order to improve their accuracy in this area, they need to revise, memorize, and practise. If you have a monolingual class, it is a good idea to look at the list of dependent prepositions on p.133 and decide which ones have a confusingly different form, and are therefore likely to cause problems for your students. Concentrate on these.

1–2 Put the students in pairs to complete the extracts, and check their answers in the tapescript on p.148.

> **a** with **b** with **c** about **d** between **e** with
> **Note:** One person / thing has a relationship *with* another. There is a relationship *between* two people / things.

3 Ask the students to complete the sentences and discuss their answers with a partner. You may wish to refer the students to the Language commentary on p.133, particularly to check how the choice of preposition affects the meaning.

> **1** angry *with* the driver
>   angry *about* the length
> **2** good *with* learner drivers
>   good *at* parking in small spaces
>   good *for* you to drive
> **3** sorry *for* him
>   sorry *about* the damage

Exploitation

1 It is best to do this in small groups of three or four.

- Give the students a few minutes to think about what to say. Let them make a few notes, if they wish, but not write full sentences.
- Ask the students to take it in turns to talk about each subject. Monitor and note errors made with dependent prepositions.
- Alternatively, you could make this a little more competitive by playing The 60 Seconds Game. See p.103 of this book for details of how to play.

2 Either ask students simply to test each other, or do the following:

1 Divide the students into groups of three or four and ask them to look at the lists of dependent prepositions in the Language commentary on p.133.

2 They should work together to write five sentences using nouns, verbs, or adjectives from these lists with the dependent preposition missing.

3 Write an example on the board: *I'm so tired I can't concentrate .... my work.*

4 Monitor and help. When they are ready, ask the students to exchange their sentences with another group.

5 Ask the students to fill the gaps without looking at the list in the book, then check their answers with the group who prepared the sentences.

17.2 But is it art?   p.128

Stage 2 consists of a reading text about gorillas creating abstract pictures. It is used as a context for looking at reference words like *this* and *these*.

Lead in

> **Aim** *To introduce and practise vocabulary used to describe a painting.*

1 Check the students understand and can pronounce the art vocabulary.

A good way of checking the *styles* is to find and bring in some pictures or postcards of various styles of art. You could check the techniques and materials by drawing or miming the words. A picture of an artist painting on canvas would be useful. *Depict* means *show, portray, represent.* For example, *the painting depicted the president as a lion.*

Note the stress on the words in the style section:

'abstract / 'classical / 'modern – on the first syllable

ex'pressionist / im'pressionist / sur'realist / sym'bolic – on the second syllable

represen'tational – primary stress on the fourth syllable.

- Put the students in pairs to discuss the questions and describe the painting.

> **Possible answers**
> **a** abstract / expressionist / modern / symbolic
> **b** you can see the brushstrokes / the colours are bright / it's probably done with oil paints / the painter has used a large paintbrush

2 Ask the students to discuss the statement as a class.

Reading

> **Aim** *To read for gist and specific information.*

1 Focus the students on the gist question, then ask them to read the text.

> It was painted by an ape: Michael.
> It was inspired by a bouquet of flowers.
> It is called *Stink Gorilla More*.

Close up

- Put the students in pairs to do the exercise. Encourage them to make guesses from the context rather than rely on their dictionaries.

1.4	*to dress* = to put on clothes / to get dressed *to dress up* = to put on clothes which are intended to make you look like someone or something you are not.
1.10	finding it difficult to make money / poor and commercially unsuccessful *to struggle* also means to fight
1.18	primates – animals like monkeys, apes, gorillas, chimpanzees

2 Read through the questions with the class then ask them to read the text again. Let them check in pairs before feedback.

a	The paintings have received critical acclaim. They have been successful.
b	They are considered to be representational, not merely random or abstract.
c	Similar characteristics to humans. The ability to joke, lie, get embarrassed, to represent reality through signs or symbols.
d	Both are symbolic representations.
e	Personal answers

Language focus: reference words (2) p.129

Aim *To revise and practise reference words and phrases.*

This section looks at how reference words and phrases like *this*, *these*, and *there* refer forwards and backwards to information mentioned in a text. It contextualizes pronouns like *it*, *mine*, *which*, and *both*, and time and place words like *that time*, *then*, and *here / there*.

- Put the students in pairs to discuss the use of reference words. Refer them to the Language commentary on p.133.
- Check answers with the whole class.

a	*this tale*	the story told in the first paragraph
	their	of the struggling artists in California
	they	the struggling artists in California
	These great apes	Michael and Koko
b	*when*	in the late 1950s
	Their	of chimps in the late 1950s
	at that time	in the late 1950s
	that	the price
c	*This*	the occasion when Koko drew a glass, etc.
d	*By then*	by the age of three

Exploitation

- Ask the students to complete the article with reference words, then check in pairs.

1 they		2 them		3 they		4 the same		5 this	
6 these similarities		7 them		8 she		9 their	
10 something		11 who							

Speaking

Aim *To discuss and extend the issues raised by the lesson.*

1–2 Put the students in groups to discuss the questions. Ask one member of each group to make notes of the group's conclusions to question 2 and report back to the whole class.

17.3 Women in the arts p.130

Stage 3 consists of a listening text in which people discuss the role of women in the arts.

Lead in

Aim *To get students talking and thinking about the role of men and women in the arts.*

1 Check that the students understand the vocabulary. You could ask check questions like: *Which word describes people who write music? (composer); Which word describes people who make art from materials like clay or metal? (sculptor).* Then put the students in pairs or small groups to think of two famous people in each category. Have a whole-class feedback. You could build up a list on the board. If students mention any artists who are not well known by the other students, ask them to give the class a little information about them.

2 Ask the students briefly to discuss the two questions. It is likely that there will be few women in their list. If so, you could briefly preview the theme of the listening by asking whether they have any ideas why there are so few women.

3 Ask the students briefly to discuss the pairs of artists.

Picasso and Morisot: Visual arts Schumann and Mozart: Music Dickens and Austen: Literature / writing novels

4 Ask the students in pairs or small groups to tell each other what they know about the pairs of artists.

- Refer the students to p.158 to check what they have said about the famous people.
- If you feel that your class will not have much to say on this subject, or will be ignorant of the people mentioned, you could approach this lead-in differently.
- Start by eliciting famous people in the categories in question 1 as a class, or bring in pictures of famous musicians, writers, and artists you think the students might know, and ask them to tell you what they do know about them.
- Introduce the students to the artists mentioned in question 3, then divide them into groups of six. Refer them to the information on p.158 about the six people mentioned in 3 and ask them to read about one of the people, making sure that each person in the group reads about a different person. When they are ready, they share three or four pieces of information about their famous person with the rest of the group.

Listening

Aim *To listen for gist and interpretation.*

1 Focus the students on the questions, then play the recording.

17.3

W1 But, you know, it's a question of if you ask, are there more famous men in the arts than women – famous in the sense that we probably know about more men than women in the arts, do you know what I'm saying?

M Well as far as classical painters, you know, you certainly don't think of women.

W1 (That's true,) but does that mean they didn't exist?

W2 Good point …

M They may have been edited, who knows?

W2 … or not had, you know, the kind of exposure that a male painter had.

M Well, look at authors like Georges Sand – women traditionally for a good number of years had to put a male pseudonym on their books (Right, exactly, yes) or they were not going to sell.

W2 Smart women who did that, boy.

M Yeah, also women were not historically given the educational advantages that men were – women were to, you know, grow up and marry off and men were sent to the universities where they were exposed to art. (Right)

W1 Do you think it's changing, now? Do you think more women are getting positions of prominence in the arts?

M Not in the business of art.

W2 Yeah, I mean what do you mean – in what field of art are you talking about?

W1 Well all different fields – let's talk about the media – what do you think about like film and TV? Do you think more and more women are …

W2 I think more and more although I heard a statistic in this documentary that, I think last year, out of the 200 or so sort of feature films, you know big feature films not independent films that were made, maybe 20 of them were directed by women.

W1 Wow!

> **a** (classical) painting / writing (authors) / TV and film direction
> **b** Historically women were not given the same educational advantages as men. Women were expected to get married. Men went to university and were more likely to be exposed to art.

2 Put the students in pairs to discuss the statements.

> **a** *edited* – omitted from the records, perhaps because they were considered to be less worthy than men
> **b** Women had to give themselves a man's name to hide the fact that they were women.

3 Focus the students on the questions, then play the recording.

17.4

J It's funny, though. If you look at say, composers, directors, theatre directors, film directors, how many of those could you name who are women?

K You mean the people who are in charge?

J Yeah. How many female composers? There are, I would say there are less female …

R (I can) Think of a few directors, a few producers.

J There are very few female, well-known female theatre directors or film directors.

R Oh yeah, comparatively.

J Comparatively.

R Of course you're right.

J Which is bizarre, because that is nothing that need be dominated by men, (No) but it just is. And I mean, even I feel that …

R But that's you … There's a parallel there with sort of I don't know, sort of business as well, do you know what I mean?

K Except that busi…

R Like the director is sort of the head of the theatre business in a sense, or the director and the producer.

J But that's become quite controversial and there are therefore a lot more women who have risen to the top because a few years ago there were a lot of people who made a lot of fuss about women being on average being paid less, and a lot of women did go to the top of businesses. But going back to art, er musicians, what about musicians? How many famous female musicians do you know?

T There are just thousands. Do you mean …?

J Of female?

T Umm.

J Female famous musicians?

R That can play instruments or singers?

K Classical musicians?

J Classical musicians …

K Well it's interesting, isn't it because …

J … or jazz musicians.

K Well I don't know I think classical music is always perhaps, well not always but is rather more balanced. It's just no one is that high profile. I mean I could, you could name classical musicians, you could name Vanessa Mae, you could name Jacqueline Du Pré, you could name, you know, there are quite a lot of people.

> **a** music (composers / classical and jazz musicians) / film and theatre directors
> **b** In both the arts and business it is men who are the organizers, the controllers, the bosses.

4 Put the students in pairs to discuss the statements.

> **a** reached senior positions in their profession or in the arts
> **b** no one is that well known

React and discuss

1 Brainstorm famous women artists to the board, or put students in pairs and give them two or three minutes to think of as many women artists as they can, then brainstorm to the board as a class. Don't worry if they can't think of many – this simply illustrates the point. Here are a few possible artists:

> **Visual arts:** Frida Kahlo (Mexican artist), Barbara Hepworth (British sculptor), Bridget Riley (British artist)
> **Literature:** Emily Dickinson, Sylvia Plath (poets), George Eliot, Simone de Beauvoir, Agatha Christie, Virginia Woolf, Maya Angelou (novelists)
> **Music:** Maria Callas (opera singer)
> **Popular arts:** Edith Piaf, Marlene Dietrich, Madonna, Whitney Houston (singers), Marilyn Monroe, Brigitte Bardot, Meryl Streep, Julia Roberts (actors), Anna Pavlova, Margot Fonteyn (ballet dancers), Martha Graham (choreographer), Jodie Foster (actor and film-maker)

2 Put the students in groups to do this, then feedback as a class.

Exploring natural speech   p.131

Aim *To look at different expressions used in conversation to check that the other person is following, or to show agreement with what is being said.*

• Put the students in pairs to discuss the words and expressions.

> a *do you know what I'm saying?* means *do you understand the point I'm making? – do you follow my argument?* It is a way of checking that the listener understands and is in broad agreement.
> *Good point* means *I agree completely;* or it could be a way of saying *that is a point that I hadn't considered before.*
> b *Right, exactly* means that you agree completely with the point just made.
> *Smart women* is a way of expressing approval for what the women did.
> c *Wow!* expresses astonishment at the statistic just mentioned.

Vocabulary: male and female words

Aim *To look at the use of non-gender specific language in English.*

• Read through the introduction as a class. You could ask whether this change to neutral, non-sexist language has taken place in the students' own language.

1 Put the students in pairs to do the exercise.

> a bar tender / barperson
> b chair / chairperson
> c author
> d firefighter
> e police officer
> f business executive / business person
> g head / head teacher
> h camera operator
> i flight attendant / member of cabin crew
> j (senior) politician

2 Do the first as an example, then students rewrite the sentences in their pairs.

> a Human beings are … creatures
> b staff
> c artificial
> d People / Human beings have
> e staffed

Exploitation

• Students remain in pairs to rewrite the news reports.

> 1 **Four police officers** went to a club in central London last night after **a bartender / one of the bar staff** had phoned to report a disturbance.
> 2 A meeting took place yesterday between a group of **flight attendants** and representatives of the management. The **chairperson / chair** reported that there was **overstaffing** in the company and that redundancies were inevitable.
> 3 Before leaving, the **manager** of the shop made a thorough search of the burning building to check that all the staff were safely out. **Firefighters** who attended the blaze praised her for her bravery. A **spokesperson** said: 'Lives could so easily have been lost.'

Speaking

Aim *To discuss the issue of male and female roles in the workplace.*

Naturally, this is a controversial area, and it is worth considering whether your students may have strongly-held views here, especially in a multi-cultural classroom. If it is a concern, just do question 1, and approach this discussion as an exchange of cultural views, rather than asking people to agree or disagree with each other.

1 Put the students in groups to discuss, but don't have class feedback at this stage.

2 In the same groups, ask students to decide whether they agree or disagree, and to think of two or three reasons why. You could appoint one person in each group as a 'secretary'.

• Either the secretary or the group as a whole presents the results.

Exploring words   p.132

This section looks at metaphorical language. Exercise 1 looks at words used metaphorically in the listening passage in Stage 1; consequently, you could insert it as a follow-up vocabulary-in-context exercise, perhaps extending it with one of the other exercises in this section. Exercises 2, 3, and 4 introduce metaphors under the headings of topic, current use, and conversational use.

1 Read through the introduction as a class, then put the students in pairs to work out the literal meanings. This exercise works well with learners' dictionaries. Ask the students to use their dictionaries to find both the literal and metaphorical meanings.

> *Trip up* literally means deliberately put your foot in the way to make someone fall. Gormley means that he wants people to be taken by surprise when people come across his work by chance.
> *Snacking* means eating between meals – usually biscuits or chocolate. *Snack* is usually a noun. *Snacking* tends to be an American usage. Gormley means that we live in a culture where thought is not required, in the way that we are fed experiences which have little intrinsic value.

2 Students remain in pairs to identify the metaphors and discuss the meanings.

> 1 *flared up* = suddenly and violently started
> 2 *set … alight* = excite
> 3 *blaze* (of publicity) = enormous amount
> 4 *burning* (ambition) = very strong
> 5 *spark off* = start
> 6 *blazing* (rows) = very strong, violent
>   *smouldering* (discontent) = literally burning slowly, so here it means that although it doesn't show itself, the discontent is there quietly under the surface
> Note that the words in brackets are very common collocations with the 'fire' words.

• Ask the students to stay in the same pairs to think of different situations in which to use the metaphors.

3 a Put the students into different pairs to discuss the meanings.

> 1 *poaching* = taking from in an underhand way (literally, hunting illegally)
>   *shore up* = support (literally, from construction, to support a building or wall with a beam (a shore) to stop it collapsing)
>   *crumbling* = failing / falling apart (literally, breaking into small pieces)
> 2 *savaged* = heavily criticized (literally, attacked by a wild animal)
> 3 *launched* = started / opened (literally, put a new ship into water, or sent a rocket into space)
> 4 *feverish* = hectic / very busy (literally, suffering from a fever – a very high temperature)
>   *turned the spotlight on* = placed attention on (literally, from the theatre, the beam of light that can be directed onto a particular small area of the stage)
>   *hole* = error / problem (literally, an empty space)
> 5 *drop their guard* = stop being vigilant (literally, from boxing, to lower your hands, allowing your opponent to hit you)

b–c Students remain in pairs to rewrite the extracts.

> **Possible answers**
> 1 The attracting of nurses … to support Britain's failing health service …
> 2 … was heavily criticized yesterday …
> 3 A murder enquiry has been started …
> 4 In an extremely busy day … the opposition focused attention on … a £10 billion deficit in their finances.
> 5 … not stop being vigilant about / to continue to watch carefully for foot-and-mouth disease …
> The versions with metaphorical language are more dramatic and colourful.

4 Play the recording, check that students have identified the metaphors, then let them discuss the meanings and the effect in their pairs. (This is not included in the tapescript section of the Student's Book.)

17.5

1 It was a great day out – the children were bubbling with excitement the whole time.

2 I've never seen him so angry. He absolutely thundered at us that we must do the whole job again, right from the start.

3 I'm fed up with the way he tiptoes round the issue. I just wish he'd come out and say what he really means.

4 We spent the whole afternoon kicking ideas around until we found something we could all agree about.

5 It was a really useful meeting. At least we managed to squash that ridiculous suggestion of Tony's.

> 1 *bubbling with excitement* = jumping up and down (like bubbles)
> 2 *thundered* = shouted (noisily, like thunder)
> 3 *tiptoes round* = carefully avoids (tiptoeing, walking very carefully)
> 4 *kicking ideas around* = discussing ideas in an unsystematic fashion (you can kick a football around)
> 5 *squash* = stop (like treading on an insect)

18 In the public eye

Theme: different sorts of fame

18.1 Infamy

How criminals deliberately seek notoriety

- **Vocabulary:** abstract nouns connected with *fame*
- **Reading:** prediction, specific information, and summarizing
- **Language focus:** sentence structure
- **Speaking and writing:** describing a favourite villain

18.2 A year in the public eye

The *Castaway 2000* experiment on TV

- **Listening:** gist and specific information
- **Exploring natural speech:** being tentative
- **Language focus:** the verb *get*
- **Speaking:** planning a new reality TV programme

Exploring words

Getting away from it all – vocabulary around the topic of *places*

Workbook

- **Language focus:** sentence structure; *get*; phrasal verbs with *get*
- **Vocabulary focus:** fame
- **Vocabulary expansion:** collocations – parts of the body; verbs – ways of looking for something
- **Listening:** getting away from it all

18.1 Infamy   p.134

Stage 1 consists of a reading text about how criminals seek notoriety. It contextualizes the use of complex and compound sentences.

Vocabulary

Aim *To introduce and practise vocabulary around the topic of fame.*

1 Put the students in pairs to look at the nouns and do the tasks. They could use a dictionary to do this.

> **a** **positive:** celebrity / fame / glory / heroism / renown
> **negative:** infamy / notoriety / villainy
> **neutral:** reputation (a reputation can be good or bad)
> **b** celebrity / fame / renown
> **c** heroism / villainy
> **d** celebrity   celebrated
>   fame   famous
>   glory   glorious
>   heroism   heroic
>   infamy   infamous
>   notoriety   notorious
>   renown   renowned
>   reputation   reputable
>   (**Note:** this has a positive meaning)
>   villainy   villainous

- In the feedback, check the difference between the words in each group. You may wish to point out the following:

> *Fame* is greater and more long-lasting than *celebrity*. For example, a great film star has fame, but a soap opera actor has celebrity.
> *Infamy* is worse and longer-lasting than *notoriety*. Hitler, for example, is infamous, whereas a soap opera star in a sex scandal might be described as notorious.
> You achieve *renown* as a singer or an artist, for example. In other words because of something you are good at.
> You achieve *glory* through war or revolution. You must be brave and victorious.
> *Heroes*, traditionally, do good, brave things. *Villains* do bad, cowardly things. Nowadays, we tend to use *hero* to describe people we look up to or admire – a footballer who wins a match, a film star in the lead role in an action film, a firefighter who risks his / her life to save a child. We use *villain* to describe someone we boo and hiss – a footballer responsible for losing a match, the bad guy in a film.
> A good way of checking further is to ask students for examples of people, and what word you would use to describe them. For example, *Picasso is a renowned artist. Napoleon was a glorious leader.*

- Alternatively, you could do this as a board presentation. Write the word *fame* on the board and try to elicit as many words as you can from the students connected with fame. Or, find pictures of a world-famous person, a minor celebrity, and an infamous killer or criminal that you think your students will know. Put the pictures on the board and ask the students to describe them or match them to the words in the book.

2 Discuss this as a class. Think of a few infamous people – historical and contemporary – relevant to your learners.

Reading

Aim *To practise prediction skills, reading for specific information, and summarizing.*

1–2 Elicit ideas from the students, then ask them to read the passage to see if they were correct.

> According to the article, the writer doesn't want to give killers notoriety because they are committing their crimes in order to be famous. They want their moment of glory – they want society's attention.

Close up

- Put the students in pairs to do the exercise. Encourage them to make guesses from context rather than rely on their dictionaries.

> 1.3 just / proportionate / equitable
> 1.29 poisonous – a *toxic idea* might have a dangerous, negative effect
> 1.47 You can't make up your mind.

3 Put the students in pairs to answer the questions.

> a Sentence 2
> b They all sought attention by committing crime. They are infamous for this reason as much as for the crimes themselves.
> c He committed crime for attention, but this is not his real name. He was probably called this in order to deny him public attention.

Language focus: sentence structure p.135

Aim *To introduce and practise complex sentences in written English.*

This section contrasts the use of simple, compound, and complex sentences. Compound sentences are two clauses independent of each other joined by a conjunction. Complex sentences, as their name suggests, consist of a main clause, and one or more other clauses which are dependent or subordinate to the main clause. There are various types of dependent clauses – relative clauses, conditional clauses, and clauses introduced by an adverb, an infinitive, or a participle. Look at the Language commentary on p.139 for more detail.

The students are introduced to these ideas in a series of recognition exercises, then given lots of practice in transforming simple to complex and complex to simple sentences.

1 Discuss sentences a–c as a class.

> Simple sentences have one part (clause), one verb, one main idea.
> Compound sentences have two clauses connected by a linking word.
> Complex sentences have more than one part and more than one verb and clauses. One or more of the clauses are dependent on the main clause.

2 Do the first as an example, then ask the students to underline the main clauses in the other sentences. Let them check in pairs before feedback. You may wish to refer the students to the Language commentary on p.139.

> The main clauses are underlined.
> a Since he wasn't a great warrior, or creative person, <u>his best chance was to gain infamy by destroying something</u>.
> b To punish his selfish act and deter others, <u>the city banned speaking of him</u>.
> c By harming innocents, <u>you're only destroying your own name</u>.
> d <u>Some of those angry ones out there</u>, who are teetering in indecision with each desperate day, <u>may even decide that it's better to help lay a few bricks</u>.
> e If they choose to join us, <u>we should try to welcome them</u>.

3 Check that the students can recognize these sorts of clauses by asking a few questions: *What kind of clause begins with 'who' or 'which'? What kind begins with 'to'? What kind begins with 'if'?*

- Put the students in pairs to label the dependent clauses in task 2. You may wish to let them check by referring to the Language commentary on p.139.

> 2a *Since he wasn't a great warrior* = d an adverb clause expressing reason
> 2b *To punish his selfish act and deter others* = e an infinitive clause
> 2c *By harming innocents* = b a clause introduced by a participle expression
> 2d *who are teetering in indecision with each desperate day* = a a relative clause
> 2e *If they choose to join us* = c a conditional clause

▶ There is an extra exercise on the effect of complex vs. simple sentences on p.143.

Exploitation

- Give the students time to read through the profiles of famous film villains first, and check vocabulary. Then, for further practice of complex sentences, ask the students to work individually to rewrite the profiles. Monitor and help.
- When the students have finished, ask a few to read out their profiles, or put the students in groups to read out their profiles to each other and to make comments.

> **Possible answers**
> a Catwoman from *Batman*
>   Protected by her nine lives, this sexy, feline queen of crime constantly has her evil eye on Batman. If she can get him to turn to crime, then he will be hers forever!
> b Cruella De Vil in Disney's *101 Dalmatians*
>   Cruella De Vil lies, cheats, and steals to get what she wants, which is the fur of Dalmatian puppies. When their owners, Roger and Anita, say the pups are not for sale, Cruella is angry and swears she she will get her hands on the dogs somehow.

Speaking and writing

Aim *To describe favourite villains, and write a profile using complex sentences.*

1 If possible, bring in some pictures of well-known villains. Alternatively, write up as many names of villains as you can think of, or elicit them from the students.

- Ask the students to choose a favourite villain and think of five or six interesting things to say about him or her. You could give them headings to consider. For example, *Why is he or she a villain? What does he or she look like? What villainous things have they done?*

- Put the students in small groups to describe their villains.

2 Ask the students to write a 40–60 word profile using their ideas in 1, and remind then to use complex sentences. Refer them to the Writing guidelines on p.150.

- You could set this for homework.

18.2 A year in the public eye

p.136

Stage 2 consists of a listening text about the reality TV programme, *Castaway 2000*. It contextualizes the many uses of the verb *get*.

Lead in

Aim *To get the students talking about the theme of the listening text, and explain what Castaway 2000 is about.*

Note

4,000 people applied to join the *Castaway* experiment – 28 adults and 8 children were chosen. The castaways spent a year on Taransay, a small, uninhabited island in the north of Scotland. TV programmes followed their progress. The castaways slept in 'pods' designed to provide shelter from 160kph winds. They had to grow their own vegetables and keep farm animals.
The Adventures of Robinson Crusoe is a famous novel about a man who runs away to sea and asks to be left on an uninhabited island and rescued five years later. *The Swiss Family Robinson* is a similar story about a family who leave Switzerland to start a new life in New Guinea. On the way they are shipwrecked and land on an uninhabited tropical island. In both stories the theme is survival through hard work and inventiveness.

- Read through the advertisement as a class.
- Check the meaning of *Want out of the rat race?* (*Do you want to escape from the competitive struggle of city life?*). You could refer back to ellipsis in Unit 12 Stage 2.
- Ask the students if *they* would be interested in taking part.

Listening

Aim *To listen for gist and specific information.*

1 Ask the students to read the questions and listen to the recording.

18.1

P So what did you think about that Castaway 2000 documentary – have you seen anything of it?

R Yeah – it was scary.

K I think it's awful.

J Yeah, I couldn't do that.

K No way!

J Never! Just to be thrown on to an island in the cold north of Scotland with a whole group of people that you don't know.

K Awful people, though, awful people!

P Is it the idea of being filmed? Is that the problem? Or, or just the experience?

J It's the fact that you can't choose who you're who you're spending time with – I think that's what I would find difficult.

K Then it's too late because you're stuck there – and there's no going back – and it's such a risk.

a The general reaction is negative, but in this first part it is only the women who express opinions.
b Being with people you haven't chosen to be with.

2 Ask the students to read the questions and listen to the recording.

`18.2`

R I did two years of agriculture at my school.

K Did you?

R Because the choice was agriculture or Latin.

K Wow!

R And my father said in his very practical Dutch way 'You'll never learn …, need to learn Latin – why learn Latin – learn about sheep.'

J So can you, do you know about farming? – I mean would you know how …

R I did then.

K But I'm sure that must still be there.

R Yeah, I'm sure it's all there, yeah.

K I think we need a therapist as well – a group therapist. (Yes)

R And do you think that you could bring that to the group?

K That would be a laugh, I'd love to try that, yes absolutely.

R I think you'd need one.

K I think definitely – definitely something.

R So we've got farming, we've got therapy covered.

J I'm very good at DIY.

P Yeah, me too.

K / R   Well, that's fantastic! / Great!

R So we don't eat anything, though at this stage.

J Eat?

R Mmm. (Can) anyone cook?

K Oh yeah, yeah, cooking – I'm sure we can all cook, can't we, I can cook, (Yeah) yeah. Grow things, I mean grow vegetables and – (Yeah) we could do that.

P Did they … Did they have to do that? Grow their own food?

K I think so, I'm sure.

R / J I don't know.

K I'm sure they did.

> **a** farming (agriculture) / therapy (psychologist) / DIY (*Do It Yourself* = practical skills – mending, building, making.) / cooking / growing food
> **b** Personal answers

3 Put the students in pairs or threes to think about how they would organize people in the experiment.

- Play the recording so that they can check their answers.

`18.3`

R So, if we're on the island – we're all faced with having to deal with new people and we all are faced with the fact that we're going to be with these people for the next, I don't know, six months, where do you start? I mean how do you, how do you put everyone into their, into their sort of hierarchal positions, and, and does it happen by itself or do you think it …?

K I don't like the sound of hierarchical – I think that would be one of the things you'd want to try and avoid, don't you think? To try and find some sort of er some sort of society that isn't built on hierarchy – that's built on skill maybe.

R Yeah – I suppose that's, that's an ideal, but maybe things would just happen.

P I think they would. I think the idea would be to perhaps all sit down, have a meeting and I suppose talk about what skills you have and try and share out certain responsibilities based on that.

J Yes.

K And there are natural leaders and natural followers which would inevitably happen – and some people might not like that, they might not like being a follower or …

J … or being led by somebody that they don't particularly like.

K Absolutely and how many leaders do you have? And … that could be very difficult.

R But what if you were in a situation where there were, you know, six people – three people considered themselves or felt that they were natural leaders, I mean, there's immediately a conflict there with the three of them and three people underneath not really knowing what to do, I mean – in some ways it's almost better to say 'OK – you're our spokesman or spokeswoman'.

P What elect somebody?

R Yeah …

> **a** Students' own ideas. Possibilities: election of leader / everyone takes turns to be leader / ask for a volunteer.
> **b** They'd have a meeting and elect someone.

Exploring natural speech

Aim *To explore ways of expressing opinions in a tentative way.*

1–2 Read through the introduction as a class, then ask the students to complete the extract with tentative words. Do one as an example.

- Let the students check in pairs then play the recording so they can check their answers. (This does not appear in the tapescript section of the Student's Book.)

`18.4`

R So, if we're on the island – we're all faced with having to deal with new people and we all are faced with the fact that we're going to be with these people for the next, I don't know, six months, where do you start? I mean how do you, how do you put everyone into their, into their sort of hierarchal positions, and, and does it happen by itself or do you think it …?

K I don't like the sound of hierarchical – I think that would be one of the things you'd want to try and avoid, don't you think? To try and find some sort of er some sort of society that isn't built on hierarchy – that's built on skill maybe.

R Yeah – I suppose that's, that's an ideal, but maybe things would just happen.

P I think they would. I think the idea would be to perhaps all sit down, have a meeting and I suppose talk about what skills you have and try and share out certain responsibilities based on that.

1 I don't know	**5** maybe
2 I mean	**6** maybe
3 sort of	**7** perhaps
4 don't you think?	**8** certain

Language focus: get   p.137

Aim *To revise and practise uses of the verb* get.

This section looks at *get* as a main verb, the use of *get* plus the past participle in causative constructions, and *get* as a phrasal verb. As a main verb, in informal, spoken English, it is regularly used as a vague alternative to more specific verbs like *achieve*, *arrive*, or *catch*. One way of understanding its use is to see it as a verb that expresses some sort of change, whether that is a change of state, (*get thinner*), change of position, (*get home*), or change of possession, (*get a present*). *Get something done* may be used causatively like *have something done*, for example, *I got the window fixed*, (= I didn't do it, but I was responsible for *causing* someone else to fix it). Note that it can also be used non-causatively, for example, *I got stuck*. Look at the Language commentary on p.139 for more detail.

1 One way of starting is to brainstorm as many phrases involving *get* as the students can think of. Write them on the board, and ask the students what different meanings and uses they think the words may have.

• Look at the two examples from the tapescript with the students and ask them to explain the meaning of *get* in those contexts.

> **a** *Get* means *receive*.
> **b** *Get on* is a phrasal verb meaning *have a good relationship*.

2 Put the students in pairs to match the uses.

> **a** becoming **b** caught **c** arrive **d** fetch
> **e** achieved **f** buy **g** catch **h** understand

3 Do the first as an example, then put the students in pairs to discuss the sentences.

> **a** *get it cleaned* = arrange for another person to clean it
> *clean it* = clean it myself
> *have it cleaned* = the same as *get it cleaned*, but a little more formal
> **b** *I must finish it* = this is me telling myself about an obligation
> *I must get it finished* = implies difficulty or slight panic on the part of the speaker
> **c** *I got my finger trapped* = this was a misfortune that happened to the speaker
> *My finger was trapped* = neutral statement of fact

4 Students remain in pairs to replace the verbs with phrasal verbs.

> **a** ... *get on* very well with my boss.
> **b** ... *getting at* me.
> **c** ... *getting up to*.
> **d** ... managed to *get by*.
> **e** ... *get round to* **answering** ...
> **f** ... *get out of* (**doing**)
> **Note:** The *-ing* form is used after *get round to* and *get out of*.

• You could use the following extra activity to round off work on the verb *get* with some prepared speaking practice.

1 Write these subjects up on the board and tell students that they are going to talk for a minute about each one.

• A person you get on well with

• A person who sometimes gets at you

• How you think you'd get by if you took part in a programme like Castaway

• Things you used to do to get out of going to school or doing homework

• Things you used to get up to as a child (things your parents didn't approve of)

• Things you never get round to doing

2 Give the students a few minutes preparation time to read through the subjects and think what to say. Then put them in pairs or threes to talk for a minute about each topic.

3 Monitor and check that they are using *get* correctly.

Speaking

Aim *To get the students to discuss, plan, and present a new reality TV programme.*

1 You could set this up by asking students as a class to describe reality programmes that have been on TV recently.

• Put the students into small groups to plan their own programme. Ask them to discuss the questions. Set a time limit – ten or fifteen minutes is realistic.

2 When they have finished, ask one student from each group to present their ideas.

• Alternatively, rather than just presenting their ideas, you could tell the students that they have to prepare a persuasive presentation of their programme to the board of a TV company. Ask them to include reasons why their programme is special. When they present their ideas, you could nominate a panel, made up of one member from each group, who have to briefly discuss and decide on the most persuasive presentation at the end.

▶ As a follow-up, or for homework, you could do the extra activity on p.143. Refer the students to the Writing guidelines on p.151 of the Student's Book.

Exploring words   p.138

Aim *To introduce and practise vocabulary around the topic of places.*

This section has two student-centred activities which introduce vocabulary, and two extended speaking activities to practise it.

1 a–d Put the students in pairs to categorize the words and discuss the questions. They could use dictionaries to do this exercise.

> **Possible answers**
>
> | City life | Country life |
> |---|---|
> | bright + | backward – |
> | bustling + | bad transport – |
> | dangerous at night – | close to nature + |
> | exciting + | conservative – / + |
> | lonely – | cut off – / + |
> | noisy – | dull – |
> | overcrowded – | isolated – / + |
> | polluted – | lonely – |
> | poor public services – | no nightlife – / + |
> | poverty – | peaceful – / + |
> | stressful – | poor public services – |
> | traffic – | poverty – |
> | unreliable public transport – | relaxed + |
> | | secure + |
> | | tranquil + |
> | | uncrowded + |
> | | unpolluted + |
> | | unreliable public transport – |
>
> **Opposites**
> bright / dull
> bustling / tranquil or peaceful
> dangerous / secure
> exciting / dull
> overcrowded / uncrowded
> polluted / unpolluted
> stressful / relaxed

2 Students remain in pairs to match the words.

> | | | |
> |---|---|---|
> | 1 | agricultural land | (country) |
> | 2 | farming communities | (country) |
> | 3 | high-rise blocks | (city) |
> | 4 | multi-storey car parks | (city) |
> | 5 | narrow lanes | (country) |
> | 6 | one-way systems | (city) |
> | 7 | open fields | (country) |
> | 8 | parking restrictions | (city) |
> | 9 | shopping malls | (city) |
> | 10 | traffic congestion | (city) |

3 This is an opportunity for the students to practise the vocabulary introduced in exercises 1 and 2.

- Let them remain in pairs to prepare things to say, and ask them to try to use as much of the new vocabulary as possible. Then divide the students into small groups, splitting the pairs, to discuss their ideas.

- A way to create more of an opinion gap is to ask the students to argue for or against living in the city or the country.

- Alternatively, you could do this as a class presentation. Ask students to prepare a short talk in pairs, then ask one member of each pair to deliver the talk to the class.

4 This sort of activity works best if you break it into stages, giving the students plenty of time to prepare what they are going to say.

- Read through the introduction as a class, then divide the students into groups of four.

- Ask them to think of three or four reasons why each option might be a good idea. You could divide the four into two pairs, and ask each pair to prepare arguments for one of the options.

- Ask the students to discuss the options and decide which one they are going to choose.

- Give the students a few minutes to think about how they are going to present their option, then ask one member of the group to make a presentation to the class.

For ease of photocopying, the answers to this section are on p.144.

Unit 1 ━━━━━━━━━━━━━━ SB p.9

Metaphors to describe people

The third speaker in **1.3** refers to Barbara Walters as a *news anchor*. This is a name for the presenter of a news or current affairs programme, especially on TV in the US.

a Match the beginnings and endings to form sentences which describe certain kinds of people.

Beginnings	Endings
1 ☐ Emma's a real *wet blanket*	a – she reorganized our office in her first week here.
2 ☐ Annie's *a mine of information*	b – she's been wonderful since Paul and I split up.
3 ☐ Paula's a complete *bag of nerves*	c – she's worried about everything at the moment.
4 ☐ Jo's a real *live wire*	d – I won't go on holiday with her again.
5 ☐ Suzy's my *shoulder to cry on*	e – I've never managed to get really close to her.
6 ☐ Julia's a bit of *a cold fish*	f – if you want to know anything about cars, ask her.

b What kinds of people do the phrases in italics describe? Do you know anyone you would describe as *a cold fish, a live wire,* etc?

Unit 1 ━━━━━━━━━━━━━━ SB p.11

Language focus practice

Complete this conversation with *all, both, either, neither,* or *none.*

Jo   I'm late for work. Can ....¹ of you drive me to the station?

Amy   I can.

Sam   So can I.

Jo   Well you can't ....² – there's only one car. But I don't mind who takes me. ....³ of you will do – as long as I get to the station on time.

Amy   We'll ....⁴ go. I'll drive – you sit in the front, Jo, and Sam can go in the back with the dog.

Sam   I don't want to sit with the dog!

Jo   Well, we can't ....⁵ sit in the front. We might crash and then ....⁶ of us would get to the station.

Unit 2 ━━━━━━━━━━━━━━ SB p.16

make and *do*

Complete this letter with an appropriate form of *make* or *do*.

I've been in this job for a month now. At first I didn't really enjoy the work and thought about leaving, but now I ....¹ quite well and I've decided to ....² a go of it.

Actually, since I started here, I ....³ amazing progress. The company paid for me to ....⁴ a computing course, which was really helpful, and ....⁵ a big difference to my self-confidence.

Unfortunately, to start with, working at the computer gave me a backache. Because I couldn't concentrate, I ....⁶ lots of mistakes. Now I've got a special chair, and that ....⁷ the trick – no more backache!

What I'd really like now is to become a computer consultant like my brother. He's really well paid – in fact he ....⁸ an absolute fortune!

Unit 3 ▬▬▬▬▬▬▬▬▬▬▬▬▬ SB p.20

It's (just) occurred to me and mind you

Work in pairs. Make conversations adding the phrases in brackets to B's replies.

1 A Don't you want to walk into town?
  B Yeah, but I haven't got an umbrella. (*it's just occurred to me*)
2 A It's really cold, isn't it?
  B Yes, and we haven't got any warm clothes with us. (*it's occurred to me*)
3 A Wasn't it fantastic on the beach yesterday?
  B It was too hot for me. I've never enjoyed sunbathing. (*Mind you*)
4 A I hate snow and ice.
  B Me too. I enjoy skiing. (*Mind you*)

Unit 3 ▬▬▬▬▬▬▬▬▬▬▬▬▬ SB p.22

Colloquial language

Work in pairs. Take turns to be Student B, whose replies should include everyday speech versions of the words underlined.

1 A *Hi. Are you ready to leave?*
  B (You are not quite ready. Ask your friend to <u>give you</u> two more minutes).
2 A *Where's John?*
  B (You're sorry, you <u>don't know</u>).
3 A *Shall we go out this evening?*
  B (You are tired. You <u>want to</u> stay in and relax).
4 A *Do you fancy a game of squash?*
  B (You can't. You've <u>got to</u> work late).
5 A *Have you seen Mandy recently?*
  B (You haven't, but you're <u>going to</u> see her this evening).

Unit 4 ▬▬▬▬▬▬▬▬▬▬▬▬▬ SB p.31

Story-telling

Work in groups of four. Make up stories beginning with one of these lines. Take turns to add the next line.

1 The students were drinking, chatting, and waiting for the next lesson to begin.
2 She climbed onto the window-sill and looked down.
3 I hadn't seen my brother for nearly seven years.

Take turns to add the next line of the story.

Example

A *The bell had rung five minutes earlier and there were still ten minutes' break.*
B *The Principal walked in and went straight to the middle of the room.*
C *She looked round, and …*

Unit 4 ▬▬▬▬▬▬▬▬▬▬▬▬▬ SB p.33

Reported speech

Rewrite these sentences in reported speech.

1 'I'll see you on Friday,' she said. (It's now the following Tuesday.)
....

2 'I'm busy at the weekend,' he said (It's the Wednesday before the weekend.)
....

3 'I still love you.' she said. (The speaker still loves him!)
....

4 'We may go to Florida for our holiday,' she said.
....

5 'I ought to stay in and work this evening,' I said.
....

6 'I must take my car to the garage,' he said.
....

7 'Would you like to come round for the evening?' she asked.
....

8 'Can you come with us?' she asked.
....

9 'Are you worried about losing data?' she asked me.
....

10 'Work harder!' she said.
....

Giving advice

1 Work in groups. Discuss one of these letters to a magazine. What advice would you give?

A

My younger brother is a very talented footballer. He'd like to play professionally when he's older, but he doesn't think he's good enough to be considered by the local football club and is too shy to apply for a trial. What can I do to help? How can I build up my brother's confidence?

B

My younger sister is a brilliant singer. I think she's good enough to become a professional – but she's not very ambitious and says she just wants to sing for fun. What should I do to persuade her to think again about singing as a career?

2 Use some of the ideas you have just discussed to write a reply to the writer of one of the letters. Refer to the Writing guidelines on p.152.

1 Make a paragraph plan, for example:

Para 1	Show understanding of the writer's situation and point of view.
Para 2	Make practical suggestions that the writer can follow up immediately.
Para 3	Say what might happen if the writer does not follow your advice.
Para 4	End on a reassuring note, expressing your hope that things turn out well.

2 Write a first draft letter. Keep a clear image in your mind of the person you are writing to. Write in a simple, friendly style which will convince the reader of your sincerity and concern.

3 Exchange letters with a partner. Read each other's letters from the point of view of the person who asked the question. Does the advice make sense to you?

4 Comment on your partner's letter. Say how you would react to the advice and comment on the style.

5 Write the final draft of your letter.

Craze vocabulary

1 Complete each sentence with an appropriate word from this list.

about	in	into	mad	of	on	with

a I was completely ballet-.........
b I was .... animals.
c I used to be a great fan .... heavy metal music.
d I was really keen .... playing with Lego®.
e I was completely obsessed .... football.
f I was always very interested .... music.
g I'm absolutely crazy .... scuba diving.

2 Work with a partner. Talk about activities you are not interested in or actually dislike.

Use some of these expressions:

- .... really annoys me.
- I can't stand / loathe / detest ....
- I'm (completely) indifferent to / unenthusiastic about ....

Language focus practice

Some verbs have different meanings depending on whether they are followed by the *-ing* form or the infinitive. What is the difference in meaning between these pairs of sentences?

1 I *forgot to meet* her at the station. / I'll never *forget meeting* her at the station.
2 On the way home I *stopped to buy* a newspaper. / I've *stopped buying* newspapers – they're so expensive.
3 I *didn't mean to offend* you. / I've got to say this, even if it *means offending* you.
4 *Remember to phone* me as soon as you get back. / I distinctly *remember phoning* her as soon as I got back.
5 Despite his injury he *went on playing* football. / Having started playing football at school, he *went on to play* for his country.
6 I *regret to tell* you that you've failed your exam. / I really *regret telling* you the exam result.

Sleep vocabulary

1 What are the differences in meaning between these sets of sleep words and phrases? Use a dictionary to help you with words you're not sure of.

a exhausted / tired / knackered / sleepy
b to go to bed / to go to sleep
c to fall asleep / to get to sleep / to drop off
d to lie down / to lie in
e have a nap / to doze
f to stay up / to be awake

2 Choose the most appropriate word or phrase.

a After the exams we went to a club and danced all night. The next day we were completely *exhausted / sleepy*.
b I didn't *go to bed / go to sleep* until 1 a.m. even though I *went to bed / went to sleep* early.
c I'd only been on the plane for 10 minutes before I *got to sleep / dropped off*.
d On Saturday mornings I often *lie down / lie in* until midday.
e Don't worry about disturbing him – he's just *having a nap / dozing* in front of the TV.
f We had so much to talk about that we *stayed up / were awake* all night.

Pairs of adjectives

1 In recording **16.2** the final action of *Chicken Run* is described as *fast and furious*. What do you think this means?

2 Here are some more similar expressions. What do you notice about them?
rough and ready / prim and proper / bright and breezy / cold and calculating / wet and windy

3 Which of the expressions might you use to describe:

a a winter's night
b a cheerful person
c a second-hand car repaired in a hurry
d the behaviour of a refined young woman
e an ambitious politician

Complex sentences

Why do we use complex sentences? What effect do they have compared with simple sentences? Read these two texts and compare ideas with a partner.

a Which text sounds more exciting?
b Which text contains more complicated ideas?
c Which text explains the connections between facts?
d Which text is easier to understand?

A
Guy Burgess worked for the British secret service at a time when British power in the world was decreasing. Blaming the upper classes for this situation, he became a Marxist who believed that the future of Britain was as a communist country. He worked as a Russian spy until the mid-1950s when, realizing the authorities suspected him, he fled to Moscow.

B
The radio crackled. It went quiet. He tried the phone. That was dead too. Was he being watched? He looked out of the window. He thought he saw a movement by the gate. He ran downstairs. Maybe he could escape through the back of the house. He took the revolver out of his pocket. He opened the back door. Instantly, he was blinded by a strong light.

Writing and speaking

You have decided to apply to take part in a programme like *Castaway*. You can apply for a real programme you know about or one of the programmes presented to the class.

1 Write a letter of application, saying why you think you should be chosen for the programme. Include the following information:

- Say why you are applying. Why does the particular programme appeal to you?
- Write about yourself. Describe your personality. List your skills and abilities. Mention any relevant experience you have already had.
- End with a summary of what you could contribute to the project.

2 Exchange letters with a partner who is applying for the same programme as you.

a Read each other's letters carefully.
b Take turns to interview each other. Ask further questions about your partner's character, experience and skills.
c Finally, decide whether your partner is a suitable candidate for the programme.

Extra material key

Unit 1 — Metaphors

a 1 d 2 f 3 c 4 a 5 b 6 e
b Personal answers

Unit 1 — Language focus

1 either **2** both **3** either **4** all **5** all
6 none

Unit 2 — *make* and *do*

1 am doing
2 make
3 have made
4 do
5 made / has made
6 made
7 did / has done
8 makes / has made

Unit 3 — Colloquial language

1 B Not quite – can you gimme two more minutes?
2 B Sorry, I dunno.
3 B No, I'm tired. I wanna stay in and relax.
4 B Sorry, I can't. I've gotta work late.
5 B No, but I'm gonna see her this evening.

Unit 4 — Reported speech

1 She said she'd see me on Friday.
2 He said he's / he was busy at the weekend.
3 She says she still loves you.
4 She said they might go to Florida for their holiday.
5 I said I ought to stay in and work that evening.
6 He said he had to take his car to the garage.
7 She asked if / whether we'd like to go round for the evening.
8 She asked if / whether I could go with them.
9 She asked me if / whether I was worried about losing data.
10 She told me to work harder.

Unit 12 — Craze vocabulary

1 a mad b into c of d on e with f in g about
2 Personal answers

Unit 15 — Language focus practice

It might be useful to draw a time line on the board.

1 *forgot to meet her* = I didn't meet her because I forgot

```
       forget           didn't meet
————————X——————————————————X————————
```

forget meeting her = I met her and I'll never forget about it

```
    meet                   forget
——————X——————————————————————X——————
```

2 *stopped to buy* = I broke my journey in order to buy

```
        stop              buy
—————————X————————————————X——————————
```

stopped buying = I didn't buy (newspapers) any more

```
              stop
———————————————X—————————————————————
              buy
```

3 *I didn't mean to offend you* = this wasn't my intention
even if it means offending you = involves offending you
(time line not relevant here)

4 *Remember to phone* = don't forget

```
      remember             phone
—————————X————————————————————X——————
```

I remember phoning = I recall the occasion

```
       phone             remember
—————————X————————————————————X——————
```

5 *went on playing* = continued
went on to play = progressed to do something else
(time line not relevant here)

6 *I regret to tell you* = I'm sorry but I have to inform you (the
speaker is going to tell)

```
       regret              tell
—————————X————————————————————X——————
```

I regret telling you = I wish I hadn't told you (the speaker
has already told)

```
        tell              regret
—————————X————————————————————X——————
```

Unit 16 — Sleep vocabulary

2
a exhausted
b go to sleep, went to bed
c dropped off
d lie in
e dozing
f stayed up

Unit 16 — Pairs of adjectives

1 The action is quick and energetic.
2 The adjective pairs have the same initial letter.
3
a wet and windy
b bright and breezy
c rough and ready
d prim and proper
e cold and calculating

Unit 18 — Complex sentences

Complex sentences allow us to express the links between facts
or ideas in a way which simple sentences do not. On the other
hand, we may choose to use simple sentences to make what
we write more immediate and dynamic.
a B   **b** A   **c** A   **d** B

Writing guidelines key

Personal profiles

Analysis – suggested answers

Profile A

1 A reference
2 To support a student's application for a course
3 A teacher / ex-teacher
4 Admissions officer / tutor at a college

Profile B

1 A letter / e-mail
2 As part of informal communication between friends / to keep someone up to date
3 A friend
4 A friend

Profile C

1 A CV / résumé
2 In support of a job application
3 An applicant for a job
4 A potential employer

Profile D

1 A biography / obituary
2 To record details of or celebrate someone's life
3 A professional writer or journalist (possibly an acquaintance of the subject)
4 A general readership – e.g. newspaper readers

Useful language – suggestions

Profile A

highly-motivated student / of an excellent standard / is rather quiet and reserved / fluent and colloquial / to communicate effectively / worked hard / the slight accent / wide vocabulary / an excellent student

Profile B

nothing special to look at - tall and slim with short dark hair / such a lovely personality / so kind / It was amazing

Profile C

All words and phrases are useful.

Profile D

a professional musician / polished musicianship / rarely out of work

Stories and narratives

Analysis – suggested answers

1 C
2 A Factual book / article about Salvador Dali
  B Letter / e-mail
3 Extract A

  The effect is to give the reader a vivid impression of places and people.

a By the use of short snappy sentences and exclamation marks [!!!]

  By the use of 'extreme' vocabulary: *You probably won't believe this... / fantastic / it was absolutely fantastic*

Useful language – suggestions

Extract A

Driving along a coast road, we passed / Next morning / Suddenly / Then

Extract B

Then

Extract C

During the first weeks at school she had rung / Now

Letters

Analysis – suggested answers

Letter A

1 Informal letter about family matters
2 Father to son
3 Least formal
4 • Writer is father (or perhaps older brother). Matt is his son. Tina is a friend of Matt. Becky is Matt's sister. Val is the writer's wife (probably second wife – therefore Matt's stepmother).
  • Possible endings: *Love / Take care / Write soon*

Letter B

1 Letter of complaint
2 Couple who stayed in hotel to hotel manager
3 –
4 • The first paragraph states the purpose of the letter. The final paragraph states what action the writer wants to follow.
  • Ending: *Yours faithfully*

Letter C

1 Letter of application (for place on music course)
2 Potential course member to course administrator
3 Most formal
4 • Topics of the five paragraphs:
    1 States the purpose of the letter
    2 The writer says why his application is appropriate
    3 The writer's qualifications and suitability for the course
    4 The writer's reassurance that this is a serious application
    5 A concluding sentence
  • Possible beginning: *Dear Mr X / Dear Ms Y* (a person's name)

Letter D

1 Reply to a request
2 University teacher to ex-student
3 –
4 • Possible ending: *Best wishes / All the best*

Useful language – suggestions

Letter A

Informal language: All verb contractions, plus: *Hi Matt / very kind of her / we fancy / loads of fantastic big houses / all cost a fortune / Better stop now*

Letter B

Formal language: *to comment on / satisfactory / the following morning / appealing / In addition to this / your response*

Letter C

Formal language: *In response to / I wish to apply / to be held / achieved Grade 8 / limited / If accepted on the course I would be a committed and enthusiastic participant / contribute / consider my application favourably*

Letter D

Semi-formal language: *good to hear from you / making use of / received / challenging / In answer to your request / you require / your project / Everyone sends their regards*

Articles

Analysis

1 **Article A:** Public interest in nature as shown by popularity of TV survival programmes
    Aimed at general readers

  Article B: Huge tidal wave threatening Britain
    Aimed at general readers

  Article C: What attracts women to certain kinds of men
    Aimed at general readers – perhaps more for women

  Article D: Problems with computers
    Aimed at users of Macintosh computers

2, 3 Personal answers

4 **Article A:** Question in headline needs an answer

  Article B: Provocative / intriguing question in headline needs an answer
    Addresses the reader directly – YOU

  Article C: Names of famous people used in the first paragraph

  Article D: The writer warns readers about problems they may have with computers. The article will help them with these.

5 Extract E is the end of Article B. The writer leaves the reader wondering, maybe worrying about future threat.

Useful language – suggestions

Article A

• The use of interesting words in the title question: *Is this <u>paradise</u> or a <u>hell</u> of a challenge?*
• *I am definitely a four-star hotel kind of girl*

Article B

• Directly addressing the reader: *If you've read this far / But don't relax too much*
• Strong stating of case: *there's no question that*

Article C

• Addressing the reader in a conversational way: *Don't ask me why / Yes, that's right*

Article D

• Conveying the idea that problems are inevitable: *Sooner or later*
• Reassuring the reader: *This isn't unusual and it certainly isn't something to panic about*

Article E

Using direct speech to quote an expert

Reports

- In comparison with articles, reports are more factual and objective. The emphasis is on conveying information clearly and effectively, so there is not the same need for reports to capture the reader's attention or to be interesting.

  Narratives usually involve a number of events in sequence.

- Personal answers

Analysis – suggested answers

1 The purpose is to report on a survey of student attitudes to the eating facilities at their college.

  It could have been written by an outside research organization; more likely to have been a group of students at the college. It was probably written for college management, or outside caterers responsible for the restaurant facilities.

2 *Variety / Range of food available*

3 Personal comments by the writer come in the conclusion, when a recommendation is made: *I suggest that the college management find a way…*

Useful language – suggestions

This report outlines / The majority of students were satisfied / Sandwiches were criticized / There was support for the idea / not a major concern / Many reported / There is a widespread feeling that / college management find

Reviews

Analysis – suggested answers

1 **a** Review C (Harry Potter)

  b Review A (Radiohead)

  c Review B (*Titanic*)

  d Review C is the most formal. Review A could be described as very informal or 'conversational'.

2 Personal answers

Useful language – suggestions

Review A

something completely new and magnificent. I firmly believe that this is one of the best albums ever released / if you haven't bought it yet, then you should / listen to it again / it's not long enough! I love the variations in time signature, and the overlapping rhythms / I just can't wait for their next album

Review B

Titanic *is a disappointment / The main problems are / Too much time is spent on / What the audience really wants to see is / the special effects are incredible / this film will not sink*

Review C

a highly readable and imaginative adventure story / this is the book you have been waiting for